North American Free Trade

North American Free Trade

Assessing the Impact

Nora Lustig, Barry P. Bosworth,
and Robert Z. Lawrence, *editors*

The Brookings Institution
Washington, D.C.

Library of Congress Cataloging-in-Publication data:

North American free trade : assessing the impact / Nora Lustig, Barry
    P. Bosworth, and Robert Z. Lawrence, eds.
        p.   cm.
    Includes bibliographical references and index.
    ISBN 0-8157-5316-0. — ISBN 0-8157-5315-2
    1. North America—Commerce.   2. Free trade—North
America.   3. North America—Commercial policy.   I. Lustig,
Nora.   II. Bosworth, Barry, 1942–   III. Lawrence, Robert
Z., 1949–
HF3211.N667   1992
382'.71'097—dc20   92-26402
                                                                      CIP

9 8 7 6 5 4 3 2 1

The paper used in this publication meets the minimum requirements of the
American National Standard for Information Sciences—Permanence of
paper for Printed Library Materials, ANSI Z39.48-1984.

Foreword

On August 12, 1992, the trade representatives of Canada, Mexico, and the United States concluded negotiations on the North American Free Trade Agreement. Implementation of NAFTA awaits formal governmental approval in each country. This will intensify the debate about the impact of the agreement, which began in mid-1990 when President Carlos Salinas de Gortari of Mexico made the formal request to pursue negotiations of a free trade agreement with the United States. Since then, research institutions and government agencies in all three countries have initiated numerous studies on the costs and benefits of NAFTA. The empirical results of these studies differ widely; indeed, in some instances they are contradictory.

To understand and resolve some of these differences, the Brookings Institution held a conference in April 1992 entitled NAFTA: An Assessment of the Research. Six papers were presented at the conference, each concentrating on a particular subject: labor markets, industry, agriculture, economywide modeling, the effect on the rest of the world, and nontrade issues. This book includes revised versions of the six papers, together with the remarks of the official commentators on each paper and the comments of a panel of two experts who presented their views in the final session. In the introductory chapter the editors, Barry P. Bosworth and Nora Lustig, both senior fellows at Brookings, and Robert Z. Lawrence, professor of international trade and investment at Harvard's John F. Kennedy School of Government, present a brief overview of the main issues and summarize the papers and discussion. Because of time constraints, the manuscript was not subjected to the formal review and verification procedures established for research publications of the institution.

The editors wish to thank the many staff members at Brookings who contributed to the project: Arianna Legovini and Suzanne M. Smith provided valuable research assistance; Charlotte B. Brady, Susanne Lane, and Annette D. Leak helped to coordinate the conference, aided by Z.

Selin Hür; Adrianne Goins, Kashif Mansori, Stephen Schwartz, and Suzanne Smith prepared discussion summaries; and Annette D. Leak, Irene Coray, Louise Skillings, and Janelle Jameson typed the final manuscript. Jonathan Preimesberger, Patricia Dewey, and Caroline Lalire edited the manuscript; Gwendolyn Stansbury proofread the pages; and Patricia Anne Deminna prepared the index.

Brookings gratefully acknowledges the financial support for this project from the Ford Foundation.

The views expressed in this book are those of the individual authors and should not be ascribed to any of the persons or organizations whose assistance and support is acknowledged above, or to the trustees, officers, or other staff members of the Brookings Institution.

BRUCE K. MACLAURY
President

August 1992
Washington, D.C.

Contents

Tables

Figure

Introduction

Barry P. Bosworth, Robert Z. Lawrence, and Nora Lustig

THE proposed North American Free Trade Agreement (NAFTA) aims at reducing and ultimately eliminating most of the remaining barriers to trade and investment among Canada, Mexico, and the United States. While it can be interpreted as a continuation of a prior trend toward increased economic integration between the three countries, NAFTA symbolizes a much larger change in economic relations, particularly between Mexico and the United States.

For Mexico it is the culmination of a dramatic shift from a previous policy that emphasized import substitution and closely regulated commercial ties with other countries. Since the mid-1980s Mexico has pursued a policy of economic liberalization, sharply reducing restrictions on trade, cutting domestic subsidies, and expanding the role of private markets.[1] In that respect NAFTA is only a formal recognition of changes that have already taken place. The agreement is still important, however, because it institutionalizes the policy changes and confers a degree of permanence on them that is critical in attracting the foreign capital and technology needed for future growth. It will be more difficult for future Mexican governments to reverse the present course and turn Mexico back toward economic isolationism. The agreement is also seen as a way to protect Mexico in the future against what it views as a highly capricious U.S. trade policy.

NAFTA is a major step for the United States. Mexico is the third largest and the most rapidly growing market for U.S. exports. Given the long and porous border between the two countries, an agreement that fosters economic prosperity and political stability in Mexico benefits the United States. NAFTA is also perceived as a model for expanding trade relations between the United States and the rest of Latin America. Yet the prospect of an agreement has heightened concerns within the United States about the ability of some domestic industries to compete in a newly expanded market. Fears center on the potential loss of jobs for less-skilled workers, a group that has already suffered large economic losses during the 1980s.

NAFTA is quite different from previous free trade regions or economic unions because it proposes to join countries that are currently at widely different stages of economic development. Most members of the European Common Market, for example, had similar levels of income per capita when they entered the European Community (EC). Likewise, levels of wages and technical proficiency are nearly identical in the United States and Canada. In those cases the main benefits of freer trade were expected to stem from efficiency gains generated by economies of scale and an intensification of competitive pressures in a broader market.

For an expansion of trade between countries with different relative supplies of capital and labor skills, however, the efficiency gains are associated more with increased specialization and reallocation of production facilities. The result could be greater dislocation of jobs in both countries than was expected from the Canadian-U.S. Free Trade Agreement (CUSFTA). There is also concern that the expansion of bilateral trade will be at the expense of trade with third countries. Thus some of the benefits to Mexico may result from a diversion of U.S. imports from other low-wage countries, and the export gains of the United States may come at the expense of other industrial countries. Finally, there are greater differences between the United States and Mexico in areas such as environmental and workplace regulations than exist between the United States and Canada. These issues are becoming increasingly important determinants of production costs and of the location of production facilities for industries such as cement, chemicals, and electronics.

The initiation of formal negotiations stimulated a large amount of research on the potential impact of NAFTA on the economies of the three member countries. The papers in this volume are intended to provide an assessment of that research, seeking to identify issues of broad consensus as well as issues on which the research remains inconclusive. They were originally presented at a conference at the Brookings Institution on April 9–10, 1992, and were subsequently modified by the authors in response to that discussion.

A consensus emerged from the conference that the direct economic effects of NAFTA will be small for both Mexico and the United States. Though this conclusion is strikingly at odds with much of the public debate that foresees large-scale relocations of production facilities, it reflects several factors. Restrictions on trade between the United States and Mexico have already been reduced to low levels: tariffs currently average about 13 percent in Mexico and about 6 percent in the United States.[2] Mexico has also significantly scaled back its system of widespread quantitative restrictions on imports, and most of the remaining nontariff barriers of both countries will be phased out gradually. Thus many of the changes in commercial relations that are often associated with NAFTA in public discussions have already occurred, and others will be spread over future years. Moreover, international trade in most manufactured products will be less affected by changes in relative prices of the magnitude that will result from the agreement than is commonly supposed. The effects on the United States will be further limited because part of the increase in imports from Mexico will come at the expense of imports from other low-wage countries rather than at the expense of U.S. production.

The conference participants agreed, however, that a static analysis of the change in commercial relations misses many of the more important dynamic elements of NAFTA. If the free trade agreement increases perceptions of a permanent shift in Mexico toward more open, liberal economic policies, the result will be a large inflow of new capital and the return of capital that fled the country in the early 1980s. Because capital is a major constraining factor on Mexican economic growth, the added inflow promises to accelerate the growth of gross domestic product (GDP) and living standards, as the dynamic models reviewed in this volume show. In effect, the free trade agreement with the United States provides an opportunity to advertise to the world the business opportunities available in Mexico. The counterpart of a net capital inflow would be a surplus of imports over exports; and since the United States accounts for about 70 percent of Mexico's trade,[3] the principal benefit to the United States will be a large trade surplus with Mexico, heavily concentrated in capital goods exports and extending over several decades.

The United States is concerned chiefly with the distributional effects of the agreement on specific U.S. industries and less-skilled American workers. The implications for particular industries will depend greatly on the specific details of the agreement, because each country maintains quantitative restrictions on imports in industries that are of key importance to the other; for example, Mexican restrictions on automobile imports or U.S. restrictions on some agricultural products. More generally, though most studies agree that a liberalization of trade with Mexico will be good for Americans as a whole, not everyone will gain—there will be important distributional consequences. Several studies reviewed in this book suggest

Table 1. Relative Size of the Canadian, Mexican, and U.S. Economies, 1990

Item	Canada	Mexico	United States
GDP (billions of dollars)	572	214	5,514
Population (millions)	26.6	86.1	250.0
Per capita GDP	21,527	2,490	22,055
Average wage per day	67.98[b]	8.11[c]	69.14[a]

Sources: Comisión Nacional de los Salarios Mínimos; World Bank, *World Development Report, 1992* (Washington, 1992); Statistics Canada; *Economic Report of the President, January 1992*; and Department of Commerce, Bureau of Economic Analysis.

a. Based on average weekly earnings for nonsupervisory workers in private nonagricultural industries.
b. Based on average weekly earnings of employees paid by the hour.
c. Average daily wages in the formal sector (covered by social security).

that the gains to better-skilled American workers will be offset by some losses to those not as skilled. The general consensus of the studies, however, is that NAFTA will raise the average wage of U.S. workers and that the effect on low-wage workers will be negligible. On the other hand, most of the research is based on comparing one equilibrium situation with another equilibrium, and transitional costs are not really captured by the existing empirical exercises. A similar problem arises for Mexico concerning rural workers who may lose as a result of liberalized trade in maize.

Again, however, it is important to distinguish between the economic effects of NAFTA and those changes that will occur regardless of a formal agreement. A widening of wage differentials by levels of education and job skills has been evident in the United States for more than a decade. And to some extent that process reflects an increased integration of the United States into a global economy in which highly skilled workers are relatively scarce and the unskilled are in surplus.[4] The United States is faced with a choice between two strategies: (1) protecting a set of industries that would continue to pay low wages to less-skilled workers, or (2) improving the skills of its existing work force so that a larger number of workers can qualify for high-productivity, high-wage jobs. The importance of this choice extends far beyond trade with Mexico. NAFTA sharpens the issue, but only marginally.

Background Information

Under NAFTA, the United States would be joined with its first- and third-largest trading partners as part of the world's largest common economic market. As shown in table 1, the combined GDP of the three countries was about $6.3 trillion in 1990, with a population of 363 million.

Figure 1. Trends in U.S. Trade with Mexico, 1970-91

Billions of 1990 dollars

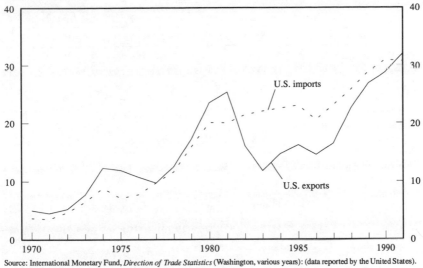

Source: International Monetary Fund, *Direction of Trade Statistics* (Washington, various years): (data reported by the United States).

By comparison, the European Community encompasses about 375 million people and produces a GDP of $5 trillion. NAFTA would be heavily dominated by the United States, however, which accounts for 87 percent of the GDP and 69 percent of the population. The real contrast is in GDP per capita and average wage rates. The United States and Canada are very similar, but in Mexico the average industrial wage is only about 10 percent that of the United States.

Historical trends in merchandise trade between Mexico and the United States are shown in figure 1. The United States generally had a bilateral trade surplus until the early 1980s, when economic collapse in Mexico led to a sharp contraction of Mexican imports. With the termination of a net inflow of capital in 1982, Mexico could no longer finance a current account deficit, and it was forced to export far more than it imported to earn the dollars required to pay interest on accumulated debt. Between 1981 and 1983 the dollar value of Mexico's imports declined by 51.6 percent, and its merchandise trade balance switched from a deficit of $3.8 billion to a surplus of $13.8 billion.[5] Trade with the United States absorbed the bulk of that adjustment simply because the United States accounts for about two-thirds of Mexico's trade. In recent years the economic situation in Mexico has improved, and the renewal of economic growth and capital inflows has made possible a large trade expansion with the United States.

Table 2. Composition of U.S. Merchandise Trade with Mexico, 1985–91
Millions of dollars

	United States					
	Exports		Imports		Trade balance	
Item	1985	1991	1985	1991	1985	1991
Foods, feed, and beverages	1,117	2,585	1,792	2,802	− 675	− 217
Petroleum	—	—	7,838	4,688	− 7,838	− 4,688
Industrial supplies (except petroleum)	4,096	8,935	1,859	3,103	2,237	5,832
Capital goods (except automotive)	4,538	11,304	2,957	6,135	1,581	5,169
Automotive vehicles, parts, and engines	1,974	5,363	2,830	7,857	− 856	− 2,494
Consumer goods (nonfood)	684	3,425	1,278	5,342	− 594	− 1,917
Other goods	977	1,525	550	1,599	427	− 74
Total	13,386	33,137	19,104	31,526	− 5,719	1,611

Source: Department of Commerce, Bureau of Economic Analysis.

Between 1986 and 1991 U.S. exports to Mexico grew at an annual rate of 22 percent and imports by 13 percent. In 1991 the United States again had a $1.6 billion trade surplus with Mexico.[6]

The composition of U.S.-Mexico trade is shown in table 2. The United States maintains a strong trade surplus with Mexico in capital goods and industrial supplies, which is offset by deficits in petroleum and consumer products. The importance of capital goods in U.S. exports is highlighted by the fact that they represent one-third of total exports to Mexico. The growth of exports of industrial supplies reflects in part the expansion of the *maquiladora* program.[7] In areas other than capital goods and oil, trade between the two countries is often distorted by specific industry quotas or other types of nontariff barriers. The United States, for example, maintains an elaborate system of quotas on imports of apparel and fruits and vegetables, while Mexico severely restricts imports of automobiles and grains. It is in these areas that the details of NAFTA will be very important in determining net economic effects.

Although Mexico has had a long tradition of restricting foreign control of its industry, foreign direct investment steadily expanded during the 1970s, from about $300 million annually to a peak of $2.5 billion in 1980–81.[8] With the onset of the economic crisis, that inflow of capital fell to $500 million in 1985. Liberalization of the ownership controls and economic recovery have been responsible for a rebound of direct investment to about \$2.8 billion in 1989–90.[9]

U.S. corporations are the dominant source of foreign involvement in the Mexican economy. On a cumulative basis, foreign direct investment in Mexico totaled about \$33 billion at the end of 1991, with about 63 percent of the participation coming from U.S. corporations. Great Britain and Germany are next in importance, each accounting for about 6 percent of the total. Until the mid-1980s foreign direct investment was concentrated in manufacturing, but in recent years it has shifted toward the service sector. Between 1985 and 1991 the industry share of cumulative direct investment fell from 78 to 58 percent.

Economic Reform in Mexico

Mexico followed an inward-looking development path throughout the post–World War II period. Rapid industrialization in the 1950s and 1960s occurred within an economic environment protected by trade barriers. Between 1950 and 1970 the Mexican economy performed remarkably well. During this period Mexico generated per capita annual growth rates of 3 to 4 percent, with an annual inflation rate of about 3 percent. This "golden age" ended in the mid-1970s, when the country faced a severe balance-of-payments crisis.[10]

New discoveries of vast oil reserves provided temporary relief. During the oil boom (1978–81) the government budget deficit soared, and Mexico, counting on continued high oil prices, borrowed heavily from abroad. In early 1982 a combination of fiscal mismanagement and adverse external shocks resulted in another balance-of-payments crisis, followed by devaluation and financial chaos. During 1982 the peso declined to one-fourth its 1981 value. Even with adjustment for inflation, the fall in the real value of the peso exceeded 30 percent. The external debt, largely denominated in dollars, rose from a manageable 30 percent of GDP in 1981 to 63 percent by 1983. In 1982 interest on the external debt absorbed half of Mexico's export revenue.[11]

The government struggled to stabilize the domestic economy between 1982 and 1985 with an International Monetary Fund–backed program that included the usual ingredients of fiscal and monetary restraint. The program failed to meet its objectives, and a new balance-of-payments crisis occurred in mid-1985. In government circles, it was increasingly believed that the failure of the stabilization program was due in part to the slowness of structural reform. Thus, starting in mid-1985, policy shifted progressively toward measures aimed at opening the economy to international markets and reducing the presence of the state in the economy. Some of the most significant elements of the Mexican economic reform were thus initiated in mid-1985 under de la Madrid and consolidated when Carlos Salinas de Gortari became president in 1988.

The changes in economic policy in recent years have been most dramatic in trade policy. In mid-1985 more than 90 percent of domestic production was protected against imports by an elaborate system of import licenses. Reference prices were used to assign arbitrarily higher tariffs on many imported products. By 1988 the domestic production covered by import licenses fell to about 23 percent, the reference price system had been eliminated, and the average level of tariffs had been reduced from 23.5 to 11 percent (production weighted). Mexico joined the General Agreement on Tariffs and Trade (GATT) in 1986. On the export side, Mexico largely eliminated direct subsidies. Industrial programs were dismantled on a more gradual basis after 1985. What remained was a set of industry-specific regulations, such as those for automobiles, that imposed export targets on importing firms.[12]

Macroeconomic policy achievements include, first and foremost, a cut in the public sector borrowing requirement from 16.9 percent of GDP in 1982 to 1.5 percent in 1991. A prime objective of economic restructuring has been to remove many of the regulatory inefficiencies that accumulated in the previous decades. Nearly three-fourths of the 1,200 state-owned enterprises have been divested, including firms in the communications, airline and, most strikingly, banking industries. Government regulation of a broad range of industries has been curtailed to stimulate competition.[13]

The results have been a renewal of economic growth, which has averaged 3.7 percent a year between 1989 and 1991, and a reduction of inflation to an annual rate of about 23 percent in 1991. Since 1986 the dollar value of Mexican non-oil exports has grown by 95 percent and total imports by 140 percent. The vast bulk of the expansion of trade has been with the United States. Furthermore, despite large social costs to the Mexican population—real wages declined by nearly 50 percent between 1983 and 1988—the public seemingly has continued to support the government's reform program. Mexico has reached a stage in which it needs a more active involvement of foreign capital and technology if it is to sustain the economic progress that has been made. NAFTA is seen as a primary means of achieving that objective by increasing the confidence of international corporations in the stability and growth potential of the Mexican economy.

Summary of the Papers

The prospect of NAFTA has generated much research on its potential economic effects in a relatively brief period of time. In particular, it has stimulated interest in computable general equilibrium (CGE) models, which provide a consistent framework for assessing the impact of changes in tariffs and their equivalents at the level of individual industries. Those models provide the basis for much of the quantitative assessment of NAFTA.

The Impact of NAFTA and CGE Models

Drusilla K. Brown surveys the results of studies of NAFTA that use applied general equilibrium modeling. The common theme of these studies is that the overall impact of a formal North American Free Trade Agreement is modest for each of the three countries. At the low end of the estimates the gains to the participating countries are in the range of 1 percent of GDP. The benefits are consistently positive for all three economies, however, with the agreement offering more to Mexico than to the United States. The models have also been useful for identifying the sectoral distribution of the gains and losses from trade liberalization and other major problem areas. The discussion did reveal, however, several shortcomings of the CGE analysis.

Although the various CGE models use similar methodologies, Brown describes how seemingly minor differences in modeling strategy can lead to significantly dissimilar results. Differences in the structure of the models, for example, lead to variations in the estimated gains to Mexico that range from 1 percent to 7 percent of GDP. She examines the implications of several key assumptions.

One issue involves the extent of product differentiation by country of origin. Models in which industry output is assumed to be a single homogeneous product, regardless of the country in which it is produced, tend to show much larger effects than models in which output is assumed to be differentiated by origin. Models that assume the latter (for example, that U.S. toothpaste is different from Mexican toothpaste) incorporate lower price elasticities for exports and imports, and they suggest that eliminating tariffs in NAFTA will have a relatively small effect on incomes—typically less than 1 percent of gross national product—although they show benefits for all participating countries. By contrast, models that assume that products are homogeneous across countries indicate larger effects, with welfare gains for Mexico in the range of 2 to 4 percent of GNP.

Brown also surveys simulations of models that assume increasing returns to scale and noncompetitive market structures. In one model (Roland-Holst and others), taking account of increasing returns raises the welfare effects of a North American free trade area (including the effects of CUSFTA) from 4.9 to 6.8 percent of GNP for Canada, 2.3 to 3.3 for Mexico, and 1.7 to 2.6 for the United States. Increased competition resulting from trade liberalization will force firms in industries with previously limited competition to reduce their price-cost margins and increase the efficiency of their scale of operation. The magnitude of estimated gains from increased competition is variable, however, because the models differ from one another in their depiction of firm behavior. In models that have more than one firm in each industry, scale economies are realized, even in sectors in which total output declines as a result of NAFTA. By contrast, in models that have only one firm in each sector, previously protected industries will experience a decline in output and a loss of scale economies.

Another key distinction among the studies is the extent to which they incorporate the impact of foreign investment. Accounting for these flows yields much larger effects on output and income. For Mexico, capital inflows equal to 10 percent of the domestic capital stock raise welfare by about 5 percent, although assumptions about how the investment is financed can make a considerable difference.

The conventional general equilibrium models assume balanced trade and are therefore unable to provide evidence on the implications of NAFTA on the trade balance, exchange rates, and capital formation. They also ignore the potential role of trade in permanently stimulating economic growth rates (as compared with one-time gains). Brown describes a more dynamic model by Young and Romero that simulates the benefits of NAFTA as (1) the removal of import tariffs on capital goods and (2) lower interest rates resulting from reduced uncertainty about the economy, both of which stimulate capital formation. Models that capture these dynamic effects and allow for their effects on productivity growth produce much larger welfare effects in the range of 10 percent of Mexican GNP. As Brown notes, these models clearly indicate that the pursuit of an agreement will indeed be worth the effort, particularly from Mexico's stand-point.

The empirical work has been useful in illustrating potential effects of NAFTA that may be quite different from what a simple application of international trade theory might suggest. In particular, standard trade theory, based on the Stopler-Samuelson theorem, concludes that removing tariffs will tend to hurt the factor of production used relatively intensively in the import-competing sector. NAFTA would be expected, therefore, to lower real wages in the United States and to lower the return to capital in Mexico. But the Stolper-Samuelson result ignores the impact of terms-of-trade effects with respect to third countries, assumes full employment of resources with flexible real wages, and ignores the possibility of scale economies. Because the models reported by Brown do not make these assumptions, they sometimes conclude that NAFTA will result in higher real wages in the United States and higher returns to capital in Mexico.

Brown emphasizes that much work remains to be done. She believes that future studies should expand the treatment of saving and investment responses, provide more analysis of the impact on the distribution of gains among different segments of the population, include macroeconomic effects such as changes in the exchange rate and interest rates, and examine the behavior of multinational corporations.

In his discussion of Brown's paper, Robert Z. Lawrence suggests that CGE modeling misses several important features of the NAFTA process. In particular, Lawrence emphasizes that the CGE models depict NAFTA simply as the removal of tariffs and quotas. This method ignores the potentially significant impacts of considerations such as policy credibility, legal regimes, and the increased harmonization of institutional practices. In addition, the models direct little attention to the potentially protectionist effect of rules of origin and changes in the administration of trade and investment rules.

In his comments, Timothy J. Kehoe observes that investment flows have generated a sharp increase in Mexican investment, GDP, and trade deficits. Policymakers have become concerned about the sustainability of this behavior, an issue that is not addressed by the CGE models. Kehoe also stresses that CGE remained at an early stage of development. He emphasizes the need for ex-post verification to achieve validation of these models. Kehoe also argues for more work on the impact of NAFTA on the behavior of financial intermediaries, policy credibility, demographic structures, and total factor productivity growth.

Lawrence, Kehoe, and other participants in the general discussion argued that because the CGE models focus only on long-term effects, they miss much of the dynamic adjustment in exchange rates, and trade and capital flows that affect the policy environment. For example, many of the studies asserted that an increase in capital inflows to Mexico will worsen the U.S. trade balance with Mexico. This is true in the long run, because the capital will ultimately generate large payments of interest and dividends to foreigners that Mexico must finance by earning a surplus on merchandise trade. But over the next several decades exactly the reverse situation should be anticipated. The inflow of capital into Mexico will finance the purchase of imports in excess of its own export earnings.

The issue of capital inflows into Mexico is crucial because of the potential to finance an accelerated growth of the domestic economy. Faster growth in Mexico will greatly stimulate the demand for imported goods, with a consequent increase in the magnitude of the effect of the agreement on trade flows between Mexico and the United States. Moreover, contrary to common practice, the gains from trade should not be measured by who exports more. The gains from freer trade will materialize as gains in productivity and real incomes, which result from a more efficient allocation of resources.

NAFTA and Labor Markets

Raúl Hinojosa-Ojeda and Sherman Robinson focus on the potential effects of NAFTA on wages and employment in Mexico and the United States. They provide a summary of results obtained in the studies that have addressed this question. The authors classify the modeling exercises into three kinds: partial equilibrium models based on historical extrapolation or regression analysis, single-country CGE model, and multicountry CGEs. The authors favor the methodology of the CGE models because they are better able to capture the effects of shifts in the sectoral structure of trade, output, and employment.

Standard trade theory predicts that liberalizing trade between the United States and Mexico should accelerate wage convergence, with the wages of unskilled workers rising in Mexico and falling in the United States. This is the issue that has caused the greatest concern in the United States. Hinojosa and Robinson find, however, that nearly all the studies predict the amount of wage convergence induced by NAFTA will be small, and in some cases the wages of unskilled workers may rise in both Mexico and the United States. In the models that allow for imperfect competition and economies of scale, increased ouput in U.S. industries may raise the wage rate of all workers, skilled and unskilled.

With two exceptions, the studies conclude that NAFTA will have a very small effect on U.S. wage structure. The first exception results from the case in which trade liberalization is accompanied by expanded migration to the United States. The removal of restrictions on trade in grains, for example, would induce a large migration of workers within Mexico from rural to urban areas, with a subsequent rise in migration to the United States. International movements of workers have a direct effect on wages that is much greater than the indirect effect operating through a liberalization of trade in the products that they produce. Thus a full trade liberalization in agricultural goods could raise Mexico-U.S. migration by 600,000 and lower the wages of unskilled workers in the United States by 3–4 percent. The second exception is a study by Edward Leamer, who argues that trade liberalization will cause a greater equalization of wage rates between the United States and Mexico than is obtained from the CGE models. The result is a much larger estimated decline in the wages of unskilled U.S. workers. Leamer's model is highly stylized, however, and it contains an implicit assumption that Mexico is comparable in size to the United States.

Hinojosa and Robinson end with a word of caution. Although CGE models suggest the long-term direction of change, they tend to understate the adjustment costs. Policymakers should therefore consider ancillary actions to facilitate adjustment and to provide means of compensating those who are displaced during the process. The authors discuss the proposal of creating a North American Development Bank and Adjustment Fund. Such a fund would focus on investments in the physical and social infrastructure as a way to facilitate integration. They argue that similar institutions were created in Europe when Greece, Spain, and Portugal were incorporated into the European Community.

In the discussion, Anne O. Krueger suggests that greater effort should be made to measure the extent of the wage gap between Mexico and the United States, after adjustment for differences in skills and productivity. The actual gap may be lower than that feared by U.S. labor and hoped for by Mexican policymakers. She also believes that NAFTA coupled with a failed Uruguay Round would produce different outcomes from NAFTA as a GATT- plus agreement. Empirical analysis, therefore, should address this issue. Finally, Krueger fears that anti-inflationary policies during the last three years in Mexico may have produced real wages in Mexico that are "too high" in dollar terms. She argues that the analysis

should place greater emphasis on the implications of macroeconomic stabilization policies as they affect nominal wages and exchange rates. That
is, fiscal and monetary variables should be included in the models. These
actions will have large effects on trade flows and, thus, on the agreement.

Michael Piore argues that the analysis of the impact of NAFTA on
migration patterns should consider which regions within Mexico would
be affected by a liberalized trade in agriculture. If the regions most affected
by labor displacement are those where there are established patterns of
migration to the United States, it will be difficult to prevent an increase
in the flow. Piore also mentions that the reform of the *ejido* system of
land ownership may have more effect on agriculture and migration than
on NAFTA.

Furthermore, using the results of a research project on the clothing
industry in Mexico City, Piore argues that the apparent cost advantage
enjoyed by Mexican manufacturing could be easily overwhelmed by the
inability to compete on the basis of quality or design. He suggests that
the actual outcomes will be less dependent on differences in labor costs
than suggested by the CGE models. Mexican firms will need time to
accumulate the business skills required to compete in an open trade regime.

NAFTA and Industry

In his review of the more specific industry effects of NAFTA, Sidney
Weintraub agrees with the conclusion of the CGE models that the direct
effects will be small, but that all three countries will experience gains in
output, employment, and wages. Mexico will gain the most, and Canada
will be the least affected. The benefits to the United States will be small
in percentage terms simply because trade with Mexico will continue to
be a small share of U.S. output. The largest increases in Mexican exports
will be in apparel products, leather, glass, and electrical machinery. Because of an increase in intra-industry trade, U.S. exports will also increase
in many of the same industries. The net gains to the United States will
be in industries such as chemicals, capital equipment, metals, and rubber
and plastic products. From the U.S. perspective the clear losers will be
the apparel and furniture industries, whereas Mexico will experience significant output and employment losses in the machinery industry.

Weintraub emphasizes, however, that the specific industry effects of
the agreement will depend on the details of the agreement in several key
industries where all three governments impose significant restrictions on

trade. This is particularly true in the automobile industry, because while Mexico is likely to obtain relatively open access to the U.S. markets, paralleling that of Canada, Mexico maintains stringent limitations on imports through local legislation and a requirement of an export offset to any imports. Rules of origin will have important implications for trade diversion of automotive imports from Europe and Asia. Mexican treatment of foreign investment is also a key question for the effects on the energy sector.

The agreement will have less implication than is often claimed for shifting labor-intensive production processes to Mexico, because the existing *maquiladora* program already permits such reallocations. Duties on apparel imports from Mexico currently average 6 percent (inclusive of the *maquiladora*), whereas Mexico's duties average 12 to 18 percent for textiles and 20 percent for apparel. Again, rules of origin will be important because of the potential to use Mexico as a backdoor way to avoid restrictions on Asian suppliers.

Furthermore, there is greater consensus among the studies in identifying the gains to Mexico than in determining the direct benefits to the United States. Weintraub points out that the conclusions of the studies are influenced by the authors' general views of international trade. Most economists strongly believe freer trade increases the welfare of the nations that participate in a regional arrangement. Thus a conclusion that the expansion of free trade principles in North America will improve overall welfare is not surprising. Concern arises only for the features of the agreement, which may result in a diversion of trade rather than an overall expansion. On the other hand, a few studies begin from the premise that more trade is not desirable and that one nation's gain may be another's loss. Those studies conclude that the United States will lose from the agreement because Mexico gains.

Finally, in comparing their results, Weintraub expresses a preference for those studies that attempt to quantify outcomes, as opposed to those that make qualitative judgments, in evaluating the impact of the agreement. The qualitative evaluations are useful, however, in providing the institutional details often overlooked in the CGE models.

In the discussion, Robert W. Crandall argues that too much emphasis has been put on industries in which Mexico might gain trade share, such as apparel, at the cost of analysis of industries, such as machinery and electronics, in which Mexico has traditionally maintained high tariffs and will import more with the agreement. He also believes that the effects of NAFTA are likely to be much smaller than those induced by the domestic economic restructuring and liberalization programs that have been initiated within Mexico. As a specific example, he argues that trade liberalization alone is unlikely to result in increased imports of steel into the U.S. market. Extensive government involvement in the Mexican steel industry has left it in an inefficient condition, with Mexico unable to fill its current quota in recent years.

Jaime Ros emphasizes a recurring conference theme that the studies placed too little emphasis on the dynamic interaction between trade, investment, and productivity growth. A liberalization of trade is expected to lead to a sharp expansion of investment and ultimately improved productivity and real wages. He expresses disappointment at the lack of evidence to date of such synergies operating in Mexico. Also, none of the studies were able to deal satisfactorily with the issue of how much additional direct investment into Mexico might result from NAFTA, even though all the authors agreed on its critical importance for judging the effects of the agreement.

NAFTA and Agriculture

Agriculture is one of the most complex issues raised in the negotiations for NAFTA. All three governments are heavily involved in their agricultural markets, and the issue has been a major sticking point in the Uruguay Round of the GATT negotiations. Until the question of NAFTA arose, comparisons of the competitive relationship of U.S. and Mexican agriculture had not been the subject of large research efforts. Furthermore, Mexico is now engaged in extensive agricultural reform. This effort, driven in part by Mexico's decision to join the GATT, incorporates reductions in tariffs and other import controls, revisions to the constitutional provisions governing land ownership, and a sharp reduction in the government's involvement in the internal market for agricultural products. Hence it is difficult to isolate the effects of NAFTA from all the other changes.

Tim Josling points out in his paper that the implications of the internal reforms in Mexico are likely to be more important for agriculture than the incremental effects of NAFTA. Similarly, for the United States the NAFTA negotiations are complicated by a parallel GATT negotiation. Until the GATT negotiations are complete, the NAFTA negotiations in agriculture will be limited largely to reductions in tariffs, leaving the quantitatively more important issues of nontariff barriers untouched.

NAFTA has stimulated four important quantitative assessments of changes in agricultural policy and six more qualitative reviews. They generally agree that the main effects would be concentrated in grains, particularly corn, where the United States has a comparative advantage, and fruit and vegetable production in northern Mexico. Health and environmental regulations, however, would have an important effect on the quantitative magnitude of the trade. Overall, there would be a net welfare gain to both the United States and Mexico; but the distribution of those gains would differ. U.S. grain producers would gain from higher exports, but consumers would face higher prices as some of the supply is exported. The opposite would be true in Mexico—producers would lose and consumers would gain. Agriculture is a case in which the net gains to the United States exceed the benefits to Mexico.

The results reinforce the conclusions from the review of labor market effects that the maize sector stands out in its potential for large displacement of Mexican farmers, with a consequent acceleration of migration to the cities. An excessively rapid pace of liberalization in that sector could cause significant economic and social disruption.

In his comment Darryl McLeod argues against a "go slow" strategy on the grounds that many of the adjustment problems were manageable, particularly if the agreement moved the three countries toward a more common structure of their agricultural policies. If Mexico substituted deficiency income payments to corn producers, as is done in the United States, for the current price support system, the price of maize could fall to U.S. levels, but with a relatively small drop in Mexican corn production. Through a gradual phaseout of the deficiency payments, Mexico could moderate the transition costs for maize producers. With fruits and vegetables there is a risk that U.S. demands for a very long transition period would delay investment in rural areas of Mexico where the problems of poverty are most severe. An export-oriented agricultural policy could attract foreign capital to some of the most needy areas of Mexico.

NAFTA and Nontrade Issues

Although the NAFTA negotiations are centered on issues of trade and investment, Robert Pastor observes that the agreement represents a political acknowledgment of a wider process of integration taking place between the United States and Mexico. It is therefore not surprising that discussion has focused on many noneconomic issues. In particular, Pastor notes that, responding to domestic pressures, the U.S. Congress has raised concerns about the environment, the social agenda, and democracy and human rights. These concerns have resonated with domestic political groups in Mexico; in both countries the NAFTA negotiations have provided interest groups with an opportunity to press their own agendas.

Although some environmentalists claim that economic growth inevitably damages the environment, Pastor quotes a study by Krueger and Grossman that finds that once per capita income reaches a threshold of about $5,000, an inverse relationship occurs between the level of pollution and income—richer countries can afford to spend more on the environment. Because the average level of income in Mexico is close to this threshold, NAFTA, through augmenting income growth, could actually lead to improved environmental conditions. Indeed, Pastor notes that recently Mexican environmental regulations have been tightened and enforcement actions increased. He cites, in particular, Mexican decisions to close a large petroleum refinery and to postpone development of a dam because of its effect on the rain forest. He does caution, however, that it is difficult to determine whether these actions have been taken for public relations purposes, or if they reflect a permanent change in policy.

Pastor is also skeptical of the claim that companies will move to Mexico because of lax environmental enforcement and, in particular, low pollution-abatement costs. He quotes calculations that indicate that the costs of complying with environmental regulations are small compared with those related to other determinants of location.

Some of the environmental concerns relate specifically to pollution along the U.S.-Mexican border. This has resulted from the rapid expansion of the *maquiladora*, the growth of which is driven by the current structure of tariff preferences. Pastor points out that NAFTA will actually reduce the tariff-related locational advantage of the *maquilas* and thus reduce the pressure on resources along the border. He argues that investment will move further into the interior of Mexico because it will be directed more toward the domestic market and because *maquila* labor tends to be transient and more expensive than workers in the interior. Pastor notes that Mexico and the United States have developed a coordinated program to deal with some of the problems in the border areas.

A second area of concern involves social issues, such as labor standards, occupational safety, and health standards. American labor organizations, in particular, are concerned that lax labor standards in Mexico will divert investment to Mexico. Pastor argues however, that it is not differences in social, labor, and environmental policies but in capabilities to implement them that cause problems on these issues. Mexico actually has extensive social legislation that reflects the close relationship between the ruling Institutional Revolutionary Party (PRI), and the Confederation of Mexican Workers. In principle, workers in Mexico enjoy more comprehensive legal protection than do their American counterparts. Unlike the Mexican and Canadian governments, for example, the U.S. government does not require paid vacations or maternity leave, and the United States alone permits businesses to hire nonunion replacement workers during a strike. The problem is that Mexico's rules are not enforced everywhere, particularly within its large "informal" sector.

The third area Pastor considers is human rights and democracy. President Salinas has emphasized that NAFTA is strictly an economic agreement (unlike the EC). Nonetheless, questions have been raised about the electoral process and other human rights abuses in Mexico. Although electoral irregularities continue to exist, opposition parties have been able to achieve victories in local elections. Also, a National Human Rights Commission has become active. Nonetheless, Pastor argues, there remains considerable range for improvements.

In the conference discussion, Gustavo Vega maintains that the extent of integration under NAFTA should be distinguished from that in the EC. For political reasons, NAFTA is likely to remain confined to trade issues rather than developing in the direction of the European Community, which has a broader political and social agenda. In particular, Vega stresses that in Mexico (and the rest of Latin America) strong concerns about national sovereignty and U.S. neo-imperialism limit the attractiveness of further political engagement. He also notes that in the EC, poorer countries were given more time to adjust to Community norms and received fiscal transfers to help defray the costs of adopting more stringent standards.

Patrick Low argues that while protectionists might use environmental concerns as an argument against NAFTA, their arguments are not particularly compelling. Not only do pollution-abatement expenditures account for a relatively small share of overall costs, but multinationals were unlikely to seek a pollution haven because of fears of future liability, scandals, and loss of goodwill. He emphasizes that firms will usually invest in clean, state-of-the art technology in Mexico simply because it is more costly to unbundle the pollution-reducing features. Low also argues that fears of a process of competitive regulation in which U.S. pollution regulations moved toward Mexico's are misplaced. Instead, Mexico is tightening its standards in the direction of those in the United States. Furthermore, the effort to improve environmental standards in Mexico will proceed at a more rapid pace with a NAFTA than without one.

Implications for the Rest of the World

In his paper Carlos Alberto Primo Braga argues that NAFTA is likely to be an "expanded" free trade agreement. That is, it will go beyond the conventional reduction of tariffs and (explicit) nontariff barriers (NTBs) and deal with the issue of market access in a broader sense. An array of domestic policies, such as local content requirements, government procurement practices, and divergences between regulatory and legal systems (competition policies, intellectual property rights, dispute settlement mechanisms, foreign investment laws, and the like) are also subjects of the negotiation. The broadness of NAFTA is not surprising given CUSFTA as precedent and the current agenda of the Uruguay Round.

In theory, the agreement could have a negative effect on the rest of the world as a result of the diversion of trade and investment away from countries that are excluded from NAFTA. The negative impact would be exacerbated if the agreement results in higher levels of protection against outsiders (that is, a "managed" NAFTA), giving rise to trade suppression. On the other hand, the agreement could have a positive effect if it leads to an acceleration of growth within the member countries, expanding their imports with other countries.

According to Primo Braga, the available studies differ in their conclusions about a net positive or negative effect for third countries, and their findings are very dependent on the specific methodology and assumptions they use. Nonetheless, they do agree that the overall effect, regardless of sign, will be small.

Though the aggregate impact of NAFTA on the rest of the world (ROW) may be small, the impact on specific sectors may be important, particularly if NAFTA becomes a managed-trade initiative. If the rules of origin discriminate against companies that rely on outsourcing or penalize firms controlled by capital from non-NAFTA countries, and if the phaseout of domestic content requirements is applied in a discriminatory fashion between established firms and newcomers, trade diversion could be significant. Primo Braga cites the sugar industry as an example and argues that if Mexico and the United States administer a joint quota system vis-à-vis the ROW, other net exporters will face significant losses. He also examines what a managed-trade NAFTA may imply for the textile, steel, and automobile industries.

As to the impact on the rest of Latin America, Primo Braga finds that available studies show that NAFTA will not lead to a significant diversion of their trade. He also notes the fact that, except for those countries that may see their existing preferences eroded (such as the U.S.–Caribbean Basin Initiative), the region has reacted favorably to the negotiation of NAFTA. This reflects their hope that NAFTA will be a building block for a broader Western Hemisphere Free Trade Agreement (WHFTA). However, Primo Braga does not believe the direct economic benefits of a hemispheric free trade agreement would be significant. Nonetheless, he acknowledges there may be other gains, such as "credibility enhancement," that are not captured by the quantitative exercises.

Primo Braga also argues that the implications of the NAFTA talks for the final outcome of the Uruguay Round are limited. In contrast, a successful completion of the Uruguay Round negotiations may ease the ratification of NAFTA in the United States, while a stalemate at the multilateral level could bolster the opposition. Regardless of the relationship between NAFTA and the Uruguay Round, the future of the multilateral system could be positively or negatively influenced by NAFTA, depending on whether the agreement becomes a building block toward freer global trade or not. If NAFTA becomes managed trilateral trade, its influence on the future of the multilateral system will be negative.

Finally, Primo Braga argues that NAFTA might contribute positively to the ongoing outward-oriented reforms in Latin America; in particular, it supports the free-trade orientation of current subregional arrangements of economic integration within Latin America. He perceives the successful completion of NAFTA as a necessary condition for the development of the trade component of the Enterprise for the Americas Initiative and any future Western Hemisphere free trade area.

Susan M. Collins, in her discussion, mentions three areas that deserve further analysis. First, more needs to be known about the implications of NAFTA for trade negotiations between the United States and other Western Hemisphere developing countries (WHD). NAFTA may result in a situation that is less favorable than if the negotiations had taken place simultaneously with the rest of WHD. Second, if international capital markets are characterized by inefficiencies and information problems, NAFTA could cause a significant problem of "investment diversion" for other countries in Latin America. Third, too little attention has been directed to the potential for effects on the service sector rates of other countries. For example, would the reorientation of business activities of Canadians and Americans be reflected in a diversion of tourism, which is a major source of foreign exchange for some countries in the Caribbean? If so, the impact would reflect a decline in their exchange rates and a terms-of-trade loss.

Jeffrey J. Schott agrees with Primo Braga that NAFTA will not cause substantial trade diversion, since existing trade barriers to the market are low. He also argues that NAFTA is likely to have a limited trade diversion effect if there is a successful Uruguay Round, because of the liberalization that would occur in textiles, automobiles, and agriculture, sectors for which the potential for trade diversion would otherwise be high. Schott believes the area of most concern should be the rules of origin, which are often used to appease sectoral interests by crafting special and more restrictive origin rules for specific industries that mask increased protection against third-country competition. This, Schott claims, has already happened in the agreement reached for textiles and apparel within NAFTA.

Panel Discussion

Carlos Bazdresch Parada begins his remarks by addressing the apparent contradiction between the minimal expected economic impact of NAFTA predicted by the modeling exercises and the intensity of the political reaction that has surrounded it. He wonders whether the expectations that preceded research about the impact of NAFTA were wrong, or did the modeling exercises fail to capture some of its more important consequences. A third possibility is that the political fuss that surrounds the prospect of NAFTA, particularly in the United States, reflects the fact that the economic issues embodied in NAFTA are only part of a process of deeper and wider integration between Mexico and the United States.

Joining others in the conference, Bazdresch Parada emphasizes the potential impact of NAFTA on cross-border movements of capital and labor and suggests that future research should concentrate more on those issues. In addition, further research is needed to analyze the short-term transitional problems.

Bazdresch also warns against a focus on managed trade in the final form of NAFTA. His concern is directed not so much toward the negative impact of such policies on trade with the rest of the world, but with the fact that the expected benefits to Mexico of more competitive domestic markets would be diluted if NAFTA allowed managed-trade arrangements. More also needs to be known about the strategic reactions of multinational corporations with headquarters outside the NAFTA countries.

Finally, Bazdresch feels it was encouraging to see the impact that the prospect of signing NAFTA had on such nontrade issues as environmental and labor concerns. In this way, Bazdresch joins others in noting that even if these issues were not included within the formal agenda with the same weight as the trade-related issues, they have acquired greater prominence than before NAFTA talks began. For Bazdresch, this shows that NAFTA is part of a much wider integration process and that the nontrade issues will come increasingly to the forefront.

In her comments, Sylvia Ostry contrasts NAFTA with regional integration in Europe and Asia. In Europe, she stresses, the central goal has been political integration. Trade liberalization begun under the Treaty of Rome was and has been followed by additional unifying measures, including actions that aim at microeconomic convergence through the standardization of regulations, and more recently the Maastricht agreement, which aims at macroconvergence and monetary union. The European Community has also attempted to develop a common environmental policy through the European Environmental Community. Ostry also stresses that the European countries share a common ideology: Europe should be run as a "social market economy."

Asian integration, by contrast, has been led by economic developments; institutional linkages and political integration remain undeveloped. Indeed, political factors divide rather than unite Asian nations. A distinctive feature of Asian integration has been the adoption by Japanese companies of an integrated intra-Asian strategy. Their Asian investments are designed to serve not only domestic markets but also export markets, supplying finished goods to North America and semifinished goods to Japan.

In North America economic integration through investment and trade has preceded the institutional arrangements that were a feature of European integration. The development of institutional arrangements has progressed further than in Asia. Unlike their Japanese counterparts in Asia, however, American firms have typically been content to set up branches in Mexico and Canada, and they have not implemented fully integrated strategies to serve the North American market.

Ostry contends that the two main problems in NAFTA relate to environmental and labor questions. She stresses the need for an institutional mechanism to deal with environmental issues. "Unless some reasonably robust international mechanism is included in the agreement and adequate financial provisions made for environmental problems, the future viability of NAFTA will remain in doubt." She also argues that pressures from migration will create continuing demands for harmonization of labor standards and even wages.

Ostry is skeptical, however, that NAFTA will follow the European path of multidimensional integration, because of a fear of U.S. political dominance by the other nations, the absence of a consensus about the economic paradigm, and the greater income disparity. She foresees, instead, intensified economic integration led by investment and continuing labor flows, with further refinement of institutional mechanisms focused on trade remedies, rules of origin, local content, and the environment, as well as, perhaps, labor standards. She is concerned, however, that the narrow focus of NAFTA on trade issues may not be conducive to progress in this evolutionary direction.

Notes

1. For a description of these reforms see Nora Lustig, *Mexico: The Remaking of an Economy* (Brookings, forthcoming).

2. Peat Marwick Policy Economics Group, "The Effects of a Free Trade Agreement between the United States and Mexico," Washington, 1991, pp. 48–50.

3. Lustig, *Mexico*, table 5-6.

4. The precise causes of the changed distribution of wages are complex and subject to strong debate. An overview of the research is provided in John Bound and George Johnson, "Changes in the Structure of Wages in the 1980s: An Evaluation of Alternative Explanations," *American Economic Review*, vol. 82 (June 1992), pp. 371–92. The authors conclude that technological changes, not trade, are primarily responsible for the widening gaps.

5. Lustig, *Mexico*, table 2-4.

6. There is a significant difference in the level of trade reported by the statistics of the two countries. Mexico excludes the trade flows that take place under the *maquiladora* program from its merchandise trade statistics, including the net revenue elsewhere in the current account.

7. *Maquiladora*, or in-bond firms, is the name given to firms that are allowed to import materials duty-free into Mexico for processing, provided that the output is exported. The United States or any other importing country applies a duty only to the Mexican value-added portion of the goods when they are exported back to the United States.

8. International Monetary Fund, *Balance of Payments Statistics Yearbook*, vol. 42 (Washington, 1992).

9. On a somewhat different accounting basis than that used in the balance of payments, new direct investment has grown from about $2.4 billion in 1986 to $3.7 billion annually in 1990–91. See Secretaria de Comercio y Fomento Industrial,

"Evolución de la Inversión Extranjera Directa en 1991," Mexico City, January 1992.

10. Lustig, *Mexico*, chap. 1.
11. Lustig, *Mexico*, chap. 2.
12. Lustig, *Mexico*, chap. 5.
13. Lustig, *Mexico*, chap. 4.

The Impact of a North American Free Trade Area: Applied General Equilibrium Models

Drusilla K. Brown

NORTH American economic integration is widely viewed as a step toward freer markets. Both Canada and Mexico were motivated to enter into negotiations with the United States by a desire to reap the benefits of specialization and exchange, the procompetitive effects of international trade, and technology transfer. Indeed, for Mexico, North American integration is only a small piece of a much grander plan designed to realize all the economic opportunities the marketplace has to offer.

However, the practice of preferential trading, in which one country gives privileged market access to a select group of trade partners, is regarded as something of an economic oddity. Preferential trading is second or third best compared with some alternative border policies.

Equally, a host of other issues are associated with the transfer of resources from one use to another during the transition to freer markets. Mexico, in particular, must consider the implications of liberalization for the alleviation of poverty, environmental degradation, the treatment of labor, relative factor prices, capital formation, and so on.

For these reasons, each proposed free trade area must be evaluated individually and empirically. The outcome of the analysis will depend on the precise nature of the current trade barriers and the trading relations of the negotiating countries with one another and with the rest of the world (ROW).

Therefore, it is desirable to evaluate quantitatively the likely effects of North American integration on wages, employment, welfare, and other important economic variables. Applied general equilibrium (AGE) modeling provides an excellent device for doing so. These are large-scale computer models that attempt to bring together the theoretical understanding of market behavior with key features of the specific economies involved.

In the last year, numerous studies of the economic effects of North American integration have been undertaken. Although these studies apparently played an important role in the public debate over the North American Free Trade Agreement (NAFTA), it is especially noteworthy that the research results reflect a wide array of conflicting conclusions. Now that the first round of modeling efforts on NAFTA is complete, this seems like an appropriate time to assess what has been learned and to ask what aspects of these models are in need of further clarification.

In this paper I first describe the basic features common to many of the AGE models; I then turn to the first generation of AGE models that are static in nature and have constant returns to scale (CRS) technology. Next I examine models that consider increasing returns to scale (IRS) technology and imperfect competition, after which I evaluate the dynamic models. Finally, I discuss some conclusions and directions for further research.

Background

All AGE models begin from basic general equilibrium international trade theory. The modeler must first explicitly specify the stock of primary factors of production, the nature of technology, and household preferences. Firms are taken to use these factors and supply output so as to maximize profits. The payments to factors are received by households, who then allocate income over goods in a utility-maximizing manner. Finally, the excess of domestic production of each good over domestic demand is exported to world markets where market-clearing prices are determined.

The modeler then performs counterfactual experiments in which one or more trade barriers are reduced. The modeler alters the trade barrier and then solves for the new equilibrium levels of all variables in the model to determine the economic impact of the policy change.

The models are made realistic in part by detailing a large number of industrial and service sectors. The tight restrictions on the number of factors and sectors found in theoretical models are not necessary in AGE models because there is no attempt to obtain an analytical solution. Rather, the modeler may specify any number of goods and factors as long as a numeric solution can still be achieved. In addition, the initial value of variables in the model, such as factor endowments, production, consumption, imports, exports, capital flows, trade barriers, and supply and demand elasticities, are set equal to the values reported in the current trade and GNP statistics.

The applied models deviate from their theoretical counterparts and from each other in several other important ways that prove to be central to the results obtained.

First, consider the specification of the production possibilities frontier (PPF). Most, though not all, models differentiate industry sales by destination—that is, goods sold to the domestic market are not identical to goods sold to the export market. In some cases, exports to different destinations are also differentiated.

For example, let Q be output by a typical Mexican industry. In a differentiated exports model, Q is composed of production for sale to the domestic market, DOM, and exports, X. X may itself be an aggregate of exports to the U.S. market, X_{US}, and exports to the ROW, X_{ROW}.

At both stages of aggregation, the modeler may decide simply to add up each of the components. A popular alternative, though, is to use a constant elasticity of transformation (CET) aggregation procedure—that is, the production possibilities curve between the exportable variety and the domestic variety within a sector is concave rather than linear.

The procedure above is used to determine aggregate industry (or firm) output, Q. The next step is to specify the technology for producing aggregate Q. Typically, production requires intermediate inputs (INT_1, INT_2, . . .) and value added. Value added, itself, is an aggregate of capital, labor and, in some cases, land. The production function for Q is usually either Leontief, Generalized Leontief (GL), the constant elasticity of substitution (CES), Cobb-Douglas, or the production function associated with a translog cost function. The value-added aggregation function is usually CES or, in some cases, Cobb-Douglas.

In most of the models, technology is CRS, though in some cases it is IRS. Scale effects are usually introduced by requiring each firm to undertake some fixed investment of capital and labor before production can begin, but then variable costs are proportional to output. Therefore, marginal cost is constant but average total cost slopes downward.

Second, consider the organization of factors markets. Firms in each sector maximize profits, thereby generating demands for factors of production and supplies of each output. Firms are almost always modeled as price-takers in the factors markets, so that factors are paid close to their marginal value product.

Various assumptions, though, are made concerning intersectoral and international factor flows. Many modelers adopt the conventional assumption that the aggregate supplies of capital and labor are set exogenously within each country and that capital and labor can flow freely between sectors in response to wage differentials. The factor prices are flexible so that both factors are always fully employed.

However, a popular alternative is to fix the real wage and allow aggregate employment to vary, thus giving the model a Keynesian flavor. A final possible configuration is to make the labor supply fixed but allow physical capital to flow freely from the rest of the world at an exogenously set world rental rate.

Third, in specifying final and intermediate demand many modelers adopt the Armington structure in which consumers differentiate goods by place of production.[1] Hence, as with the production side, the demand structure is nested. Consumers first allocate expenditure across goods without regard to the place of production. The utility function at this stage is usually Cobb-Douglas, though increasingly the almost ideal demand system (AIDS) is used and some models adopt the linear expenditure system.[2] Consumers then allocate expenditure on each good across the competing national suppliers. Typically, the aggregator at this level is a CES function, though, again, AIDS has been used.

Product differentiation of some sort is a common feature of many AGE models. The first generation of modelers originally incorporated the Armington structure to accommodate cross-hauling, a prevalent characteristic of the trade data.

However, since those early models, modelers have found that product differentiation on both the import and the export sides tends to dampen the response of the domestic price system to fluctuations to the landed price of foreign goods. This point can be understood by comparing the mechanics of price determination in the models of differentiated products with those of homogeneous products.

Equilibrium prices for traded goods are usually determined in world markets, where demand for each variety of a good must equal supply. The number of prices for each industry in each country depends on the extent to which product differentiation is imposed. In the most parsimonious models, products are treated as homogeneous across all suppliers, so there will be only one price per industry worldwide, implying that the domestic price system moves in tandem with prices determined on world markets.

At the other end of the spectrum, firms differentiate between domestic sales and exports and between exports to the United States and the ROW, and consumers differentiate between domestic goods and imports from each national source. In this case each industry in each country will have three different prices: one domestic market price and two export prices. In a three-country model, there will be nine prices for goods in each industry. Thus, fluctuations in export and import prices will be imperfectly transmitted to domestic consumer prices.

Fourth, none of the models faithfully incorporate all the countries of the world. The easiest models to construct are those that detail the production and demand structure of only one country, usually Mexico or Canada. The most extensive models include a detailed structure of Mexico, Canada, the United States, and other important trade partners. Countries that are not modeled explicitly are usually captured with ad hoc export supply and import demand functions that depend only on relative prices. In some cases, the small North American assumption is made such that prices of goods offered or purchased by the ROW are fixed exogenously.

Fifth, as with the conventional trade models, the static models can be closed by imposing the condition that household expenditure equals after-tax payments to factors. In this case, Walras' Law will also require that the current account balance remain at the base level. However, the more sophisticated models attempt to endogenize savings, investment, international transfers, and government behavior. Such models could exhibit changes in the trade balance.

Finally, models also differ in their choice of a numeraire good. Normally only one is required. However, some modelers find it easier to interpret results if the domestic price level in each country is held at the base level. Introducing a numeraire for each country will also require the specification of an exchange rate. It should be kept in mind, though, that such exchange rates do not necessarily play a role in determining the real outcome of the model. For the exchange rate to affect the real outcome, some price in the model must be set exogenously.

Static Models with CRS Technology and Perfectly Competitive Goods Markets

First-generation AGE models applied to the study of international trade policy were static in nature and characterized by constant-returns-to-scale technology and perfect competition. This section reviews the results of five studies, though in several cases, the basic model has been subsequently elaborated upon by the authors in order to improve the analysis of particular sectors of the economy. Characteristics of the models specific to each study are detailed in table 1.

Perhaps the most conventional of the five is the U.S. model developed by Roy Boyd, Kerry Krutilla, and Joseph McKinney.[3] Production and demand follow the structure as laid out in the previous section, and capital and labor are taken to be freely mobile between sectors but not between countries. The special characteristic of this model is the detail in the utility function. The income distribution is divided into six strata, giving rise to six different household types. In addition, both the labor-leisure and utility-maximizing savings choices are modeled. Finally, this is the only model in its class that takes supply from and demand by the ROW to be less than perfectly elastic.

The model of David Roland-Holst, Kenneth Reinert, and Clinton Shiells bears a close resemblance to that of Boyd and others,[4] though without the detail on the demand side. There are two important distinctions between the two models, however. First, Roland-Holst and others retain the assumption that labor is intersectorally mobile but impose the condition that the real wage paid to labor is exogenous. Second, the Mexican and Canadian economies are modeled explicitly, but ROW import demand and export supply are perfectly elastic.

The KPMG Peat Marwick model shares the rigid real Mexican wage assumption with Roland-Holst and others, but adds considerably more detail to savings and investment behavior.[5] Investment demand includes both real capital formation and the holding of inventories. In addition, debt repayment, labor remittances, and profit repatriation are included. The international payments and investment features make the model suitable for considering the effect of international capital flows. A second special feature of the Peat Marwick study is the choice of the production function. The upper stage is Generalized Leontief, a specification that allows factors of production to be both substitutes and complements.

Raúl Hinojosa-Ojeda and Sherman Robinson have tailored their model to address questions concerning the effects of liberalization on different classes of labor.[6] The labor force is classified into four separate groups: rural, urban unskilled, skilled, and white collar. Urban-rural migration is permitted in Mexico within the rural and urban unskilled groups so as to maintain a prespecified wage differential. Similarly, U.S.-Mexican migration holds the base period ratio of real wages constant in these two labor categories in the two countries, as measured in a common currency. Hinojosa and Robinson have also used the AIDS aggregation function, rather than a CES function, to disaggregate demand by place of production. The authors hope that the choice of a more flexible functional form will relax some of the restrictions imposed by the CES specification.

Of the five models discussed in this section, the work by Irene Trela and John Whalley is the most distinctive.[7] Their model is designed specifically to analyze the effects of removing bilateral quota restrictions between the United States and Mexico on textiles, apparel, and steel. The model is special in two respects. First, the Armington assumption is not

Table 1. Static Models with Constant Returns to Scale Technology

Item	KPMG Peat Marwick	Hinojosa and Robinson	Roland-Holst, Reinert, and Shiells I	Trela and Whalley	Boyd, Krutilla, and McKinney
Countries	Mexico, U.S.	Mexico, U.S.	Mexico, Canada, U.S.	U.S., Canada, Mexico, other exporters	U.S.
Sectors	44	7	26	I: 4 textiles, 1 other; II: steel, 2 others	12
Base year	1988	1988	1988	1986	1984
Demand					
Government	Deficit exogenous	Exogenous	...	...	Cobb-Douglas utility
Investment	Inventory prop. to output; net investment prop. to capital stock	Exogenous	...	...	Equal to savings
Intermediate	From profit maximization	From profit maximization	From profit maximization	...	...
Final				*Textiles (steel)*	
Level 1	AIDS	Cobb-Douglas	LES	Textiles (steel)/other—CES	6 HH types
Level 2	Dom/imp—CES[a]	Dom/imp by source—AIDS[b]	Dom/imp by source—CES[b]	Composite textile group—CES	Goods/leisure—CES
Level 3	Imp: diff. by partner—CES[c]	...	...	Each textile: VER/non-VER—CES	Good:Dom/imp by source—CES[b]
Supply				*Textiles (steel)*	
Level 1	Dom/exp—CET[d]	Dom/exp—CET[d]	Dom/exp.—CET[d]	Textiles (steel)/other—CES	...

	U.S. MFRs[e]	U.S. non-MFRs/MEX all				
Level 2	Exp. diff. by partner—CET[c]	...	...	...	Composite textile group—CES	...
Level 3	...	...	...	...	Each textile group: VER/non-VER—CES	...
Technology	U.S. MFRs[e]	U.S. non-MFRs/MEX all				
Level 1	K/L/mat./energy—GL[f]	VA/intermed.—Leont.[g]	VA/intermed.—Leont.[g]	VA/intermed.—Leont.—	VA/intermed.—CES[g]	VA/intermed.—CES[g]
Level 2	Materials: Leont.; Energy prod.: Leont.; CRS	VA: K/L—Cobb-Doug.[h]	VA: K/L—CES;[b] CRS	I: CRS	VA: K/L—CES;[h] CRS	VA: L/K—CES;[h] K: physical K/land—CES; CRS
Labor market	MEX: rigid real wage; U.S.: full employment		Rural and urban unskilled: international mobility in response to U.S.-MEX wage difference; skilled, white collar: intersectoral mobility to preserve wage difference	Rigid wage	Intersectoral mobility in response to wage difference—adjustment cost	Intersectoral mobility
Capital market	MEX: full employment; U.S.: full employment		Intersectoral mobility to preserve base period rent difference	Full employment	Intersectoral mobility	Intersectoral mobility
Land market	None		Rural: sector specific	...	Intersectoral mobility	...
Goods markets	Perfect competition; ROW prices exogenous	Perfect competition; ROW prices exogenous	Perfect competition; ROW prices exogenous	I: Perfect competition; ROW prices exogeneous	Perfect competition	Perfect competition; MEX/ROW elastic supply/demand

Table 1 (*continued*)

Item	KPMG Peat Marwick	Hinojosa and Robinson	Roland-Holst, Reinert, and Shiells I	Trela and Whalley	Boyd, Krutilla, and McKinney
Trade policy	Tariffs, quota ad valorem equivalent	Tariffs, NTB ad valorem equivalent	Tariffs, NTB ad valorem equivalent	U.S. tariffs, bilateral VERs on steel, textiles, apparel	Tariffs
International transfers	Debt repayment, labor remittances, profit repatriation exogenous	...	...	...	...
Savings	Set to balance current account	Residual to balance investment	...	From utility maximization	...
Exchange rate	Endogenous	Two numeraires: P_{US}, P_{MEX} requires nominal exchange rate	Three numeraires require nominal exchange rates	...	...

Sources: Carlos Bachrach and Lorris Mizrahi, "The Economic Impact of a Free Trade Agreement between the United States and Mexico: A CGE Analysis," KPMG Peat Marwick, Washington, February 1992; Raul Hinojosa-Ojeda and Sherman Robinson, "Alternative Scenarios of U.S.-Mexico Integration," Working Paper 609 (University of California, Berkeley, Department of Agricultural and Resource Economics, April 1991); David Roland-Holst, Kenneth A. Reinert, and Clinton R. Shiells, "North American Trade Liberalization and the Role of Nontariff Barriers," Mills College, April 1992; Irene Trela and John Whalley, "Bilateral Trade Liberalization in Quota Restricted Items: U.S. and Mexico in Textiles and Steel," University of Western Ontario, Department of Economics, May 1991; and Roy G. Boyd, Kerry Kruhilla, and Joseph A. McKinney, "The Impact of Tariff Liberalization between the United States and Mexico: A General Equilibrium Analysis," Ohio University, Economics Department, February 1992).

a. CES function used to aggregate the domestic and imported variety of each good.
b. The domestic and imported varieties of each good are differentiated by source and aggregated using a CES (AIDS) aggregation function.
c. Imports (exports) are differentiated by partner using a CES (CET) aggregation function.
d. CET function used to aggregate the domestic and exported variety of each good.
e. Manufacturing sectors in the United States.
f. Production is a CES (Leontief) function of value added and intermediate inputs.
g. Production is a CES (Leontief) function of value added and intermediate inputs.
h. Value added is a CES (Leontief) function of capital and labor.

maintained. Within each subcategory of textiles, apparel, and steel, all suppliers worldwide are assumed to produce an identical product. Second, the bilateral quotas are not modeled using ad valorem equivalents, as with all other models. Rather, the model is solved incorporating quantitative restrictions that may or may not be binding.

A selection of results on the economic effects of a U.S.-Mexican agreement or NAFTA from the static perfectly competitive models is presented in tables 2 and 3. Table 2 reports factor returns and real income, and table 3 reports trade figures. A few points of interest are immediately apparent. Consider, first, the impact of a trade agreement on real income in Mexico, as reported in column 4 of table 2. Roland-Holst and others calculate the effect of a three-country agreement removing tariffs only. Mexico's welfare as measured by real income rises by a mere 0.11 percent and U.S. welfare (column 8) rises by 0.07 percent. The studies that also consider nontariff barriers (NTB) produce a larger gain for Mexico and for the United States. Both Peat Marwick and Hinojosa and Robinson estimate a welfare gain from U.S.-Mexican bilateral tariff and NTB liberalization of 0.3 percent, and Roland-Holst and others find Mexican welfare rising by 2.28 percent.[8]

On the basis of the small welfare gains from trade liberalization reported here and elsewhere, many researchers suggest that negotiating a trade agreement may not be worth the trouble. However, it should be noted that the assumption of national product differentiation incorporated into all four of the studies just mentioned constrains the response by the domestic sector to relaxation in border controls and limits the scope for gains from specialization in production—that is, Armington models are predisposed to small welfare effects.

In contrast, Trela and Whalley take products to be homogeneous across all suppliers. They estimate that Mexican welfare would rise by 1.2 percent simply as a consequence of the removal by the United States of quota restrictions on Mexican textiles and apparel, with another 1.6 percent welfare gain due to the liberalization of import restrictions on steel.

The static welfare gains are also considerably greater in experiments in which trade liberalization is accompanied by additional foreign direct investment into Mexico. The Peat Marwick study reports that Mexican employment could rise by as much as 6.6 percent if enough new capital flows into Mexico after trade liberalization to hold the return to capital fixed. The necessary capital inflow for this purpose would raise Mexico's capital stock by about 7.6 percent. Hinojosa and Robinson also perform

Table 2. Static Models with Constant Returns to Scale: NAFTA and Income

Percent change

Model	Mexico				United States			
	Wage[a] (1)	Employment (2)	Rent (3)	Real income (4)	Wage[a] (5)	Employment (6)	Rent (7)	Real income (8)
KPMG Peat Marwick								
Tariffs and NTBs	...	0.85	0.60	0.32	0.02	...	0.03	0.02
Tariffs/NTBs and K-inflow	...	6.60	0.0	4.64	0.03	...	0.07	0.04
Hinojosa-Ojeda and Robinson								
Tariffs and NTB	R: -0.2; US: -0.2; S: 1.0; WC: 1.0	...	1.1	0.3	R: 0.3; US: 0.4; S: 0.0; WC: 0.0	...	0.0	0.0
Tariffs, NTBs, and K-inflow[b]	R: 9.2; US: 9.2; S: 7.4; WC: 8.8	...	-1.2	6.4	R: -0.4; US: 0.7; S: 0.1; WC: 0.3	...	1.2	0.1
Tariffs, NTBs, K-inflow, and endogenous migration	R: 4.7; US: 4.7; S: 7.7; WC: 9.1	...	-0.9	6.8	R: 1.8; US: 1.8; S: 0.0; WC: 0.2	...	1.1	0.1
Roland-Holst, Reinert, and Shiells I								
NAFTA tariffs	...	0.33	0.45	0.11	...	0.08	0.10	0.07
NAFTA tariff and NTB	...	1.49	5.18	2.28	...	1.88	2.43	1.67
Trela and Whalley								
Textiles	...	...	...	1.2	...	...	...	0.01
Steel	...	...	...	1.6	...	...	...	0.01
Boyd, Krutilla, and McKinney								
U.S.-MEX tariff removal	...	...	...	...	0.01	...	-0.01	...

Sources: See table 1.   a. See table 1.   b. Exogenous capital inflow identical to Peat Marwick study.

the experiment of allowing the Mexican capital stock to grow by 7.6 percent and find a Mexican welfare gain of 6.4 percent.

The difference in results with capital flows obtained by these two studies is at least in part due to the treatment of capital ownership. The Peat Marwick study assumes that the new capital is foreign owned. As a result, in the years after installation, Mexico would have to have a trade surplus to pay for profit repatriation. Notice in column 3 of table 3 that Mexico's trade balance with both the United States and the ROW soars under the capital inflow scenario. Hinojosa and Robinson, however, assume that the new capital is domestically owned. Therefore, no trade surplus is required, and the concomitant welfare-reducing deterioration in Mexico's terms of trade is also absent.

Among the most difficult issues concerning a U.S.-Mexican agreement are the likely implications for relative and absolute factor rewards. Considerable attention has been focused on the return to labor in the United States, particularly unskilled labor. Indeed, with Stolper-Samuelson–type forces at work, the expected real return to at least one factor should fall in each country with liberalization.

The United States, as the labor-scarce country, would, according to this reasoning, suffer a decline in real wages and Mexico would experience a decline in the return to capital. The theoretically expected decline in the return to capital in Mexico is a particular cause for concern because the models suggest that the lion's share of the welfare gain for Mexico would be caused by a capital inflow.

However, the gloomy predictions of the Stolper-Samuelson theorem do not present themselves in table 2. For example, the Peat Marwick study shows that tariff and NTB removal will indeed raise the U.S. rental rate (0.03 percent) relative to U.S. wages (0.02 percent), but real U.S. wages nonetheless still rise. Hence, U.S. labor gains from the agreement. Moreover, the rental rate in Mexico rises by 0.6 percent. A similar result obtains in the Roland-Holst and others study. Tariff removal raises the return to Mexican capital by 0.45 percent. Hinojosa and Robinson show a decline in the return to some factors, but in the tariff-NTB removal experiment, the factor that loses is unskilled and rural labor in Mexico.

These unexpected results, of course, can readily be traced back to the underlying assumptions of the models. A number of mechanisms are at work in the factor markets that can easily undermine Stolper-Samuelson mechanics.

One confounding influence at work stems from the assumption about the rigid wage for Mexico in the Peat Marwick study and for both Mexico

Table 3. Static Models with Constant Returns to Scale: NAFTA and International Trade
Percent change

	Mexico				United States			
Model	Imports (1)	Exports (2)	Trade balance (3)	Exchange rate (4)	Imports (5)	Exports (6)	Trade balance (7)	Exchange rate (8)
KPMG Peat Marwick								
Tariffs and NTBs	U.S. 5.39 ROW: 0.38	U.S.: 4.22 ROW: -0.28	U.S.: 1.63 ROW: -3.06	... ...	MEX: 4.22 ROW: 0.0	MEX: 5.39 ROW: 0.03	MEX: -1.81 ROW: 0.14	... ...
Tariffs/NTBs and K-inflow	U.S.: 5.21 ROW: 0.27	U.S.: 12.94 ROW: 18.06	U.S.: 26.88 ROW: 76.39	... ...	MEX: 12.94 ROW: -0.20	MEX: 5.21 ROW: 0.16	MEX: -20.79 ROW: 1.32	... ...
Hinojosa-Ojeda and Robinson								
Tariffs and NTBs	U.S.: 2.03 ROW: 0.06	U.S.: 2.17 ROW: -0.08	... ...	-0.6 ...	MEX: 2.17 ROW: 0.01	MEX: 2.03 ROW: 0.15	... ...	0.0 ...
Tariffs, NTBs, K-inflow	U.S.: 2.83 ROW: 0.73	U.S.: 2.76 ROW: 0.80	... ...	1.8 ...	MEX: 2.76 ROW: 0.58	MEX: 2.83 ROW: 0.51	... ...	-0.5 ...
Tariffs, NTBs, K-inflow, endogenous migration	U.S.: 2.86 ROW: 0.75	U.S.: 2.75 ROW: 0.86	... ...	2.3 ...	MEX: 2.75 ROW: 0.20	MEX: 2.86 ROW: 0.09	... ...	-0.6 ...

Roland-Holst, Reinert, and Shiells I						
NAFTA tariffs	Total: 1.15 NAFTA: 1.56	Total: 1.12 NAFTA: 1.99	−0.21 ...	Total: 0.36 NAFTA: 1.33	Total: 0.27 NAFTA: 1.34	−0.09 ...
NAFTA tariffs and NTBs	Total: 14.74 NAFTA: 21.12	Total: 13.06 NAFTA: 14.23	−3.51 ...	Total: 8.95 NAFTA: 36.13	Total: 8.05 NAFTA: 27.17	−0.37 ...
Trela and Whalley[a]						
Textiles	...	...	...	MEX: n.a. CND: −36.3	... ...	... ...
Apparel	...	...	...	MEX: 3,775.7 CND: −100.0	... ...	... ...
Steel	...	...	...	MEX: 3,416.7 CND: −38.1	... ...	... ...
Boyd, Krutilla, and McKinney						
U.S.-Mexican tariff removal	...	...	MEX: 19.0	MEX: 27.0	...	...

Sources: See table 1.   n.a. Not available.   a. CND is Canada.

and the United States in Roland-Holst and others. The removal of tariffs and NTBs lowers consumer prices, thereby raising the real wage. To return the real wage to its predetermined level, the fall in consumer prices must be counterbalanced by a fall in the marginal product of labor. Consequently, production must become generally more labor intensive. As a result, the marginal product of capital rises along with the total employment of labor.

Moreover, in a differentiated products model, the country that enjoys a terms-of-trade gain may also see a rise in the real return to both factors. To see this point, recall that when products are differentiated by national origin, the price of each domestically produced variety of a good need not equal the price of the imported variety. A terms-of-trade gain, then, may manifest itself as a rise in the price of many or all domestically produced varieties relative to imports. Therefore, a rise in the price on the world market of the variety of each good being produced domestically relative to the variety imported could pull up the *value* of the marginal product in terms of imported goods, even for a factor whose marginal product is falling. A U.S. terms-of-trade improvement in the Peat Marwick tariff-NTB experiment is likely to be the reason that the real returns to both capital and labor rise in the United States.

The key point here is that fairly innocuous looking modeling assumptions, such as nationally differentiated products and a rigid real wage, can mask some of the distributional consequences of trade liberalization. Hinojosa and Robinson clearly demonstrate that if factor markets are allowed to clear, the ROW supply and demand equations are relatively inelastic, and technology is constant returns to scale, then the return to at least one NAFTA factor must fall.

A final point worth noting concerns the effect of the agreement on the rest of the world. The negative consequences of an agreement for the ROW are not expected to be very important. U.S. tariffs and nontariff barriers against Mexico are already quite low, thus minimizing the distortion effects associated with a preferential tariff. Mexico's trade barriers are higher, but a very large fraction of Mexico's trade is already directed toward the United States. Consequently, there is very little trade with the ROW to divert.

The Trela-Whalley results are perhaps the most instructive on this point. Trela and Whalley consider two of the sectors in which U.S. trade barriers are most noticeable, and they explicitly model the economies of Canada and the other countries covered by the bilateral restrictions. Furthermore, their assumption that goods are treated as homogeneous across producers predisposes the model to exhibit strong negative consequences for the ROW.

The impact on Mexico of the elimination of bilateral import quotas is pronounced. U.S. imports from Mexico of apparel rise by 3,775.7 percent and of steel by 3,416.7 percent, and Canada's access to the U.S. market is disrupted, as can be seen in table 3. However, the welfare and production effects on the ROW are small by comparison. Canadian production of textiles and steel fall by 0.1 percent and 4.1 percent, respectively, apparel is unaffected, and Canadian welfare falls by 0.01 percent. For other countries covered by these quota agreements, production of textiles, apparel, and steel fall by 0.2 percent, 0.6 percent, and 0.002 percent, respectively, and welfare falls by 0.034 percent.

Static Models with Increasing Returns to Scale

The static CRS scale models have been criticized on a number of accounts. Nearly all the first-generation AGE trade modelers impose some type of product differentiation on the utility and production functions. The modelers follow the empirical observation that, given the current level of international trade barriers, national economies are not as specialized in production as a homogeneous products world would require. The conclusion is that there must exist nationally specific factors of production that give rise to nationally differentiated products.

The assumption of national product differentiation is particularly attractive for the current international environment because the analysis of preferential trading is required. As a result, our models must be configured to allow for identification of the bilateral trade flows that are to receive preferential treatment. National product differentiation, by identifying each country's exports as a separate product, allows the models to solve explicitly for all the bilateral trade flows. Models of homogeneous products seem less attractive for this purpose because they are not able to solve uniquely for bilateral trade. Moreover, preferential trading in a homogeneous products model will completely eliminate some bilateral trade, an implausible outcome.

However, the fact that national product differentiation is a convenient assumption does not make it a good assumption for empirical analysis. Concern with the implications of nationally differentiated products was first raised by Bob Hamilton and Whalley, and John Shoven and Whalley, and later by Drusilla Brown.[9] All these researchers discovered that the optimal tariff in these models tends to be very high for small, as well as large, countries.

National product differentiation implies that each country has a monopoly in the market for its own national variety. Monopoly power is ignored by its perfectly competitive firms, leaving wide scope for government intervention.

A second property of national product differentiation is that it severely constrains the possibility for intersectoral specialization as a result of liberalization. Consumers place a high premium on consuming all the different varieties of a good. To satisfy world demand, all countries must continue to follow the traditional allocation of production across sectors.

That these models are characterized by a high optimal tariff is not in itself a criticism of the Armington assumption. However, most recent work in international trade theory suggests that the low degree of international specialization in production is not a consequence of nationally specific factors but rather of the existence of IRS technology and imperfect competition.

Notably, it has demonstrated that national product differentiation with CRS technology provides a poor approximation to a model with imperfect competition and IRS technology. The reasons are fairly clear, as discussed in Brown and Robert Stern.[10]

First, to the extent that product differentiation exists, each imperfectly competitive firm will be aware that the demand schedule is less than perfectly elastic and will incorporate this information into its pricing decisions. Firms are exercising whatever market power is associated with product differentiation, so little room is left for government in this regard, particularly in small countries. Second, greater intersectoral specialization is possible even in differentiated products. Exiting firms in one country can relocate in another country, which gives rise to greater intersectoral specialization. Smaller optimal tariffs combined with greater potential for intersectoral specialization in the imperfectly competitive models will considerably enhance the potential gains from liberalization.

Perhaps an even more important criticism of the CRS models comes from Richard Harris and others.[11] In the Canadian context, import protection is thought to foster collusive behavior by imperfectly competitive firms, resulting in high price-cost margins and low scale of production. Liberalization, then, would lead to large welfare gains associated with the realization of economies of scale in production.

The second generation of AGE models, therefore, addresses some of these criticisms concerning technology and market structure. The essential features of each model are described in table 4. David Cox and Harris, Horacio Sobarzo, Roland-Holst and others, and Brown, Deardorff, and Stern introduce increasing returns to scale by adding to the input requirements a fixed input of capital and labor for each firm.[12] Marginal cost is constant, but average total cost slopes downward.

Four different market structures have been adopted for analyzing the behavior of firms. The Harris-Cox model of Canada uses an amalgamated pricing rule, combining focal pricing and monopolistic competition. Under the focal pricing hypothesis, firms are assumed to collude around an easily observable price, the focal price. Freedom of entry, however, guarantees that the focal price is also equal to average total cost.

The focal price chosen for the Canadian market is the landed price of imports. The role of trade liberalization, then, is to lower the focal price by the amount of the tariff and force all firms down the average total cost curve to a higher scale of production.

Note that economies of scale can be realized by a firm even if total industry production is falling. The intensification of competition from imports will still raise the output of each of the surviving firms. In fact, the realization of economies of scale is likely to be greatest in the most closely protected sectors.

Under the assumption that firms are monopolistically competitive, each firm calculates the elasticity of its demand curve and then sets a profit-maximizing markup of price over marginal cost. Again, entry drives profits to zero. The role of trade liberalization here is to lower the price of imports, so that domestic firms perceive more competition from foreign firms. The consequent rise in the perceived elasticity of demand causes firms to cut the price-cost margin. To break even with a lower margin, firm output must rise.

Cox and Harris assume that the imperfectly competitive firms calculate both the focal price and the markup price and then set the price equal to an average of the two. Firms in Sobarzo's model of Mexico behave similarly.

Roland-Holst and others take a slightly different approach to modeling the price-setting behavior of imperfectly competitive firms. In one version of their model of Canada, Mexico, the United States, and the ROW, the market structure is taken to be contestable—that is, firms' price at average total cost. It is worth pointing out that the assumption that average total cost declines monotonically when the market structure is contestable im-

Table 4. Static Models with Increasing Returns to Scale

Item	Cox and Harris	Sobarzo I, II, III	Brown, Deardorff, and Stern I, II	Roland-Holst, Reinert, and Shiells II
Countries	Canada	Mexico	Canada, Mexico, United States, other	(See table 1)
Sectors	9 NTs; 10 Ts[a]	21 Ts; 6 NTs[a]	23 Ts; 6 NTs[a]	...
Base year	1981, 1989	1985	1989	...
Demand				
Government	...	...	...	...
Investment	...	= Foreign plus domestic savings	...	...
Final				
Level 1	Cobb-Douglas	Cobb-Douglas	Cobb-Douglas	...
Level 2	Dom/Imp by source—CES	Dom/Imp by source—CES	Dom/Imp by firm	...
Technology				
Level 1	Intermed./K/L—Cobb-Douglas	Intermed./VA—Leontief	Intermed./VA—Leontief	...
Level 2	NTs CRS-Ts IRS	VA: K/L—Cobb-Douglas CRS and IRS	VA: K/L—CES CRS and IRS	II: IRS

Labor market	Intersectoral mobility	I./II. Rigid real wage; III. Intersectoral mobility	Intersectoral mobility	...
Capital market	Perfect international mobility	I./II. Intersectoral mobility; III. International mobility	I. Intersectoral mobility; II. International mobility	...
Goods markets	U.S., MEX, ROW exogenous export price; end: import demand from C-D utility differentiated by source; Ts: monopolistic competition, focal pricing, free entry	North A., ROW exogenous export price; End. import demand differentiated by source; oil price exogenous; perfect competition; monopolistic competition; focal pricing, free entry	End. imp demand/exp supply; NTs, agriculture: Perfect competition; other Ts: monopolistic competition; free entry	II. Cournot/Contestable
Trade policy	Tariffs and NTBs	...	Tariffs	Tariffs, NTB ad valorem equivalent
International transfers	...	...	Rent remitted on Foreign Capital	...
Savings	...	Fixed share of income	...	...
Exchange rate	...	I. Trade balance exogenous; II./III. exchange rate exogenous	Trade balance exogenous	...

Sources: David Cox and Richard G. Harris, "North American Free Trade and Its Implications for Canada: Results from a CGE Model of North American Trade," *World Economy* (forthcoming); Horacio E. Sobarzo, "A General Equilibrium Analysis of the Gains from Trade for the Mexican Economy of a North American Free Trade Agreement," El Colegio de Mexico, Centro de Estudios Económicos, December 1991; Drusilla K. Brown, Alan V. Deardorff, and Robert M. Stern, "A North American Free Trade Agreement: Analytical Issues and a Computational Assessment," *World Economy*, vol. 15 (January 1992); and Roland-Holst and others, "North American Trade Liberalization."

a. NTs = nontradable goods; Ts = tradable goods.

plies that there is only one firm in each industry. In the second version of the Roland-Holst and others model, firms engage in Cournot competition, maximizing profits taking the output of all other firms as given.

Although the contestable markets version of the Roland-Holst and others model looks similar to the focal pricing model, the potential for the realization of economies of scale is greatly diminished. The fact that there is only one firm in each industry implies that firm output expands only if industry output expands. Therefore, the closely protected sectors that decline once tariffs are removed will lose scale economies. Significant scale gains will emerge only in the important export sectors.

The implications of the contestable markets hypothesis for scale economies are softened a bit by the assumption concerning the functioning of the factor markets. Roland-Holst and others take the real wage measured in terms of the domestic price level to be exogenous. Tariff removal lowers the domestic price level, thereby raising the real wage. The labor market adjusts by expanding employment. Consequently, the economies of all three countries in NAFTA become larger. In principle, then, domestic production in all industries can rise and thus realize economies of scale. Trade diversion has a similar effect of expanding total demand within NAFTA at base period prices, which further contributes to scale gains.

A common weakness of the three models just described is that the assumption of national product differentiation is retained. To remove any concern associated with national product differentiation, Brown and others have constructed a model of Canada, the United States, Mexico, a group of another thirty-one industrial countries, and the ROW. The market structure in the manufacturing sectors is monopolistically competitive and product differentiation exists only at the firm level.

Detailed results for various liberalization scenarios are reported in tables 5 and 6. Roland-Holst and others provide the most direct comparison between the CRS and IRS models. The CRS version of their model predicts welfare gains from trilateral tariff and NTB removal for Canada, Mexico, and the United States of 4.87 percent, 2.28 percent, and 1.67 percent, respectively. By comparison, their IRS model with contestable markets predicts welfare gains of 6.75 percent, 3.29 percent, and 2.55 percent, respectively.

Similarly, Brown and others find that modeling scale economies with a monopolistically competitive market structure considerably raises the gains from NAFTA. They find that trilateral tariff removal plus the relaxation of some U.S. NTBs against Mexico's exports of agriculture, food, textiles, and apparel will raise Mexican welfare by 1.6 percent. This

Table 5. Static Models with Increasing Returns to Scale: NAFTA and Income
Percent change

Model	Real income	Real wage	Employment	Rent rate
Roland-Holst, Reinert, and Shiells II				
Cournot				
Canada	4.08	. . .	7.29	13.57
Mexico	2.47	. . .	1.73	5.77
United States	1.58	. . .	1.79	2.49
Contestable				
Canada	6.75	. . .	11.02	20.74
Mexico	3.29	. . .	2.40	6.57
United States	2.55	. . .	2.47	3.40
Cox and Harris: Canada				
CUSFTA	3.1	5.5	. . .	. . .
NAFTA	0.03	0.4	. . .	. . .
Hub and spoke	0.002	−0.0	. . .	. . .
Sobarzo: Mexico				
I. Exogenous wage, K-stock	2.0	. . .	5.1	6.2
II. Exogenous wage, K-stock exchange rate	2.3	. . .	5.8	6.6
III. Exogenous exchange rate, rental rate	2.4	16.2	. . .	0.0
Brown, Deardorff, and Stern				
NAFTA: tariffs and NTBs				
Canada	0.7	0.4	. . .	0.4
Mexico	1.6	0.7	. . .	0.6
United States	0.1	0.2	. . .	0.2
ROW	−0.0	−0.1	. . .	−0.1
NAFTA: tariffs, NTBs, and MEX K-inflow				
Canada	0.7	0.5	. . .	0.5
Mexico	5.0	9.3	. . .	3.3
United States	0.3	0.2	. . .	0.2
ROW	−0.0	−0.0	. . .	0.2

Sources: See table 4.

is the case even though in their model both capital and labor are assumed to be already fully employed. Therefore, all the welfare gain for Mexico is the result of intersectoral specialization, the realization of scale economies, and the removal of consumption distortions.

Sobarzo and Cox-Harris, using the amalgamated pricing rule, show welfare results that are larger still. Sobarzo finds that the removal of U.S.-Mexican tariffs would raise Mexican welfare by between 2.0 and 2.4 percent, and Cox and Harris find that the removal of U.S.-Canada tariffs

Table 6. Static Models with Increasing Returns to Scale: NAFTA and International Trade
Percent change

Model	Terms of trade	Canadian imports	Mexican imports	U.S. imports	Exchange rate	Trade balance
Roland-Holst, Reinert, and Shiells II						
Cournot						
Canada	. . .	Total: 18.71; NAFTA: 27.87	. . .	. . .	3.11	. . .
Mexico	. . .	. . .	Total: 15.01; NAFTA: 21.25	. . .	−2.71	. . .
United States	. . .	. . .	. . .	Total: 8.31; NAFTA: 33.71	−0.25	. . .
Contestable						
Canada	. . .	Total: 24.18; NAFTA: 35.07	. . .	. . .	6.89	. . .
Mexico	. . .	. . .	Total: 17.70; NAFTA: 23.82	. . .	−4.20	. . .
United States	. . .	. . .	. . .	Total: 12.34; NAFTA: 46.44	−1.04	. . .
Cox and Harris: Canada						
CAFTA	−0.9	. . .	. . .	. . .	. . .	. . .
NAFTA	0.01	. . .	. . .	. . .	. . .	
Hub and spoke	−0.0	. . .	. . .	. . .	. . .	
Sobarzo: Mexico						
I. Exogenous wage, K-stock	. . .	. . .	. . .	. . .	NA: 3.0 ROW: 0.3	0.0
II. Exogenous wage, K-stock exchange rate	. . .	. . .	. . .	. . .	0	5.6
III. Exogenous exchange rate, rental rate	. . .	. . .	. . .	. . .	0	18.3
Brown, Deardorff, and Stern						
NAFTA: tariffs and NTBs						
Canada	−0.5	. . .	. . .	. . .	. . .	. . .
Mexico	−0.1	. . .	. . .	. . .	. . .	. . .
United States	0.2	. . .	. . .	. . .	. . .	. . .
NAFTA: tariffs, NTBs, and MEX K−inflow						
Canada	−0.5	. . .	. . .	. . .	. . .	. . .
Mexico	−2.5	. . .	. . .	. . .	. . .	. . .
United States	−0.0	. . .	. . .	. . .	. . .	. . .

Sources: See table 4.

and NTBs would raise Canadian welfare by 3.1 percent. It is difficult, however, to sort out how much of the greater gain is the result of the use of focal pricing rather than monopolistic competition. Unlike Brown and others, both Cox-Harris and Sobarzo assume that at least one factor is in perfectly elastic supply. Cox and Harris assume that foreign capital can be imported at the world interest rate. Sobarzo alternates between perfectly elastic supply of domestic labor and perfectly elastic supply of foreign capital.[14]

Brown and others also consider the effects of a capital inflow and find that foreign direct investment has a powerful impact on Mexico's gains from liberalization. Under the assumption that foreign direct investment expands Mexico's capital stock by 10 percent, NAFTA raises Mexico's welfare by 5.0 percent and raises real wages in Mexico by 9.3 percent. In a similar experiment, Sobarzo (III) finds that Mexican welfare rises by 2.4 percent and wages rise by 16.2 percent. Thus, as with the perfectly competitive models, the reform of the rules concerning foreign direct investment in Mexico dominates the barriers to goods trade in determining the gains from NAFTA.

As for the effects of NAFTA on factor returns, once again expectations based on the Stolper-Samuelson theorem have not been confirmed. Real returns to or employment of both factors rise in all countries participating in the liberalization experiments. As with the CRS models, factor market distortions play a role here.

However, even in the Brown and others model, in which there are no factor market distortions, both the return to capital and labor rise. Here the realization of economies of scale is playing a role in raising both returns.

In monopolistic competition, each factor is paid a wage, w, according to

$$w = MR \times MP = (1 - 1/e) P \times MP,$$

where MR is the firm's marginal revenue, MP is the factor's marginal product, $e > 0$ is the firm's perceived elasticity of demand and P is price. Tariff liberalization, by lowering the landed price of imports, raises the firm's perceived elasticity of demand.

A more elastic demand curve has the well-known effect of inducing the firm to cut its price-cost margin, thus sliding down the average total cost curve and realizing economies of scale. Both factors share in the benefits as the real wage, w/P, rises. As a result, the return to a factor could rise even if its marginal product is falling.

Finally, the IRS models also lend further support to the notion that the impact on the ROW will be small. For example, Harris and Cox compare the impact on Canada of a hub-and-spoke arrangement whereby the United States and Mexico negotiate a separate agreement, excluding Canada, to an agreement that extends the Canadian-U.S. treaty to include Mexico. One might expect that Canada would be most likely to suffer the trade-diverting effects of a U.S.-Mexican agreement. Indeed, Canada gains marginally more with NAFTA (0.03 percent) than with a hub and spoke (0.002 percent), but in each case the impact is negligible. Curiously, a U.S.-Mexican agreement that excludes Canada actually raises Canada's welfare, a result confirmed by Brown and others.

Dynamic Models

Like the first generation of AGE models, the second generation also has its critics. There are many interesting and important questions concerning NAFTA that the static IRS and CRS models cannot address. The issue of labor market dynamics is particularly important in the Mexican context. The static models also are not able to provide evidence on the implications of an agreement for the trade balance, exchange rates, and capital formation. To address these questions, a model must include a dynamic dimension that attempts to model intertemporal utility and profit maximization and attitudes toward risk and uncertainty.

Moreover, recent theory in international trade and macroeconomics (for example, Gene Grossman and Elhanan Helpman, Paul Romer, and Nancy Stokey) places great emphasis on the importance of the endogenous determinants of economic growth and the role that the opportunity to trade internationally plays in accelerating growth.[15] As a practical matter, endogenous growth is potentially of enormous importance to Mexican economic development. Calculations by Timothy Kehoe suggest that liberalization today could raise Mexican output per worker in twenty-five years by 51 percent above what it otherwise would have been.[16]

The static modeling approach described earlier can be extended to analyze questions of dynamics. The most straightforward, but least satisfying, approach is to specify a time path for one or more of the exogenous variables of the model and then re-solve the static model for each period incorporating the new values of the exogenous variables. A second approach is to endogenize the growth of some of the variables in the system.

For example, interest-sensitive investment in one period can lead to the augmentation of the capital stock in the next period.

A third possibility is to solve all periods of the model simultaneously, which requires intertemporal optimization by firms and consumers. This approach is the most satisfying but the most difficult to execute.

The characteristics of the dynamic models are described in table 7. Leslie Young and José Romero have constructed the most nearly neo-classical of the growth models for Mexico.[17] The key feature of their model is the existence of two tradable capital goods (machinery and vehicles) and one nontradable capital good (buildings). Firms make investment decisions such that in the steady state, capital is earning its marginal value product. The path of capital acquisition is set to maximize the value of GNP subject to the condition that each industry's capital stock achieves the steady-state level in eleven years. Capital leaves a sector through depreciation.

Young and Romero's contribution is especially important because their model of the capital goods market captures the negative growth consequences of import tariffs on capital goods. However, the more conventional welfare-reducing aspects of trade restrictions are also incorporated.

A second important feature of the Young-Romero model is that domestic and foreign goods are perfect substitutes. The domestic price is taken to be the world price plus import tariffs.

These two modeling choices together should predispose the model to welfare gains that are larger than reported from static CRS models. Indeed, Young and Romero find that the removal of Mexican tariffs would raise the steady-state level of gross domestic product by 2.6 percent, as shown in table 8. Young and Romero also evaluate the effect of Mexican tariff removal along with a reduction in the real interest rate from 10.0 percent to 7.5 percent that might emerge if an agreement were to reduce uncertainty about the economy. In this case, Mexican welfare rises by 8.1 percent. Thus, Young and Romero lend further support to the view that issues concerning capital formation in Mexico are central to the welfare gains from an agreement.

The Santiago Levy and Sweder van Wijnbergen model has been specifically designed to analyze the adjustment issues for agricultural labor in Mexico.[18] Products in the rural sector are disaggregated into maize (raw and tortillas), basic grains, fruits and vegetables, other agricultural goods, and livestock. The model also carefully disaggregates households into six groups: landless rural workers, subsistence farmers who own two hectares of rain-fed land, rain-fed farmers who own the remainder of the

Table 7. Dynamic Models

Item	Young and Romero	McCleery and others	Levy and van Wijnbergen
Countries	Mexico	Mexico, U.S., ROW	Mexico
Sectors	9 final/intermed. Ts; 3 capital goods: 2Ts, 1 NT	1 T, 1 NT	Urban: T, NT; rural: 5 Ts, 1 NT
Base year	1988	1988	1989
Transition to steady state	11 years	...	...
Demand			
Intermediate	Shepard's lemma	...	...
Government investment	Investment to maximize GNP, subject to condition that K stock achieves steady-state level in 11 years	International allocation to equalize risk adjusted returns	Government invests in irrigation infrastructure
Final			
Level 1	Cobb-Douglas	Linear expenditure system	6 HH types classified by factor ownership; rural/MFR/services—Cobb-Douglas; rural: 5 rural goods—CES; maize: raw/tortillas—CES
Level 2	Linear	Import consumption proportional to income	
Level 3	...	...	
Technology			
Level 1	K/L/intermed.—translog	Exportable: K/MFR L/imported intermed.—CES[a] NT good: K/skill. L/unskill. L/Land—CES[b]	Intermed./VA—Leontief
Level 2	K; machinery, buildings, vehicles—translog; intermed.: 9 intermed.—Cobb-Douglas; CRS	CRS: I. productivity growth exogenous; II. productivity growth function of investment	Urban—VA: K/L—Cobb-Douglas; rural—VA: land/labor—Cobb-Douglas; CRS

Labor market	Population growth rate—exogenous; steady-state sectoral allocation: base ±20%	International labor flow exogenous; labor force growth exogenous; 3 types of labor—full employment	Urban, rural; mobility preserves utility difference between landless rural and urban workers; Population growth exogenous
Capital market	Machinery, vehicles tradable; buildings intersectoral mobility; all depreciable	FDI in MEX: 50% from U.S. domestic I;[c] 50% from U.S. other FDI;[d] world i rate exogenous	Capital sector specific; K-stock growth exogenous; Hicks neutral change exogenous
Land market	. . .	Sector specific	Rain-fed and irrigated
Goods markets	ROW prices exogenous	Price of oil rise to 75% of 1982 level by 2000; law of one price for tradables holds	World price exogenous for Ts; perfect competition
Trade policy	Mexican tariffs	. . .	Production consumption tax and subsidies; Tortivale program
International transfers	. . .	MEX receives exogenous new loans annually; migrant remittances; pays debt service and profits on FDI	. . .
Savings	. . .	Trend savings rate exogenous, interest sensitive	By urban capitalists proportionate to income

Sources: Sources: Leslie Young and Jose Romero, "Steady Growth and Transition: A Dynamic Dual Model of the North American Free Trade Agreement," University of Texas, Austin, February 1992; Robert K. McCleery and others, "An Intertemporal, Linked, Macroeconomic CGE Model of the United States and Mexico, Focusing on Demographic Change and Factor Flows," Economic Development and Policy, East-West Center, Honolulu, February 1992; and Santiago Levy and Sweder van Wijnbergen, "Transition Problems in Economic Reform: Agriculture in the Mexico-U.S. Free Trade Agreement," Boston University, December 1991.

a. Production of the exportable good is a CES function of capital, manufacturing labor, and the imported intermediate input.
b. Production of the nontraded good is a CES function of capital, skilled labor, unskilled labor, and land.
c. Fifty percent of the new capital stock in Mexico is diverted from capital installed in the United States.
d. Fifty percent of the new capital stock in Mexico is foreign direct investment diverted from other developing countries.

Table 8. Dynamic Models: NAFTA and Income
Percent change

Model	Real income		Land prices	
Young and Romero: Mexico				
Complete liberalization	Gain over base steady state:	2.6	. . .	
Liberalization and interest rate reduced from 10% to 7.6%	Gain over base steady state:	8.1	. . .	
Levy and van Wijnbergen: Mexico				
Maize liberalization	Mexico:	0.6	Rain-fed land:	−23.5
	Subsistence farmers:	−3.3	Irrigated land:	1.6
	Landless rural workers:	−1.6		
	Rain-fed farmers:	−5.7		
	Irrigated farmers:	2.8		
	Urban workers:	1.6		
	Urban capitalists:	1.8		

Sources: See table 7.

rain-fed land and part of the land used for livestock, owners of irrigated land, urban workers, and urban capitalists. Rural-urban migration is assumed to hold the relative utility between landless rural and urban workers equal to its value in the base level. Three other key assumptions are that technology is constant return to scale, domestic-traded goods are perfect substitutes for foreign-produced goods, and world prices are set exogenously.

Although the model has a multiyear time horizon, it does not actually have any intertemporal dynamics. In each period, markets are assumed to clear, given world prices, domestic policy, current endowments, and technology. However, several parameters of the model evolve exogenously over time. The exogenous changes are population growth, Hicks-neutral technological change, growth of the urban capital stock, government spending, and world prices. In addition, border controls, consumption subsidies, and government investment in irrigation infrastructure evolve exogenously.

Results in table 8 indicate the welfare and factor price effects of completely eliminating all taxes and subsidies to maize and tortillas. First note that the overall welfare gains for Mexico are positive, approximately 0.6 percent of GDP. However, unlike in most of the previous models, the distributional effects are noticeable. Subsistence farmers, landless rural workers, rain-fed farmers, and owners of rain-fed land suffer a decline in earnings. Most maize is grown on rain-fed land. The decline in maize prices due to liberalization, therefore, lowers its return. For a similar reason, rural wages fall, though wages do not fall as much as land prices, since rural labor has the option of migrating to the urban sector. Subsistence farmers are hurt the most because of a fall in wages and a fall in the price of their land. Interestingly, the fall in rural wages allows owners of irrigated land to adopt a more labor-intensive process, thereby raising the return to irrigated land.

The assumptions of perfect competition and homogeneous products in this model contribute to results that conform more closely with textbook expectations. Welfare gains are both large and unevenly distributed.

Levy and van Wijnbergen then use the model to evaluate the possibility of phasing in maize liberalization over a five-year period. The efficiency gains over this period are smaller because they are postponed, but the loss is small.

Robert McCleery, alone, attempts to incorporate the recent literature on endogenous economic growth.[19] However, like Levy and van Wijnbergen, his model does not attempt to incorporate any dynamic optimizing behavior of economic agents. The model consists of two goods produced in the United States and Mexico, using CRS technology. Tradable good 1 consists primarily of manufacturing and agribusiness. U.S. production of good 1 may be consumed domestically, consumed in Mexico, or used as an intermediate input in Mexico. Good 1 in Mexico is used only for final consumption in both countries. Nontradable good 2 consists largely of services and subsistence agriculture. Mexican- and U.S.-produced goods are not differentiated by consumers, so that the law of one price must hold. However, the expenditure share on imports is held constant as a fraction of income. The demand structure and production functions are detailed in table 7.

There are three types of labor: manufacturing workers, high-wage nonmanufacturing workers, and low-wage manufacturing workers. The demand for high-wage workers is largely driven by capital formation in each sector. Residual labor is employed as low skilled. Factor payments are based on marginal value product, but wages and the return to capital are not equalized across sectors.

Capital flows between the United States and Mexico within each sector respond to risk-adjusted interest-rate differentials. Half the capital is assumed to come from the U.S. capital stock and half from U.S. investments in other newly industrializing countries. Saving is determined as a fraction of income, but the marginal propensity to save is a function of interest rates. Mexico's balance of payments condition, then, requires that its debt service, imports for final consumption and intermediate inputs, and capital imports be financed with exports, migrant remittances, and new finance.

The model is solved each period for prices, employment, consumption, and trade flows, given the exogenous variables. Over time, the price of oil and the U.S. and Mexican labor forces grow exogenously, and the capital stock is determined endogenously. In the first set of simulations, productivity growth is also taken to be exogenous. In subsequent runs, though, U.S. productivity is taken to be an increasing function of the production of capital goods, and Mexican productivity is a function of the import of capital goods.

The model is then used to chart the path of the U.S. and Mexican economies between 1993 and 2000 under various liberalization experiments. Free trade is shown to raise Mexican welfare by 1 percent by the year 2000 and to upgrade 350,000 jobs in the United States from low wage to high wage. However, as one might expect with a homogeneous products model and CRS, the gains are not uniform across factors of production.

A second experiment allows for the possibility that an agreement might also improve investor confidence, so that the interest differential between the United States and Mexico declines. Under this scenario, the U.S. welfare gain is still positive. Mexico's gain rises to 3.2 percent of GDP by 2000. Once again, the evidence is that capital inflows into Mexico play a much greater role in raising Mexican welfare than does the removal of border controls on goods trade. The gains across factors are uneven but accrue primarily to the poorest segments of the Mexican population.

Finally, McCleery considers the possibility of still greater gains from endogenizing productivity. Under the scenario of free trade, improved investor confidence, and endogenous growth, Mexico's welfare would be 11 percent above the baseline by 2000. Low-wage labor is again the beneficiary, with one million new high-wage jobs created and a 14 percent increase in the return to low-wage labor.

Conclusions and Directions for Future Research

I have attempted to provide an overview of the likely effects of the formation of NAFTA as reported by economy-wide AGE models and to evaluate the role that various modeling assumptions play in explaining the cross-model differences in results. First, the differentiated product–CRS models show small welfare gains of less than 1 percent of GNP, though the welfare effects are positive for the participating countries. Models that take products to be homogeneous across producers, incorporate IRS, or both, show welfare gains for Mexico in the range of 2 to 4 percent. The addition of international capital flows suggests still larger welfare gains for Mexico of 4 to 7 percent. Finally, endogenizing productivity growth produces much larger welfare effects, possibly in the range of 10 percent of Mexican GNP. These models clearly indicate that the pursuit of NAFTA will indeed be worth the effort, particularly from Mexico's standpoint.

Second, nearly all the models confirm that understanding the behavior of capital is central to evaluating the effects of NAFTA for Mexico. In view of the fact that all the models, to some degree, handle capital formation in an ad hoc fashion, there is more work to be done in this area. More careful treatment of the savings and investment decisions and the market for capital goods would be welcome additions to this literature.

Third, questions concerning the likely impact of an agreement on factor prices and the distribution of gains across different segments of the population remain unanswered. Models range from predicting that the poorest segment of the Mexican population would be hurt by an agreement because of the liberalization of the maize market, to predicting that the poorest segments of the Mexican population have the most to gain from NAFTA because of endogenous productivity growth. The models produce no consensus on this point.

Finally, there are two very important issues that the current class of economy-wide AGE models are not equipped to address at all. For one thing, these models provide virtually no information on the likely effects on the nominal exchange rate and the trade balance. The only information available on the macroeconomic dynamics of an agreement is provided by the INFORUM-CIMAT model, which links a macro-forecasting model to individual industry models.[20] A second very important issue that is not broached by any of the economy-wide models concerns the behavior of multinational corporations. Multinationals dominate international trade in North America and are likely to be the most important conduits of foreign direct investment and technology. Yet, Linda Hunter, James Markusen, and Thomas Rutherford are the only modelers to attempt to deal with multinational behavior, doing so in the context of their study of the automobile industry.[21] Their results are particularly notable in that they suggest that multinationals tend to reduce the distorting effects of import protection.

Comment by Timothy J. Kehoe

Drusilla Brown, in surveying the results of various applied general equilibrium studies of the potential impact of North American economic integration, provides more than a survey. She also analyzes the economic intuition behind the central results of each study and the differences among them. For estimating the impact of policy changes such as those involved in NAFTA, applied general equilibrium models have become the tool of choice; indeed this sort of model is virtually the only tool currently used to measure the global impact of NAFTA. Having worked on and off in applied general equilibrium modeling for the past twelve years, and having long been convinced of the superiority of this approach over obvious alternatives, such as large-scale macroeconomic models, I am pleased by these developments. Yet I think it essential to bear in mind that this sort of approach to policy analysis is still at a fairly early stage in its development.

As Brown stresses, it is important that these models do not become black boxes. Since there is still no widespread agreement on model structure, it is essential to relate the results that a model generates to the underlying assumptions on structure. Brown's paper is a major contribution in this direction. It is worth stressing, however, that a more complex model is not necessarily a better model. Ultimately, there is a need to choose among alternative model structures on the basis of how well they are able to match up with empirical evidence. In this respect, NAFTA will provide an ideal empirical test for the applied general equilibrium models used to analyze it. As Brown points out in her paper, these models must incorporate dynamic phenomena if they are to capture much of the actual impact of a change like NAFTA. They may also need to incorporate, even in simple ways, some stochastic phenomena, particularly to model the effect of NAFTA on investor confidence in Mexico.

Empirical Validation

Although much energy and resources have gone into constructing applied general equilibrium models and using them to perform policy analyses over the past two decades, it is surprising how little effort has gone into evaluating the performance of such models after such policy changes have actually taken place. Only by showing that a model can replicate

Table 9. Comparison of Spanish Model's Prediction with the Data
Percent change in relative price[a]

Sector	Actual, 1985–86	Model	Adjusted model
Food and nonalcoholic beverages	1.8	−2.3	1.7
Tobacco and alcoholic beverages	3.9	2.5	5.8
Clothing	2.1	5.6	6.6
Housing	−3.2	−2.2	−4.8
Household articles	0.1	2.2	2.9
Medical services	−0.7	−4.8	−4.2
Transportation	−4.0	2.6	−6.6
Recreation	−1.4	−1.3	0.1
Other services	2.9	1.1	2.8
Weighted correlation with 1985–86[b]	1.000	−0.079	0.936

Source: Timothy J. Kehoe, Clemente Polo, and Ferran Sancho, "An Evaluation of the Performance of an Applied General Equilibrium Model of the Spanish Economy," Working Paper 480 (Federal Reserve Bank of Minneapolis, 1991).

a. Change in sectoral price index deflated by appropriate aggregate price index.

b. Weighted correlation coefficients with actual changes 1985–86. The weights used, from top to bottom, are 0.2540, 0.0242, 0.0800, 0.1636, 0.0772, 0.0376, 0.01342, 0.0675, and 0.1617, respectively; these are the consumption shares in the model's benchmark year, which is 1980.

and, to some extent, predict the principal developments that occur in the economic system that it intends to represent can the effort put into a large-scale quantitative model be justified.

One approach to empirically validating a model is to investigate how well it tracks the impact of policy changes and exogenous shocks after these shocks have occurred.[22] Another approach is to compare predictions with actual outcomes. The problem with the second approach is that the actual data can be significantly affected by unforeseen exogenous shocks that occur concurrently with the foreseen policy change. Applied general equilibrium modelers of the Canadian-U.S. Free Trade Agreement complain, for example, that it is difficult to compare their predictions with the economic experience of the last several years because of the recession in both countries. Since applied general equilibrium models have very explicit structures, however, it should be possible to disentangle the impacts of different shocks and policy changes using the model.

Kehoe, Polo, and Sancho take a step in this direction.[23] They assess the performance of a model of the Spanish economy built in 1984–85 to analyze Spain's 1986 entry into the European Community. The first column of table 9 shows the percentage changes in relative prices that actually took place in Spain between 1985 and 1986. The second column shows the model predictions. In each case the prices have been deflated by an appropriate index so that a consumption-weighted average of the changes sums to zero: these sorts of models are designed to predict changes in relative prices, not those in price levels. Notice that the model fares particularly badly in predicting the changes in the food and nonalcoholic beverages sector and in the transportation sector. There are obvious historical explanations for these failings: in 1986 the international price of petroleum fell sharply and poor weather caused an exceptionally bad harvest in Spain. Incorporating these two exogenous shocks into the model yields the results in the third column in table 9, which correspond remarkably to the actual changes.

Kehoe, Polo, and Sancho perform similar exercises comparing model results, both with and without the exogenous shocks, with the actual data for changes in industrial prices, production levels, returns to factors of production, and major components of GDP. In general, the unadjusted model does somewhat better in predicting the actual changes in these variables, and the adjusted model does somewhat worse. Overall, however, the exercise shows that this sort of model can well predict the changes in relative prices and resource allocation that result from a major policy change.

To be sure, the principal policy change that occurred in Spain in 1986 was a tax reform that converted most indirect taxes to a value-added tax, in accord with EC requirements. The process of trade liberalization began in 1986 and is captured in the model: unlike the modeling exercises evaluated by Brown, however, the work on Spain did not concentrate on trade issues. Consequently, the results from the Spanish model do not help us much to discriminate among the various model structures discussed in Brown's paper.

One way to evaluate these different modeling strategies would be to modify the Spanish model to incorporate alternative assumptions about product differentiation, returns to scale, and market structure. Alternative versions of the model could then be used to "predict" the impact of the trade liberalization that has occurred in Spain in recent years and the results compared with the data. Similarly, and more to the point, the different models used to analyze the impact of NAFTA could be evaluated by using them to "predict" the impact of the policy changes and exogenous shocks that have buffeted the three North American economies over the past decade.

In any case, if NAFTA is implemented, it will be possible in less than a decade to go back and see which models performed better in predicting its effects. One difficulty with doing so is that of comparing sectoral disaggregations across models. Modelers have an obligation to provide a correspondence between the sectors in their models and accessible statis-

Table 10. Growth Rates of GDP in Mexico and Spain, 1980–91
Real change in percent a year

Year	Mexico				Spain			
	GDP	Investment	Exports	Imports	GDP	Investment	Exports	Imports
1980	8.3	14.9	6.1	31.9	1.5	1.3	0.6	3.8
1981	8.8	16.2	11.6	17.7	−0.2	−3.3	8.4	−4.2
1982	−0.6	−16.8	21.8	−37.9	1.2	0.5	4.8	3.9
1983	−4.2	−28.3	13.6	−33.8	1.8	−2.5	10.1	−0.6
1984	3.6	6.4	5.7	17.8	1.8	−5.8	11.7	−1.0
1985	2.6	7.9	−4.5	11.0	2.3	4.1	2.7	6.2
1986	−3.8	−11.8	5.3	−12.4	3.3	10.0	1.3	16.5
1987	1.7	0.1	10.1	2.0	5.6	14.0	6.1	20.2
1988	1.4	5.8	5.0	37.6	5.2	14.0	5.1	14.4
1989	3.1	6.5	3.0	19.0	4.8	13.8	3.0	17.2
1990	3.9	13.4	5.2	22.9	3.6	6.9	3.2	7.8
1991	3.6	8.5	5.1	16.6	2.4	1.6	8.4	9.4

Sources: Instituto Nacional de Estadística, Geografía e Informática, Mexico; and Instituto Nacional de Estadística, Spain.

tical sources. The consumption-good sectors in the Spanish model, for example, correspond to those in the consumer price index published by the Spanish government, and the industrial sectors correspond to those in the national income accounts. Furthermore, details on this correspondence have been published.[24]

Intertemporal Factors

As Brown points out, and as I have stressed elsewhere,[25] the dynamic impact of NAFTA is likely to dwarf the static impact analyzed by most applied general equilibrium models. Perhaps the main impact of the entry into the EC on the Spanish economy, for example, has been a sharp increase in foreign investment closely related to increases in GDP and imports. From 1980 to 1985 investment in Spain actually fell by 1.0 percent per year (as shown in table 10). In contrast, since its entry into the EC in 1986, investment has grown by 10.0 percent a year on average. Similarly, GDP growth has increased from 1.4 percent average in 1980–85 to 4.1 percent in 1986–91, and import growth has increased from 1.3 percent to 14.2 percent. A similar pattern can be seen to emerge in Mexico with the "apertura," or openness policy, that began to take effect in 1988 and 1989.

NAFTA would be expected to reinforce this pattern, with substantial increases in GDP fueled by foreign and domestic investment and with even more substantial increases in imports leading to large trade deficits.

In both Spain and Mexico, many, if not most, of the current discussions of economic openness in the press, among academic analysts, and in policy circles concentrate on the sustainability of these investment booms and the corresponding trade deficits. Interestingly, none of the models discussed by Brown deal explicitly with the issues involved. Robert McCleery mentions the pattern in the data in a footnote, but most of the relevant variables are assumed to be exogenous in his model.[26]

In many of the models, the most dramatic effects of NAFTA are those that result from increases in foreign investment in Mexico. Yet in all these models, even in the dynamic ones, this process is modeled as exogenous. A fully specified dynamic general equilibrium model is the ideal tool for analyzing capital flows. The essential question that such a model needs to address is: if the post-NAFTA capital stock in Mexico is large and the corresponding interest rate low, why is the pre-NAFTA capital stock small and the corresponding interest rate high? One possible answer is that a high interest rate in Mexico has been the result of relatively closed capital markets and of inefficient, oligopolistic financial intermediaries. There is indeed some evidence to support this view.[27] To follow this approach, one would model explicitly how NAFTA would result in more competition and lower prices in the financial intermediation market.

An alternative answer to the question why the pre-NAFTA interest rate in Mexico is higher than it is in the United States or Canada is that there is a risk premium on investing in Mexico because of fears of inflation or changes in government policies. To follow this approach, one would model how NAFTA would lock Mexico and its two northern neighbors into policies that would help guarantee economic stability in Mexico, which would lower the risk premium and, consequently, the interest rate. Modeling this satisfactorily would require including some stochastic features in the model: exactly what is it that potential investors, inside and outside Mexico, fear, and how does NAFTA lower the probability of this occurring?

There are, of course, other intertemporal factors that should be built into a complete analysis of the impact of NAFTA. One obvious factor is differences in the rates of population growth and in the demographic structures among the three countries. In Mexico, for example, because of a high rate of population growth, half the population is currently under the age of twenty, while in Canada and the United States the population is aging (see table 11). Modeling how the three countries will interact over time requires explicit modeling of borrowing, lending, and human capital accumulation decisions.

Table 11. Population by Age Group, 1990
Percent

Age	Mexico	United States
0–15	41.0	23.2
16–24	19.2	13.0
25–64	35.6	51.2
65 and over	4.2	12.6

Sources: Instituto Nacional de Estadística, Geografía e Informática, Mexico; and Department of Commerce, Bureau of the Census, United States.

Yet another intertemporal factor that should be built into a dynamic analysis of the impact of NAFTA is total factor productivity growth. Using simple econometric estimates based on cross-country data, I have calculated that openness in Mexico could lead to a 50 percent increase in total factor productivity in manufacturing in Mexico within twenty-five years, over and beyond other effects.[28] This work is still at a preliminary stage. The sizes of the numbers involved, compared with those in the studies analyzed by Brown, indicate that this is a fruitful direction for future research.

Comment by Robert Z. Lawrence

This is a very informative paper that does what it intended to do. Not only does Brown summarize the results of the various models, but she gives the reader some useful insights into why they differ. In particular, she makes clear the considerable degree to which fairly innocent modeling assumptions can affect results. Indeed, making assumptions that products are differentiated by country of destination or origin, or both, and that returns to scale are constant will reduce the size of the effects of NAFTA. Together these assumptions limit the degree to which countries specialize because of increased trade opportunities. This leads to results that suggest NAFTA has small effects on welfare, and, implicitly, on adjustment, even in the case of Mexico. As Brown notes, however, work following recent theoretical developments captures more realistic features, such as investment flows, imperfect competition, scale economies, product differentiation, endogenous growth, and uncertainty and indicates effects that are considerably larger.

I do not wish to criticize the overall CGE modeling framework. The great virtue of models is that they usually rest on solid theoretical grounds and are thus far more credible than the ad hoc polemical calculations that often characterize advocacy pieces in trade research. Since Brown has done such a good job of showing what these models capture, in my comments I discuss what they leave out.

A spurious criticism sometimes lodged against these models is that they typically assume full employment. In many policy discussions the question arises about the impact of policy on net job loss. I have heard it argued that models which assume full employment cannot capture employment effects. However, they are able to indicate the sectoral reallocation of labor induced by NAFTA and thus, implicitly, the extent of employment adjustment. By contrast, the more Keynesian models that assume permanent and variable unemployment are not well suited for analyzing the medium-term effects of trade policy.

What is NAFTA? In the models summarized by Brown it is a policy that would remove the tariff and nontariff barriers in North America. But in several respects, I believe this characterization is inadequate and tends to understate NAFTA's impact both on North America and the rest of the world. Admittedly, some features of NAFTA are difficult to quantify, but they could actually be more significant than those that have been quantified in the models. I feel they should not be overlooked in appraising the merits of an agreement.

The first relates to the issue of policy credibility. Implicitly all policies in the models are assumed to be credible and permanent. However, particularly so far as Mexico is concerned (and to some degree so far as the United States is concerned) without NAFTA these policies would be less credible. President Salinas could have unilaterally reduced tariffs and investment barriers in Mexico—indeed he did to a large extent—but he would not have had the effects of NAFTA in convincing foreign and domestic investors that his policies were likely to persist. Some have tried to embody this effect by lowering risk premiums on aggregate investment, but I think doing so fails to capture the major effects on sourcing decisions that multinational corporations are likely to undertake when changes are credibly permanent. I would argue that the elasticity parameters of adjustment are likely to be considerably larger when changes are credible.

A second issue is that NAFTA is about much more than the simple removal of border barriers. As seen in the deliberations over NAFTA, when a poor country lowers its border barriers it raises concerns not simply about competition between workers of different wages but also about the effects of different institutional practices and legal regimes. These relate to rules for intellectual property, pollution, worker safety, and so on. The result is that to allow free trade, the governments have to agree to a much greater degree of integration than is reflected simply by the removal of border barriers. In many cases, this will again lead to much greater responses than the models estimate. As a result of NAFTA, for example, Mexico has introduced a new regime for the protection of intellectual property rights. Mexico has also radically transformed its sectoral industrial policies in automobiles and informatics and technology transfer. Mexico will also be importing U.S. rules and standards, a change that will eventually mean much easier and less costly access for products and capital flows on both sides of the border. In some cases, however, tougher standards could raise costs, and some Mexican industries could find expansion more difficult than the models estimate.

A third feature of NAFTA of particular concern to U.S. consumers and producers in third countries relates to the definition of rules of origin. In textiles, automobiles, and semiconductors, U.S. producers see NAFTA as an opportunity to increase domestic protection and to gain an advantage, particularly against Asian competitors. Tough, protectionist rules of origin could well take away what the lowering of tariffs and nontariff barriers seem to provide. Trade diversion from third countries could be more significant than the estimates that ignore the effect of such rules.

A fourth aspect, which is missing from the models but was central to the U.S.-Canadian trade negotiations, concerns the administration of trade and investment rules. Indeed a major reason for the Canadian-U.S. Free Trade Agreement was the Canadian fear of the arbitrary and protectionist administration of U.S. trade laws. Likewise the United States sought easier access for investment in Canada. To be sure, the goals were not fully achieved, but nonetheless their impact could potentially be greater than the removal of tariffs worth a few percentage points.

A fifth aspect relates to the geographic incidence of the effects. This issue demands considerable more work and detail in the models. Nonetheless, as Paul Krugman has pointed out, NAFTA is likely to have a dramatic effect on the geographic development of Mexico—in particular, in alleviating some of the centripetal forces that the inward-looking strategies of the past set up around Mexico City and in redistributing growth toward the north of the country. Likewise in the United States, NAFTA's effects appear small in relation to the U.S. economy but could be large in certain regions and communities. These locational aspects deserve more attention.

The final consideration, which I am particularly concerned about and which could in principle be modeled but has not been, concerns the impact of the real exchange rate and its dynamics. There is a consensus that the most important effects of NAFTA are on capital flows. This implies that if NAFTA is successful, there will be an adjustment in the North American capital stock that could be associated with large shifts in the real exchange rate. Yet the CGE models examine only the comparative static long-run effects and fail to track the effects of this stock adjustment. Over the long run, Mexico, as a debtor country, will probably have to run larger trade surpluses (or smaller deficits), and thus the real value of the peso will have to be weaker than it would otherwise be. However, the transition path is more complex. In the short run, to effect the capital transfer to Mexico, the real exchange rate of the peso would have to rise and of course Mexico would have to sustain a larger trade deficit. These effects imply that, in the short run, the Mexican adjustment to NAFTA is more difficult and larger than implied in the CGE models, since the traded-goods sector will be hit by a strong currency as well as liberalization. On the other hand, the inflationary adjustment in Mexico may be eased. For the United States, the process is the mirror image. The dollar will be weaker, the trade surplus with Mexico larger, and thus the impact on adversely affected sectors smaller than the CGE models suggest. Indeed, in anticipation of NAFTA there has been a larger Mexican trade deficit, a larger U.S. trade surplus with Mexico, and a stronger peso. This sort of adjustment is not beyond the capacity of modelers to perform, and I believe just such an analysis should be undertaken as a guide to policy.

Notes

1. Paul Armington, "A Theory of Demand for Products Distinguished by Place of Production," *International Monetary Fund Staff Papers*, vol. 16 (March 1969), pp. 159–78.

2. Angus Deaton and John Muellbauer, *Economics and Consumer Behavior* (Cambridge University Press, 1980).

3. Roy G. Boyd, Kerry Krutilla, and Joseph A. McKinney, "The Impact of Tariff Liberalization between the United States and Mexico: A General Equilibrium Analysis," Ohio University, Economics Department, February 1992.

4. David Roland-Holst, Kenneth A. Reinert, and Clinton R. Shiells, "North American Trade Liberalization and the Role of Nontariff Barriers," Mills College, April 1992.

5. Carlos Bachrach and Lorris Mizrahi, "The Economic Impact of a Free Trade

Agreement between the United States and Mexico: A CGE Analysis," KPMG Peat Marwick, Washington, February 1992.

6. Raúl Hinojosa-Ojeda and Sherman Robinson, "Alternative Scenarios of U.S.-Mexico Integration: A Computable General Equilibrium Approach," Working Paper 609 (University of California, Berkeley, Department of Agricultural and Resource Economics, April 1991); and Sherman Robinson and others, "Agricultural Policies and Migration in a U.S.-Mexico Free Trade Area: A Computable General Equilibrium Analysis," Working Paper 617 (University of California, Berkeley, Department of Agricultural and Resource Economics, December 1991).

7. Irene Trela and John Whalley, "Bilateral Trade Liberalization in Quota Restricted Items: U.S. and Mexico in Textiles and Steel," University of Western Ontario, Department of Economics, May 1991.

8. Roland-Holst and others adopt a structure similar to that of Peat Marwick, yet the welfare effects associated with tariff and NTB removal obtained by Roland-Holst and others are over six times larger. It is difficult to account for the discrepancy, though a likely explanation is that Roland-Holst and others incorporate much larger NTBs than found by Peat Marwick.

9. Bob Hamilton and John Whalley, "Optimal Tariff Calculations in Alternative Trade Models and Some Possible Implications for Current World Trading Arrangements," *Journal of International Economics*, vol. 15 (November 1983), pp. 323–48; John B. Shoven and John Whalley, "Applied General Equilibrium Models of Taxation and International Trade," *Journal of Economic Literature*, vol. 22 (September 1984), pp. 1007-51; and Drusilla K. Brown, "Tariffs, the Terms of Trade, and National Product Differentiation," *Journal of Policy Modeling*, vol. 9 (Autumn 1987), pp. 503–26.

10. Drusilla K. Brown and Robert M. Stern, "Computational Analysis of the U.S.–Canada Free Trade Agreement: The Role of Product Differentiation and Market Structure," in Robert Feenstra, ed., *Trade Policies for International Competitiveness* (University of Chicago Press, 1989), pp. 217–45.

11. Richard Harris, "Market Structure and Trade Liberalization: A General Equilibrium Assessment," *American Economic Review*, vol. 74 (December 1984), pp. 1016–32.

12. David Cox and Richard G. Harris, "North American Free Trade and Its Implications for Canada: Results from a CGE Model of North American Trade," *World Economy*, vol. 15 (January 1992), pp. 31–44. Horacio E. Sobarzo, "A General Equilibrium Analysis of the Gains from Trade for the Mexican Economy of a North American Free Trade Agreement," El Colegio de México, Centro de Estudios Económicos, December 1991; and Drusilla K. Brown, Alan V. Deardorff, and Robert M. Stern, "A North American Free Trade Agreement: Analytical Issues and a Computational Assessment," *World Economy*, vol. 15 (January 1992), pp. 11–30.

13. H. Eastman and S. Stykolt, "A Model for the Study of Protected Oligopolies," *Economic Journal*, vol. 70 (June 1960), pp. 336–47.

14. Both Sobarzo and Cox and Harris have performed sensitivity analyses on the pricing rule and have found that focal pricing produces considerably greater welfare gains from liberalization than does monopolistic competition.

15. Gene M. Grossman and Elhanan Helpman, "Product Development and International Trade," *Journal of Political Economy*, vol. 97 (December 1989), pp.

1261–83; Paul M. Romer, "Endogenous Technological Change," *Journal of Political Economy*, vol. 98 (October 1990), pp. S71–102; and Nancy L. Stokey, "Learning by Doing and the Introduction of New Goods," *Journal of Political Economy*, vol. 96 (August 1988), pp. 701–17.

16. Timothy J. Kehoe, "Modeling the Dynamic Impact of North American Free Trade," Working Paper 491 (Federal Reserve Bank of Minneapolis, Research Department, March 1992).

17. Leslie Young and Jose Romero, "Steady Growth and Transition in a Dynamic Dual Model of the North American Free Trade Agreement," University of Texas, Austin, February 1992.

18. Santiago Levy and Sweder van Wijnbergen, "Transition Problems in Economic Reform: Agriculture in the Mexico-U.S. Free Trade Agreement," Boston University, December 1991.

19. Robert K. McCleery, "An Intertemporal, Linked, Macroeconomic CGE Model of the United States and Mexico, Focusing on Demographic Change and Factor Flows," Economic Development and Policy, East-West Center, Honolulu, February 1992.

20. INFORUM, *Industrial Effects of a Free Trade Agreement between Mexico and the USA*, report prepared for the U.S. Department of Labor (University of Maryland, 1990).

21. Linda Hunter, James R. Markusen, and Thomas F. Rutherford, "Trade Liberalization in a Multinational-Dominated Industry: A Theoretical and Applied General Equilibrium Analysis," University of Colorado, December 1991.

22. Kemal Dervis, Jaime de Melo, and Sherman Robinson, *General Equilibrium Models for Development Policy* (Cambridge University Press, 1992), chap. 10; Shantayanan Devarajan, and Hector Sierra, "Growth without Adjustment: Thailand, 1973–1982," World Bank, Washington, 1986; and Brian Parmenter and others, "Structural Change in the 1970's: Historical Simulations with ORANI-F," IAESR Working Paper, (University of Melbourne, 1990).

23. Timothy J. Kehoe, Clemente Polo, and Ferran Sancho, "An Evaluation of the Performance of an Applied General Equilibrium Model of the Spanish Economy." Working Paper 840 (Federal Reserve Bank of Minneapolis, 1991).

24. See Timothy J. Kehoe and others, "Una matriz de contablidad social de la económica española," *Estadística Española*, vol. 30 (1988), pp. 5–13.

25. Kehoe, "Modeling the Dynamic Impact."

26. McCleery, "An Intertemporal, Linked, Macroeconomic CGE Model."

27. See for example, Garber and Weisbrod, "Opening the Financial Services Market in Mexico," Brown University, 1991.

28. Kehoe, "Modeling the Dynamic Impact."

Labor Issues in a North American Free Trade Area

Raúl Hinojosa-Ojeda
Sherman Robinson

THIS paper surveys research on labor issues in a North American free trade area involving the United States, Mexico, and Canada. The main focus is on the possible evolution of employment, wages, and labor-related institutions, especially in the United States and Mexico. These labor issues involve much more than simply trade relations, which are the primary concern of the trilateral NAFTA negotiations and also of the Uruguay Round of multilateral world trade negotiations under the General Agreement on Tariffs and Trade (GATT). The impact of NAFTA on labor must be analyzed in the context of the complex relationship between trade, investment flows, technological change, and migration, as well as labor practices and social and political institutions within and across the three countries. Ultimately, given the initial wide gap in income levels across the region, the key question concerns the potential convergence or divergence of wages and productivity across the three countries and among socioeconomic groups within them. Will the creation of NAFTA lead to a pattern of convergence based on rising Mexican productivity and wages, or will the primary result be a worsening of the distribution of income within the United States?[1] What additional resources and institutions are needed to facilitate Mexican growth and a smooth transition to a new and mutually beneficial integration arrangement?

Dramatic change has already started in Mexico because of the collapse in the 1980s of the pattern of inward-oriented, import-substituting industrialization (ISI) that had been pursued since World War II. The ISI development strategy was already largely exhausted before the large discoveries of oil in the mid-1970s, and the debt crisis of the 1980s confirmed Mexico's inability to continue on that path. From the mid-1980s, Mexico has undergone a major program of macroeconomic stabilization and structural adjustment and has shifted to an outward-looking development strategy with trade providing the major engine of growth. This shift in strategy can potentially provide important benefits for Mexico and, with renewed growth, an expanding market for U.S. exports.[2] Labor market problems, however, pose special difficulties for Mexico as it shifts its development strategy. Through the 1990s Mexico faces a demographic bulge, which will lead to high labor force growth just as the economy requires major restructuring.

The United States, too, is facing a period of significant structural change. A decade of macroeconomic imbalances (including declining savings, increased government deficits, and large swings in trade deficits), slow productivity growth, unemployment problems, stagnation in real wages, and increasing inequality has created an environment of uncertainty and a loss of confidence by labor, investors, and consumers. Considerable industrial restructuring has occurred, and all indications are that further changes will be required as the economy adjusts to continuing changes in the world economy and the macroeconomic environment.

In facing these changes, the United States and Mexico are finding their futures increasingly linked through an already extensive web of economic, social, and political interdependence. Although this interdependence is clearly asymmetrical in many areas, the United States and Mexico never-theless share by far the most extensive and complex network of linkages of any two countries on opposite sides of the North-South divide. Mexican-U.S. interdependence includes the largest trade relation and the largest debtor-creditor relation between any two developed and developing countries, the largest foreign investment flows, the largest in-bond coproduction relations (*maquiladoras*), and the longest contiguous border with the highest levels of border crossings and border commerce, both legal and illegal. Since the debt crisis erupted in 1982, and especially with the inauguration of the Salinas and Bush administrations, Mexico and the United States have begun a dramatic new phase of liberalized opening in the areas of trade and foreign investment, which has culminated in the NAFTA ne-gotiation. Even before the 1980s, official observers had often noted the centrality of this relationship for the national security interest of both countries, an importance that is expected to increase with the decline of the cold war and the rise of a multipolar world order.[3]

Factor market linkages, especially labor flows, actually represent a more extensive linkage between the two economies than does trade. Trade and investment flows have been comparatively freer than labor flows, which have been more socially and politically sensitive and subject to more legal controls. Migration issues have explicitly been excluded from the current NAFTA negotiations. However, the future patterns and levels of labor migration will be an important influence not only on relative

Table 1. U.S.-Mexican-Canadian Trade, 1989

Item	Mexico	United States	Canada
GDP (billions of U.S. dollars)	200.7	5,156.4	488.6
GNP per capita (U.S. dollars)	2,010.0	20,910.0	19,030.0
Trade flows as share of GDP (percent)			
Total exports	16.9	7.0	27.8
To Mexico	. . .	0.5	0.1
To United States	13.9	. . .	17.4
To Canada	0.7	1.5	. . .
Total imports	18.0	9.5	27.6
From Mexico	. . .	0.5	0.3
From United States	12.4	. . .	15.9
From Canada	0.2	1.6	. . .

Sources: World Bank, *World Development Report, 1991*; and International Monetary Fund, *Direction of Trade Statistics, 1991*.

wages and the pattern of trade and employment but also on the future pattern of sectoral production, productivity growth, corporate profitability, investment spending, and international competitiveness. Some U.S. and Mexican labor market segments are now so linked that employment levels, working conditions, and wages exist in a delicate balance that spans both sides of the border, and the social compacts in both countries have become intimately interdependent. Unilateral attempts to close off or penalize labor flows not only have been ineffective but usually result in perverse feedback effects in other markets, besides raising divisive issues of cultural diversity, national sovereignty, and regional security. Any comprehensive trade and investment agreement must at least implicitly address the likely pattern of migration and its related impact on the economic interests of different groups, including the sectoral pattern of employment and the resulting patterns of income inequality, with obvious social and political feedbacks.

While there are many potential benefits from the creation of NAFTA, successful integration of the North American economies poses serious challenges for the three countries. Mexico, in particular, faces many special problems because of its initial position.

—There are wide disparities in the economic sizes of the three economies, with Mexican gross domestic product at less than 4 percent of U.S. GDP and less than 40 percent of Canadian GDP (table 1). U.S.-Mexican trade represents a much larger share of Mexican GDP (16.9 percent) than of U.S. GDP (0.6 percent). From size differences alone, one expects that the effects of NAFTA, both positive and negative, will be much greater for Mexico and Canada than for the United States.

—Development disparities *between* North American countries are much

Table 2. Comparative Data for Selected Countries, Selected Years and Periods, 1965–89

Country[a]	GDP (billions of U.S. dollars), 1989	Population (millions), 1989	Per capita GNP U.S. dollars, 1989	Per capita GNP Growth rate (percent), 1965–89	Average annual growth rate (percent) GDP, 1980–89	Average annual growth rate (percent) Agriculture, 1980–89	Average annual growth rate (percent) Industry, 1980–89	Share of GDP (percent) Savings, 1989	Share of GDP (percent) Exports, 1965	Share of GDP (percent) Exports, 1989
United States	5,156.4	248.8	20,910	1.6	3.3	3.2	2.9	13	6	12
Canada	488.6	26.2	19,030	4.0	n.a.	n.a.	n.a.	23	19	25
Mexico	200.7	84.6	2,010	3.0	0.7	0.8	0.4	18	8	16
Germany	1,189.1	62.0	20,440	2.4	1.9	1.6	0.0	27	19	35
Spain	379.4	38.8	9,330	2.4	3.1	n.a.	n.a.	22	10	19
Greece	39.9	10.0	5,350	2.9	1.6	0.3	0.9	9	9	24
Portugal	44.9	10.3	4,250	3.0	2.5	n.a.	n.a.	21	27	36
Yugoslavia	71.8	23.7	2,920	3.2	1.3	1.0	1.4	53	22	34
Turkey	71.6	55.0	1,370	2.6	5.1	3.0	6.3	21	6	22
Egypt	31.6	51.0	640	4.2	5.4	2.6	4.8	7	18	22
Brazil	319.2	147.3	2,540	3.5	3.0	3.0	2.7	26	8	7
Venezuela	43.8	19.2	2,450	-1.0	1.0	3.4	1.4	27	26	34
Argentina	53.1	31.9	2,160	-0.1	-0.3	0.3	-1.1	19	8	16
Chile	25.3	13.0	1,770	0.3	2.7	4.1	3.0	24	14	38
Colombia	49.4	32.3	1,200	2.3	3.5	2.6	5.0	24	11	18
Japan	2,818.5	123.1	23,810	4.3	4.0	0.4	5.2	34	11	15
South Korea	211.9	42.4	4,400	7.0	9.7	3.3	12.4	37	9	34
Thailand	69.7	55.4	1,220	4.2	7.0	4.1	8.1	29	16	36
Philippines	44.4	60.0	710	1.6	0.7	2.0	-0.8	18	17	25
Averages										
Lower-middle income	…	…	1,360	2.0	2.5	2.1	2.6	23	15	25
Upper-middle income	…	…	3,150	2.6	3.2	3.0	3.2	30	20	24
High income	…	…	18,330	2.4	3.0	1.5	2.1	22	13	23

Source: World Bank, *World Development Report, 1991*. n.a. Not available. a. Countries are arranged in regional groups in order of decreasing per capita GNP.

wider than between any other group of countries that have attempted to integrate their economies. Groups such as the European Community (EC) and the European Free Trade Association (EFTA) started with far smaller differences in per capita (and total) GDP than that between Mexico and the United States (table 2).

—Income distribution disparities *within* the United States and Mexico are also much wider than within member countries of the EC. An important element in U.S. income inequality is the widening gap between the incomes of white Americans and those of Hispanics and other minority populations, both U.S. born and immigrant.[4]

—Because of demographic trends, Mexico's labor supply is growing at about 3 percent a year, far more rapidly than labor in the United States, and the rate will decline only slowly for the rest of the decade. This rapid growth will place strains on the Mexican labor market and lead to migration pressures both within Mexico (rural-urban) and internationally.

—The large differences in initial income highlight problems of reconciling labor and environmental standards across the region, especially the need for, and the difficulties in achieving, integrated government investment and regulatory policies. Migration is very sensitive to labor market conditions in both countries as well as to differences in incomes between them. Capital flows are potentially sensitive to environmental standards as well as to differences in economic conditions. The costs of achieving integrated labor and environmental standards will be relatively higher for Mexico, the poorest of the three countries, and will require public infrastructure investment to provide an environment conducive to complementary private investment.

—Mexico starts with a debt overhang of about $100 billion, which is the second highest (after Brazil) among developing countries. No other developing country that has made a successful transition to an open development strategy started with such a large debt burden.[5]

—After a decade of crisis management and policy focus on stabilization, Mexico has neglected its physical and social infrastructure and must generate renewed investment in social overhead capital. Such social investment is necessary to complement private investment, which together are required to generate productivity growth. Achieving rapid productivity growth, in turn, is a crucial element determining the success of the new development strategy.[6]

—Taking advantage of the opportunities provided by increased integration in North America requires that the economies be able to reallocate labor and capital within and across sectors. To achieve these reallocations quickly and efficiently, policies are needed to minimize the adjustment costs to workers and communities that necessarily accompany displacement of labor and capital.

—Establishing a free trade area is a necessary part, but only a part, of the policy package that will enable Mexico to shift its development strategy. If the new strategy is to succeed, Mexico's domestic and foreign capital needs will expand greatly. It will need to mobilize resources for a major investment effort and be able to reenter world capital markets. The creation of a free trade area should improve confidence for private investors, including Mexicans who have maintained large investments abroad during the last decade. Under existing institutional arrangements, however, and given Mexico's debt overhang, more will be needed, especially to finance large-scale social overhead investments.

Demographics and Labor Market Linkages

Historically, the U.S. and Mexican labor markets have been closely linked. Mexican migrant labor has had a large impact on the U.S. economy through increasing the supply of labor—an effect probably greater than that arising from increased U.S.-Mexican commodity trade, direct foreign investment, or financial transactions. At least 10 percent of the growth of the U.S. labor supply since World War II is due to Mexican migrants, and Mexicans working in the United States represent close to one-sixth of the Mexican work force (table 3).

Typical of a rich and a poor country, the United States and Mexico are at different points in their demographic transition. In the United States the population growth rate has declined and the population is aging. In Mexico the age structure is much younger, the population growth rate is higher, and the labor force growth rate is higher still (as the younger population enters the labor force). In this environment, Mexican migration has historically provided the United States with an important source of labor, especially in the Southwest, and has also served as a safety valve for Mexico, providing employment opportunities for workers displaced by the structural changes accompanying Mexican industrialization.[7]

Several writers have pointed out that Mexico and the United States have shown a labor market complementarity over the postwar period, due both to demographic trends and to changes in the sectoral structure of production in the two countries.[8] For a variety of reasons, the close links between the U.S. and Mexican labor markets will undoubtedly persist

Table 3. Mexican Contributions to the U.S. Population and Labor Pool, Selected Years, 1940–90

Thousands unless otherwise specified

Item	1940	1950	1960	1970	1980	1990
1. Total U.S. population	132,457	151,868	179,979	203,984	227,217	249,660
2. Total Mexican population	19,654	25,791	34,923	48,225	66,847	85,782
3. Total Mexican origin population in the United States	377	450	1,735	4,532	8,740	13,495
4. U.S. labor force	41,870	63,379	71,489	84,889	108,544	126,424
5. Mexican labor force	5,858	8,345	10,213	14,489	22,092	31,027
6. Annual flow of legal temporary workers	0	150	420	47	20	120
7. Cumulative stock of undocumented workers (beginning in 1940)	0	100	200	316	1,095	2,298
8. Cumulative stock of legal immigrant workers (beginning in 1940)	0	46	286	673	1,230	2,172
9. Total "Mexican" workers in U.S. work force[a]	0	296	906	1,036	2,345	4,590
10. Total Mexican origin labor force in United States	335	571	1,308	2,063	3,498	8,742
11. "Mexicans" working in United States as percent of Mexican labor force	n.a.	3.55	8.88	7.15	10.61	14.79
12. "Mexicans" working in United States as percent of U.S. labor force	n.a.	0.47	1.27	1.22	2.16	3.63
13. Total Mexican origin labor force as percent of U.S. labor force	0.80	0.90	1.83	2.43	3.22	6.91

Sources: U.S.-Mexican labor force totals for 1940, 1950, 1970, 1980, and 1990 are from the census data on economically active population (including unemployed). The 1960 census figure was adjusted to correct for overcounting rural workers. For details see Clark W. Reynolds, "A Shift-Share Analysis of Regional and Sectoral Productivity Growth in Contemporary Mexico," working paper, International Institute for Applied Systems Analysis, Laxenburg, Austria, 1979. The estimates in row 6 are based on the number of legal temporary workers (including braceros from 1942 to 1964, H-2 from 1952, and SAW/RAW from 1986). Estimates in row 7 are estimates of undocumented workers during the previous five-year period (one-quarter of undocumented immigrants deported reduced by one-fourth for nonparticipants in the work force) and are adjusted by estimates published by Jeffrey Passel and Karen A. Woodrow, "Geographic Distribution of Undocumented Immigrants: Estimates of Undocumented Aliens Counted in the 1980 Census by State," *International Migration Review*, no. 18 (1984), pp. 642–71; and Manuel García y Griego, "The Mexican Labor Supply, 1990–2010," in Wayne A. Cornelius and Jorge A. Bustamante, eds., *Mexican Migration to the United States: Origins, Consequences, and Policy Options* (University of California at San Diego, Center for Mexican Studies, 1989), vol. 3, pp. 49–94. Row 8 is based on Immigration and Naturalization Service, *Yearbook of Immigration Statistics*, with demographic growth calculated along with a 0.68 labor force participation rate and a 0.05 attrition rate.

n.a. Not available.

a. "Mexicans" in the United States refers to all legal and undocumented immigrants from Mexico who entered this country between 1940 and the present and their progeny, regardless of place of birth. This is clearly not the same as "people of Mexican origin" as detailed in the census and Current Population Survey, which comprises all legal and undocumented immigrants and their descendants who came to the United States before 1940. The second group is about one and one-half times as large as the first.

well into the next century, regardless of whether a free trade area is established:

—Even under the most optimistic productivity growth scenarios, the United States will face a serious shortfall in labor supply well into the next century as its native population increasingly ages and continues to shrink.[9]

—Mexico, on the other hand, even under optimistic scenarios of resumed growth, will produce a dramatic labor force surplus into the next century.[10]

—Deeply rooted social networks have now been established where binational codependence has become a way of life for many communities (and productive sectors) on both sides of the border. These networks will continue to operate as long as the large wage gaps persist, barring dramatic and highly unlikely changes in migration policies.[11]

—The gap in relative wages across the two countries will remain quite wide for the relevant time period, regardless of any forces that would promote convergence.[12]

While recognizing that social and political factors are important in determining the stock, flow, and wages of migrant workers, Francisco Alba concentrates on the economic and demographic factors affecting the demand for and supply of migrant workers.[13] Examining the historical relation between migration and development from the 1940s and 1950s, he compares demographic trends forecast for Mexico and the United States up to the year 2000, trends that initially appear to indicate a harmony of interests. During the 1940s and 1950s there was a relatively stable pattern of migration, with demand concentrated in agro-industry in the southwestern United States and supply originating in central Mexican rural communities. This particular "escape valve" mechanism has since undergone important changes. The demand for labor has shifted away from agriculture in the United States, which was rapidly mechanized in the postwar period, toward the expanding service and light-manufacturing sectors in U.S. cities. Meanwhile, similar structural changes in the Mexican economy, with rapid industrialization and a relative decline in agriculture, have created a supply of labor more complementary to the U.S. demand.

This apparent complementarity of changes in supply and demand conditions on both sides of the border, however, does not necessarily indicate a harmony of interests. Within the United States, persistent macroeconomic problems have led to unemployment and slackness in labor markets, with concomitant political pressure to control immigration and use trade policy to protect domestic employment. Moreover, Mexico's demographic profile, though complementary to that of the United States, is also similar to that of Caribbean and other Latin American countries, which are increasingly sending migrants to the United States and competing with Mexican migrants.

Alba argues that the best solution for both countries is not to continue the migration process as it now exists. Rather, he favors policies to increase trade in goods and services between the two countries. In his view, dismantling protectionist policies and encouraging trade would allow for rapid employment creation in Mexico and technological evolution in the United States as export industries expand.

Saul Trejo Reyes also discusses Mexican economic policy and U.S.-Mexican relations in the context of recent trends of Mexican labor force growth and employment.[14] Even though population growth in Mexico slowed from 3.4 percent a year during the 1970s to 2.7 percent in the 1980s, the labor force is still growing at about 3 percent a year. Given rapid industrialization and resulting internal rural-urban migration, most of Mexico's population growth has been in urban areas, with almost no net rural growth expected in the future. The shift to the cities has also been accompanied by a rapid growth in the tertiary sector. Labor force participation rates have also increased, in large part because of a rise in female participation rates.

Since the 1982 crisis there has been a shift in employment in Mexico from large firms to the informal sector, with a large increase in open unemployment. Employment in sectors producing capital and intermediate goods has been particularly hard hit. Using a macroeconomic growth model of the Mexican economy, Trejo Reyes generates three alternative scenarios for future employment growth for the period 1985 to 2000. With optimistic assumptions, but without explicitly considering NAFTA or Mexico's shift in development strategy, he projects an annual GDP growth rate of 5 percent. In this scenario there is a "deficit" in employment for the existing and future labor force of about 8 million by the end of this period. Under the assumption that the changes in development strategy currently under way in Mexico are only moderately successful, these scenarios project increased internal pressure on urban labor growth as well as increased pressure for undocumented migration to the United States.

The results of these demographic studies indicate that even if Mexico succeeds in achieving a shift in development strategy, there will be increased strains on its labor markets and increased migration pressure over the next decade. The severity of this pressure will depend largely on three factors: how successful Mexico's shift to the new, open development strategy is and its effect on the eventual structure of the economy; how rapidly Mexico can restructure its economy, generate new investment, and achieve rapid growth; and macroeconomic developments in the United States. The last factor is largely independent of questions relating to the formation of NAFTA and so should be seen as an exogenous factor in any analysis of NAFTA, which is the approach taken in existing studies. The first two factors have been the focus of a number of studies.

Modeling the Effects of NAFTA on Labor Markets

The announcement by the presidents of Mexico and the United States of their intention to negotiate a free trade agreement between their two countries sparked a veritable growth industry of economic modeling of NAFTA. Some of the policy debate over the last two years has been characterized by the selective and uncritical citing of one or another study to justify apparently preconceived positions on the impact of NAFTA on employment and the structure of the economies in both countries. Some of the positions have been quite strident, with few qualifications, belying President Harry Truman's view that he wanted a one-armed economist who could not keep saying "on the other hand." In surveying empirical work on the labor-market implications of NAFTA, we focus in this section on differing assumptions and discuss how the various approaches are linked to different theoretical and empirical models.

Table 4 presents examples of various types of modeling approaches that have been used to analyze the effect of establishing a free trade area and have either focused on labor issues or have discussed implications for labor as part of a wider analysis. There are three types of models represented: (1) partial-equilibrium models based on historical extrapolation or regression analysis of key relationships; (2) single-country computable general equilibrium (CGE) models; and (3) multicountry CGE models.

Extrapolation-Regression Models

The first model in this group is by Gary Hufbauer and Jeffrey Schott for the Institute of International Economics (IIE).[15] They have developed what they call a historical model that is largely based on a comparative analysis undertaken by the World Bank of thirty-one episodes of trade liberalization.[16] This study, like many before it, indicates that developing countries which successfully shift from an inward-looking, import-substitution development strategy to an outward-looking, trade-oriented strategy tend to do very well. Although the Asian tigers represent extreme cases, the desirability of shifting to an open development strategy has become part of the conventional wisdom in development economics.

Using some rather simple, even simplistic, relationships drawn from the World Bank study, Hufbauer and Schott seek to project Mexican performance under the new strategy. In their model, they simply postulate that Mexico will rapidly increase its trade, increase the trade share in GNP, increase foreign capital inflows, and accelerate the growth rate of GNP. These assumptions are not related to any specific notions of what NAFTA will or will not include. The magnitudes are based on the experiences of comparable countries and are imposed as macroeconomic trends. Hufbauer and Schott then assume a fixed ratio of trade with the United States to total Mexican trade, and their trends generate an improvement in the U.S. trade balance. Finally, they estimate changes in employment as a function of the change in trade balance, and so forecast an improvement in U.S. employment of 130,000 jobs, which they note is very small compared with total U.S. employment of more than 115 million.

The underlying model of employment is not spelled out but must be some kind of Keynesian trade multiplier. The multiplier is based on "net exports," defined as additional exports minus additional imports of consumer goods. Hufbauer and Schott assume that this multiplier is six times as high in Mexico as in the United States.[17] In the NAFTA scenario, Mexican capital inflows increase, which implies a decrease in the current account balance (and, presumably, an appreciation of the real exchange rate). However, they assume that much of the increased inflow of imports consists of capital goods, and so they manage to generate an increase in their "net export balance" measure. The result is an increase in Mexican employment of 609,000, which represents 2 percent of aggregate Mexican employment by 1995.

The IIE historical model has the virtue of applying to Mexico some rough empirical lessons gleaned from comparative work. The experience of other countries can provide some indication of the best that Mexico might expect from successfully shifting development strategy. The model, however, has no discernible roots in trade theory. The use of short-run, Keynesian macroeconomic trade multipliers in a model seeking to analyze the long-term benefits of trade liberalization seems inappropriate. Since the model involves only aggregates and macroeconomic trends, it cannot

Table 4. Properties of NAFTA Models

Model	Model characteristics	Sectoral structure	Factor markets	Migration
		Extrapolation-regression models		
Hufbauer and Schott (Institute of International Economics)	Macro trends based on average behavior of countries that have shifted to an open development strategy; no consistency framework	Macro only	Employment effects based on elasticities with respect to change in net trade balance	No migration
Prestowitz and others (Economic Strategy Institute)	Macro trends based on assumptions about the impact of NAFTA on Mexico; new investment in Mexico assumed to increase exports to United States and imports from United States; sectoral structure and trade diversion estimates based on historical shares; balance of trade determined from separate export and import projections	Sectoral results for six industries	Employment effects based on fixed employment to trade ratios; aggregate employment effects determined by changes in balance of trade	No migration
Koechlin and others	Cross-country econometric model to estimate increase in direct foreign investment in Mexico from the United States resulting from NAFTA; assumes increase in DFI lowers aggregate U.S. investment	Macro only	Assumes fixed aggregate capital-labor ratio; employment change then depends on investment change	No migration
Leamer	Regression equations, estimating and testing various propositions from neoclassical trade theory regarding the impact of increased trade on low-skilled wages in the United States; two-	Commodities at one-, two- and three-digit SIC aggregation levels	Theoretical model distinguishes capital, skilled, and unskilled labor; regression model relates changes in factor	No migration

	country, two-and-three-factor, three-good theoretical models provide motivation for regression equations		prices to changes in product prices
INFORUM	Two-country (Mexico and United States), linked, economy-wide, multisectoral, macroeconomic regression model; model uses fixed input-output coefficients and determines cost prices, but has no market-clearing equilibrium conditions	Seventy-eight sectors in the U.S. model, and seventy-four in the Mexican model	Labor demands, differentiated by detailed occupational categories, are determined by sectoral employment coefficients, given sectoral demand projections	No migration

Single-country static CGE models

Levy and van Wijnbergen (World Bank)	Static CGE model of Mexico; detailed treatment of agriculture, income distribution, and agricultural policies; tradable/nontradable specification	Seven sectors focusing on maize and agriculture; one nontraded sector, one industrial sector	Two land types (irrigated and rainfed), capital, urban labor, and rural labor	Rural-urban migration. Depends on real income differential between rural and urban workers
Sobarzo	Static CGE model of Mexico; focus on imperfect competition and economies of scale in manufacturing sectors; Armington specification; in one version, the balance of trade is fixed and the exchange rate adjusts; in two other variants, the exchange rate is fixed and the balance of trade adjusts	Twenty-seven sectors, of which twenty-one are traded; one agricultural sector	Capital and labor; sectoral capital stocks and the wage are fixed in two versions, while in third the wage is flexible and capital is intersectorally mobile	Implicit rural-urban migration, as labor can move from agriculture to other sectors

Table 4 (continued)

Model	Model characteristics	Sectoral structure	Factor markets	Migration
		Multicountry static CGE models		
U.S. International Trade Commission	Highly stylized, two-country (United States and Mexico), CGE model; Armington specification for tradable good	Two sectors, a tradable and nontradable	Capital and two labor categories, skilled and unskilled; capital is sectorally fixed	International migration of unskilled workers, using an elasticity of migration with respect to international wage differential
KPMG Peat Marwick	Three-country CGE model (United States, Mexico, and rest of world); competitive markets; Armington specification	Forty-four sectors, focusing on manufacturing; four agricultural sectors	Capital and labor; fixed wage in Mexico	Implicit rural-urban migration, as labor can move from agricultural sectors to other sectors; no international migration
Hinojosa and Robinson	Three-country CGE model (United States, Mexico, and rest of world); competitive markets; policies represented by tariff, tax, and subsidy equivalents; Armington specification	Seven sectors, with one agricultural sector	Land, capital, and four labor categories; various assumptions about factor mobility	Rural-urban migration within Mexico; Mexican-U.S. migration for rural and urban unskilled labor; migration depends on wage differentials
Robinson and others	Three-country CGE model (United States, Mexico, and rest of world); competitive markets; explicit modeling of agricultural and trade policies in both countries; Armington specification	Eleven sectors, with four agricultural sectors	Land, capital, and four labor categories; various assumptions about factor mobility	Rural-urban migration within Mexico; Mexican-U.S. migration for rural and urban unskilled labor; migration depends on wage differentials

Brown, Deardorff, and Stern	Five-region CGE model, including United States, Mexico, and Canada separately; monopolistic competition and increasing returns to scale in most tradable sectors; goods differentiated by producer rather than by country of origin	Thirty sectors, of which twenty-three are tradable; one agricultural sector	Capital and labor, both intersectorally mobile	Implicit rural-urban migration, as labor can move from agriculture to other sectors; no international migration
Roland-Holst, Reinert, and Shiells	Four-country CGE model (United States, Canada, Mexico, and rest of world); increasing returns and average-cost pricing in some sectors; Armington specification	Twenty-six sectors, with one agricultural sector	Capital and labor, both intersectorally mobile; fixed wage in all three countries	Implicit rural-urban migration, as labor can move from agriculture to other sectors; no international migration

Dynamic CGE models

Levy and van Wijnbergen (World Bank)	Dynamic CGE model of Mexico; model of transition period (nine years) terminating with steady-state balanced growth; tradable/nontradable specification	Seven sectors focusing on maize and agriculture; one nontraded sector, one industrial sector	Two land types (irrigated and rainfed), capital, urban labor, and rural labor	Rural-urban migration, depending on real income differential between rural and urban workers
Hinojosa and McCleery	Stylized, dynamic, two-country CGE model of Mexico and United States; tradable/nontradable specification	Two sectors, one traded, one nontraded	Capital and two labor categories: "high wage" and "low wage"; land is included in Mexico	Mexican-U.S. migration depends on real income differential; some linkage between the two labor markets within both countries
McCleery and Reynolds	Stylized, dynamic, two-country CGE model of Mexico and United States; tradable/nontradable specification; capital accumulation, with investment determined by savings	Two sectors, one traded, one nontraded	Capital and two labor categories: "high wage" and "low wage"; land is included in Mexico	No migration; some linkage between the two labor markets within both countries

Sources: See text notes for complete sources of models.

capture any of the structural changes and gains from trade liberalization predicted by neoclassical trade theory. Since most of the gains and strains arising from trade liberalization will involve shifts in the sectoral structure of trade, output, and employment, predictions of the IIE model about employment effects are questionable at best.

The second extrapolation model is the Economic Strategy Institute (ESI) model by Clyde Prestowitz and others.[18] Like the IIE model, the ESI model starts from a number of assumptions about the macro impact of the formation of an FTA. The authors assume, for example, that Mexico will increase investment in export-oriented industries by $25 billion to $46 billion and that imports from the United States will expand with Mexican income, equaling 2 percent of the increase in Mexican output. They determine the composition of imports by assuming fixed shares and an assumption about the course of import substitution in Mexico in intermediate goods and components. On employment, they state: "The potential employment effects were then estimated by using the standard economic formula holding that $1 billion worth of trade represents 30,000 jobs."[19] Their employment relation is thus based on a fixed net-trade coefficient, similar to the treatment in the IIE model. They also separately estimate the employment impact in six industries because of new capital spending in Mexico, but this analysis does not use the labor-trade deficit relation.

Two scenarios are run with the ESI model, assuming low ($25 billion) and high ($46 billion) investment increases in Mexico. Prestowitz and others then generate growth paths to 1999, including the balance of trade (given their assumptions about export and import coefficients). In both scenarios, the United States runs a trade surplus with Mexico until 1996–97, when it shifts to a deficit. In the high growth scenario, in 1999 the deficit is $30 billion, and given their employment coefficients, "more than 900,000 American jobs are destroyed."[20]

In economic structure, the ESI model is similar to the IIE model. Both assume a variety of fixed-coefficient macroeconomic relationships and are driven by exogenous trends. They differ in their assumptions about those trends and the magnitudes of the employment coefficients. The ESI model is subject to the same criticisms as given to the IIE model.

The third extrapolation-regression model is that of Timothy Koechlin and others.[21] This model focuses on investment and employment effects. The chain of causation is as follows: (1) NAFTA will generate increased foreign investment in Mexico; (2) much of the increased investment will come from the United States; (3) increased U.S. investment in Mexico will reduce aggregate investment in the United States; and (4) given fixed capital-labor ratios in the United States the decline in U.S. investment will lead to a decline in aggregate employment.

Koechlin and others use cross-country data and some regression analysis to put empirical content into each of these causal links. They estimate that the establishment of NAFTA would generate an increase in U.S investment in Mexico of $3.5 billion to $5.9 billion a year, or $31 billion to $53 billion cumulatively over the period 1992–2000. Assuming a corresponding decline in U.S. investment, and given projections of the capital-labor ratio, they estimate that between 29,000 and 49,000 jobs will be relocated in the first year of NAFTA, and a total of between 290,000 and 490,000 jobs through the year 2000.[22]

Whereas steps 1 and 2 in their chain of reasoning seem plausible, steps 3 and 4 are highly questionable. The figure of $3 billion-$6 billion dollars a year is a tiny fraction of aggregate U.S. investment, and even a small fraction of the current U.S. trade deficit. Macroeconomic adjustments in the United States over the next decade are generally projected to be large, with the current account deficit projected to decline dramatically. The projected changes in U.S. investment in Mexico are tiny compared with these shifts. From a different perspective, the changes in U.S. investment in Mexico postulated by Koechlin and others represent a tiny part of the U.S. capital market and should have a negligible effect on interest rates or returns to capital in the United States. There is no theoretical or empirical reason to think that these investment changes will have any effect at all on aggregate investment. In fact, EC experience after Spanish and Irish accession suggests that NAFTA should increase direct foreign investment (DFI) into the United States.[23]

Even assuming a change in investment in the United States, the assumption of a fixed aggregate capital-labor ratio is suspicious in the short run and insupportable in the medium to long run. Even assuming limited substitution possibilities in sectoral production, which is empirically unwarranted, changes in the sectoral structure of production arising from changes in trade policy will lead to changes in the aggregate capital-labor ratio. Even though changes in the sectoral structure of employment are to be expected as a result of changes in trade and investment policy, the argument put forward by these authors that, in the aggregate, jobs will "relocate" from the United States to Mexico with an increase in commodity trade and investment flows is theoretically and empirically unsustainable.

The optimistic IIE model and the pessimistic analyses by Prestowitz and others and Koechlin and others are striking in their lack of theoretical underpinnings. There is, after all, a large body of neoclassical trade theory that seeks to explain what will happen when one adds or removes barriers to trade between countries. The Heckscher-Ohlin, Stolper-Samuelson, Rybczynski, and factor-price equalization theorems represent milestones in the theoretical analysis of the impact of trade on economic structure in a general equilibrium setting. One might well expect empirical work on trade liberalization to draw on this extensive and rich theoretical literature.

The final study in this group, by Edward Leamer, does draw extensively on this body of theoretical work.[24] Leamer starts from a small, neoclassical, trade-theory model and then seeks to estimate the important linkages implied by the theory. He first argues that labor and capital migration between the United States and Mexico will lead to a tendency toward equalization of factor prices across countries; he then draws on the factor-price equalization theorem to argue that free commodity trade should lead to equalization under a free trade agreement, even in the absence of factor mobility. The result, he argues, is that unskilled wages in the United States should fall because of the increase in international trade, and that this tendency will be accelerated by the creation of a U.S.-Mexican free trade area. Consistent with trade theory, he does not argue for changes in aggregate employment but instead analyzes the effect of trade on wages.

Although this approach is consistent with the long-run focus of neoclassical trade theory, the relevant empirical questions are (1) is the Mexican economy big enough relative to the United States for changes in trade to have a significant aggregate effect on the United States? and (2) what are the relative sizes of indirect effects on wages and profits arising from changes in product prices compared with direct effects arising from labor and capital mobility between the two countries? While acknowledging that Mexico is very small relative to the United States, and hence that short-term aggregate effects should be tiny, Leamer attempts to estimate the effects of an empirical scenario in which Mexico becomes much larger. Under this scenario, he assumes that U.S. rates of protection would continue to rise for the rest of the world but would be prevented from rising vis-à-vis Mexico because of NAFTA; and that Mexico is able to increase its level of productivity to OECD levels rapidly (Italy is used as the proxy) and thus grow very quickly and capture a large U.S. market share through trade diversion from the rest of the world.[25]

Starting from this Mexico-becomes-Italy scenario, Leamer then analyzes, using disaggregated data at the two- and three-digit SIC levels, the effect of changes in relative prices on sectoral trade and production and on wages. He extends his model to include nontradables and seeks to estimate the relationship between changes in factor returns to changes in prices (Stolper-Samuelson) and changes in output to changes in factor supplies (Rybczynski). He argues that the major differences in capital-labor ratios between the United States and Mexico will have an impact on factor prices with trade liberalization. In the long run, he thinks the creation of NAFTA should increase the capital rental and the wage of skilled labor in the United States and lower that of unskilled labor. His empirical results generate a wide range of estimates, but he concludes, "Earning reductions on the order of $1000 per year [for low-skilled labor in the U.S.] seem very plausible."[26]

Compared with the first three studies examined, Leamer's work has strong theoretical underpinnings. His empirical work is characteristically careful, yet is clearly speculative and highly contingent on an extreme scenario. He recognizes these problems, emphasizes the wide range of estimated effects, and describes his empirical results on factor returns as conjectural and uncertain "both because there is econometric uncertainty in the estimates and also because the precise economic theory that underlies the computation is not compelling."[27] Given his assumptions, his empirical results are consistent with trade theory. One could probably not expect to do better theoretically without moving to a full general equilibrium model. The underlying driving scenario that Mexico becomes large relative to the United States, however, has to be seen as a very long-run projection.

A step toward the construction of a computable general equilibrium model is provided by the INFORUM model.[28] This study is conducted with a two-country (Mexico and United States), linked, multisectoral, macroeconomic regression model. The linked model uses a seventy-eight-sector input-output matrix for the United States and a seventy-four-sector matrix for Mexico. Through macroeconomic projections based on an econometric macro model, the model generates output, exports, imports, consumption, and income by industry. The models also estimate trends in the coefficients of the input-output matrices. The connection between the two models occurs through import-share functions. Labor requirements are determined by sectoral labor coefficients, which change over time. The INFORUM model does not have any behavioral supply responses to price changes. The model is used to generate a base run scenario with the 1990 level of protection and two alternative NAFTA scenarios: (1) the elimination of tariffs only; and (2) no tariffs and lowered nontariff barriers in textiles, agriculture, autos, and computers.

The INFORUM results indicate that the effects of removing tariffs are larger than the effects of removing the few nontariff barriers they consider, and the stimulus to U.S. exports is greater than to Mexican exports, both bilaterally and to the rest of the world. The second result is implausible, is not supported by any of the other NAFTA models, and is difficult to explain in the model. The authors' explanation is as follows: "This extra boost to [U.S.] exports comes about because the reduction of tariffs with Mexico lowers cost of production in the U.S., which then competes more effectively in other foreign markets."[29] It is difficult to see how this mechanism would operate in their model, which lacks profit-maximizing supply behavior by producers. In any case, the postulated mechanism is certainly empirically implausible. Given their result, they find that the employment effect is a slight net increase in U.S. employment and a net decrease in Mexican employment (of 0.5 percent).

The INFORUM model is not a full general equilibrium model, since it is essentially demand driven, with no market-clearing, price-adjustment mechanisms. It is best seen as a sophisticated, multisectoral, essentially Keynesian macroeconometric model. As such, it is not a good vehicle for examining trade liberalization effects that work through product and factor-price mechanisms, as described by neoclassical trade theory.

Computable General Equilibrium (CGE) Models

The trade-focused CGE models used to analyze NAFTA are all firmly rooted in neoclassical trade theory.[30] Single-country CGE models determine relative domestic prices and a real exchange rate that clear product markets and factor markets and also satisfy a balance-of-trade constraint. Besides domestic relative prices, the multicountry CGE trade models also solve for relative world prices that clear world product markets for traded goods and a set of real exchange rates such that each country satisfies its balance-of-trade constraint. All market-clearing equilibrium conditions are in terms of flows. The models solve only for relative prices, with the absolute price level set exogenously by a choice of numeraire. The models have no financial variables and do not include money, assets, or asset markets. Their roots are Walrasian, not Keynesian.

All the models include tradables and nontradables, and many specify imperfect substitutability between imported and domestic goods—the Armington assumption. The Armington specification treats all domestic goods as "semitradables" and can be seen as an extension of the standard neoclassical model with nontradables.[31] The approach is widely used in empirical trade models because it yields a more realistic empirical picture of the links between domestic and international prices than do models that assume an extreme dichotomy between tradables and nontradables.

Although all are rooted in neoclassical trade theory, the CGE models developed to analyze the impact of the formation of NAFTA vary widely in their sectoral focus; treatment of labor markets, including migration; assumptions about technology and industrial organization; treatment of policy instruments; and specification of structuralist rigidities such as immobile factors, fixed wages, and barriers to migration. Our focus in this paper is on the treatment of labor and the conclusions the various models draw regarding the effect of the formation of NAFTA on labor markets.

The two single-country, static CGE models referred to in table 4 differ widely in their treatment of labor markets. The Horacio Sobarzo model, in some variants, assumes a fixed wage, with aggregate employment determined endogenously, and sectorally fixed capital stocks.[32] Though perhaps useful for analyzing short-run impact effects, such a model is ill suited for analyzing the medium- to long-run impact of NAFTA. In the model variant with a variable wage, aggregate employment fixed exogenously, and intersectorally mobile capital, NAFTA coupled with capital stock growth in manufacturing leads to a decline in agricultural labor in Mexico of about 8 percent, as the increase in manufacturing draws labor out of agriculture. Total employment is fixed by assumption, and the average real wage rises by 16 percent. Real GDP rises by 8 percent because of the increase in aggregate capital and the exploitation of economies of scale in manufacturing.

The second Mexico-specific CGE model, by Santiago Levy and Sweder van Wijnbergen, provides a much more detailed specification of the agricultural sectors and of rural-urban migration.[33] They explicitly model agricultural support policies, including protection for the maize sector and food subsidies for the urban poor. They include rural-urban migration, with migration adjusting to maintain an exogenously specified real income differential between rural and urban households. They explore a number of scenarios in which the maize sector is liberalized, allowing free trade, and various compensation polices are simulated that are designed to soften the impact on the poor.

Liberalization in the maize sector leads to significant rural-urban migration, of about 650,000 to 700,000 workers. Total rural employment is 6 million, of which 29 percent (or 1.7 million) is in the maize sector. Without compensation, Levy and van Wijnbergen find the distributional effects of trade liberalization to be regressive, but it is possible to design feasible compensation packages that largely offset the income losses to the poor. On the basis of several simulated scenarios, they argue that one can design targeted adjustment programs that achieve substantial efficiency gains from trade liberalization but that ameliorate the regressive distributional impact of removing protection from low-income maize farmers.

In a dynamic version of their model, Levy and van Wijnbergen explore different transition paths to free trade over a nine-year adjustment period.[34] They explore the effect of introducing trade liberalization and domestic policy changes instantaneously or more gradually, analyzing the effect of the speed of reform on migration. They find that if liberalization is done all at once, in the first year, the efficiency gains are large but that migration is also very large early on, with 700,000 migrants from the rural sector in a single year. Such migration would seriously strain the social and political system. Under all liberalization scenarios, cumulative rural-urban migration over nine years is about the same, 1.9 million workers. A gradual liberalization scenario, however, provides a smooth time path of migration, with annual rates of about 200,000 rural-urban migrants a year. Note that in a base scenario without liberalization the model generates a cumulative migration of 1.2 million workers from the rural sector. Their model embodies the underlying demographic trends discussed earlier. Mexico faces major structural change in its labor markets, with or without trade liberalization.

Hinojosa and Robinson and Robinson and others explore some of the same labor-market issues as Levy and van Wijnbergen but in the context of a two-country, U.S.-Mexican trade model.[35] In particular, Robinson and others use a similar breakdown of the agricultural sectors, separating out maize, fruits and vegetables, and other program crops (relevant for capturing U.S. agricultural policies). They use the same type of migration function as Levy and van Wijnbergen but differentiate the labor force by skill category and add Mexican-U.S. migration. Their results are also broadly consistent with those of Levy and van Wijnbergen. They find that complete trade liberalization increases bilateral trade and leads to efficiency gains for both countries but induces large rural out-migration from Mexico. In a full liberalization scenario, more than 800,000 workers leave the rural sector, and more than 600,000 migrate to the United States. Most of the migrants to the United States go to the urban labor market (for example, Los Angeles) rather than to agriculture. Robinson and others also explore a variety of partial liberalization scenarios, seeking policy packages that will provide a less socially disruptive transition path to free trade. They find that it is feasible to design such transition policy packages.

Robinson and others explore how much growth is required in Mexico to absorb the labor released from agriculture, without increased migration to the United States. For example, a 25 percent increase in the Mexican aggregate capital stock relative to the United States eliminates the increased Mexican-U.S. migration induced by complete trade liberalization. Such a growth differential is consistent with the experience of other semi-industrial countries that have successfully shifted to an open development strategy. The policy problem for Mexico is that trade liberalization in maize releases labor quickly, whereas the increased growth required to absorb that labor in industry takes longer.[36] Consistent with Levy and van Wijnbergen, these results indicate that Mexico will need a lengthy transition period and must allocate resources to agriculture during the transition. Undue haste in introducing free trade in agriculture may not be desirable for either country when the social and economic costs associated with increased migration are weighed against the benefits of increased trade growth.

Hinojosa and McCleery present a dynamic U.S.-Mexican CGE model with a game-theoretic component that implicitly takes into account the nature of sociopolitical institutions for the regulation of distributional conflicts between workers and capitalists in both countries.[37] While the model is highly aggregated and stylized, it incorporates international migration as well as rural-urban migration within Mexico. The authors use their model to develop three alternative scenarios for Mexico: a continuation of the current "neoliberal" opening; a reversal toward neoprotectionism; or the adoption in both countries of a "managed interdependence" strategy. Although the names are more evocative, the scenarios are similar to those explored in Robinson and others, with similar results.

The model results point to the long-term superiority of a free trade agreement leading to increased trade, while also indicating a short-run deterioration in workers' welfare that poses serious obstacles to the neoliberal strategy. Compared with policies directly affecting capital and labor markets, changes in trade policies usually have smaller effects on production and welfare. An FTA by itself is not capable of entirely reducing the trend toward increased illegal migration, as some have claimed. Migration, in fact, will increase in the absence of significant capital inflows to raise employment and wages in Mexico. An attempt to close off either economy from exchange with the other (the protectionist alternative) emerges as the worst long-term welfare option for most workers' groups in both countries. The dilemma, however, is that, in the short run, this option is superior for those workers benefiting from direct protection. Of the three alternative scenarios, only managed interdependence can provide for continued growth, increased international exchange, and a basis for strategically agreed-upon social pacts in both countries. The key to this approach is developing a combination of debt, trade, and migration policies that maximize growth and welfare on both sides of the border.

McCleery and Reynolds present a model that is similar to the one developed by Hinojosa and McCleery, but that disables the migration equations and the Stakelberg tie between workers and capitalists.[38] The first scenario removes tariffs and again demonstrates that simply eliminating official tariffs has little effect on either economy. The new elements introduced in scenarios two through four are (1) a consideration of endogenous capital flows in response to the reduced risk of investing in Mexico under NAFTA, (2) the possibility of more labor-intensive production in Mexico after removing factor and product market distortions, and (3) a simulation of one possible avenue of productivity growth for the U.S. economy resulting from NAFTA.

Unfortunately, a stylized, two-country, two-factor model cannot properly deal with these interesting questions. In the second scenario, capital flows to Mexico induced by NAFTA are assumed to reduce U.S. investment, thus reducing employment in the high wage (also tradable and capital-intensive) sector in the United States. As discussed earlier, it is implausible to assume that increased U.S. investment in Mexico will have a significant effect on the U.S. capital market or on aggregate investment. In the third scenario, a change in the mix of products produced and exported is proxied by a reduction in the (exogenous) capital-labor ratio in the tradable sector. The approach is understandable in a two-sector model but is not really satisfactory, given that it is feasible simply to specify more sectors.

Further, there is an empirical question about the strength or even direction of the assumed effect. Trade liberalization favors labor-intensive sectors in Mexico, but new foreign investment is already increasing capital-labor ratios. Consider, for example, the recent series of extremely capital-intensive investments in the automobile sector in Mexico.[39] The fourth scenario is useful in showing that if productivity gains through learning by doing, increased research and development, or other spillover effects of increased capital goods production in the United States are present, the gains from free trade (with capital movements) will be larger and more evenly distributed between capital owners and labor income. The productivity parameter, however, is not estimated but assumed. Such issues are treated in a more satisfactory way, both theoretically and empirically, in the Deardorff, Stern, and Brown model.

Although only a few of the CGE models include international migration or an adequate treatment of rural-urban migration within Mexico, they all include enough labor-market structure to determine the effect of trade liberalization on market-clearing wages. In general, given the wide disparity in country sizes and levels of GDP, one would expect trade liberalization to have a much larger impact on Mexico than on the United States. As carefully discussed by Leamer, trade theory predicts that, with the removal of trade barriers, unskilled wages should fall in the United States and rise in Mexico, because Mexican exports are intensive in unskilled labor. The theoretical model, however, does not predict magnitudes, and its predictions become ambiguous given preexisting domestic distortions in both countries. The issue becomes an empirical question: how large are the various effects?

The International Trade Commission (ITC) model, which is the most stylized and closest to standard trade theory, does yield a fall in the wage of unskilled labor in the United States, and a rise in Mexico, after trade liberalization.[40] On the U.S. side, however, the effect is tiny. This empirical result is robust and is replicated in all the CGE models. In the absence of significant migration, the impact of the FTA on the aggregate U.S. labor market is insignificant. For example, Hinojosa and Robinson, in an experiment designed to replicate the scenario in the ITC model, find that wages of rural and urban unskilled workers in the United States decline by a tenth of a percent and that other factor returns do not change at all.[41] The KPMG Peat Marwick model, which has forty-four sectors but only one labor category, finds that trade liberalization actually raises the real wage in the United States, but only by 0.02 percent.[42] If the authors fix the wage and, instead, generate the change in demand for workers, they find that aggregate employment in the United States rises by 0.04 percent, or 40,800 jobs. David Roland-Holst, Kenneth Reinert, and Clinton Shiells, also using a model with one labor category and a fixed wage, find that trade liberalization across the United States, Mexico, and Canada raises aggregate employment in the United States by only 0.09 percent.[43] Brown, Deardorff, and Stern, find that the wage gap between U.S. and Mexican workers narrows, but that U.S. workers also gain (largely through pro-competitive effects that lead to exploitation of economies of scale in major U.S. industries).[44]

Evidently, the sorts of indirect effects that drive the Stolper-Samuelson and factor-price equalization theorems are empirically small for the United States, especially since the trade policy change affects a small share of total U.S. trade. There are certainly significant price and quantity changes (winners and losers) at the sectoral level in all the models, but these do not translate into significant changes in the aggregate factor markets. Perhaps with more disaggregation of labor categories, one might find a larger effect, but the question then arises about how valid it is to segment the labor market into many nonsubstitutable categories. These empirical results contrast with those from Leamer discussed earlier.

The models with international migration find more significant wage changes resulting from changes in trade policy. For example, Robinson and others find that a full trade liberalization scenario, which yields Mexico–United States migration of about 600,000 workers, leads to a decline in rural and urban unskilled wages in the United States of 3–4 percent. Wages are sensitive to changes in aggregate labor supplies. International movements of factors have a direct effect on factor returns that is much larger than the indirect effects working through price changes in product markets. These direct effects of migration also largely drive the results from the Hinojosa-McCleery model.

Policies, Politics, and Institutions

Economists tend to assume that changing incentives, such as eliminating import protection, automatically leads all the relevant actors to change supply and demand behavior, as the free market equilibrium model postulates. Actual economies are more complex. Social and political institutions are fundamental for determining whether, how, and how rapidly economies will adjust and reallocate resources in response to a major policy change such as trade liberalization. A major shift in development strategy requires active participation by all large institutional forces, whose interests must then be considered. Labor-related institutions, such as unions and governmental labor agencies, are crucial to ensuring the rights of workers, their participation in bargaining for improved income distribution, and their willingness to support the policy shift. The harmonization of labor-related institutional developments across countries, and a recognition of their complementarity, is fundamental if there is to be a "high wage" convergence based on rising productivity and wages in both countries. In addition, reliance on private capital markets to conduct all elements of potential restructuring and investment is unrealistic. The need for social-overhead investment, infrastructure investment, and the existence of potential real and pecuniary externalities (including environmental externalities) implies that multilateral and public sources of investment funds have an important role to play and can be very beneficial in the integration.

Institutional issues are difficult to integrate into traditional economic modeling. Some attempts have been made, nevertheless, within a U.S.-Mexican framework. Koechlin and others, for instance, incorporate a labor discipline model of wage determination into their analysis.[45] Institutions in the labor market are conceptualized as determining the cost of job loss through wages forgone over an average period of unemployment between jobs, during which time benefits are received. These benefits, in turn, affect work effort and the wage employers are willing to pay. The U.S. equilibrium wage is also affected by the unemployment rate and, in their analysis, is expected to increase due to U.S. investment shifts to Mexico. In Mexico, the equilibrium wage falls as labor is assumed to be displaced from agriculture in an FTA, and the fallback wage is determined by informal-sector employment rather than unemployment benefits.[46]

Hinojosa and McCleery motivate the game-theoretic elements of their model as reflecting the operation of such institutions as unions, employer associations, and the legal system.[47] The bargaining game is seen as essential for reaching long-term, dependable (that is, credible) agreements or social pacts over wage, investment, and employment levels. The weaker the institutions, the less likely are actors to enter into accords that might allow for the more efficient reallocation of resources. If trade liberalization is not accompanied by policies to provide social "safety nets," retraining, and adjustment assistance, workers and capitalists in the losing sectors can be expected to resist politically. Even if overall social welfare may be increased and the proposed FTA passes the compensation test, it may fail in the political process if the losers are not compensated.

There have been some proposals to develop new institutions in North America to facilitate the movement toward greater integration, assist in resource reallocation, and compensate affected communities. One proposal, which indicates the sorts of problems that need addressing, is the creation of a new institution, a regional North American Development Bank and Adjustment Fund (NADBAF).[48] This institution would serve two functions: as a regional investment bank, it would lend funds to finance long-term development projects; as an adjustment fund, it would provide short- to medium-term assistance to facilitate the reallocation of resources required to generate productivity increases in the region.

The underlying assumption is that there will be no serious shortage of private investment funds but that there is a real need to mobilize resources for long-term investment in social overhead capital and in areas where private markets cannot work properly (that is, when there are environmental externalities). Institutions with functions similar to the proposed NADBAF were established in Europe, as the European Community expanded to include relatively less developed countries like Greece, Spain, Ireland, and Portugal. Institutions like the European Regional Development Fund and the European Social Fund have been very successful in facilitating the integration of poorer new members into the EC. North America can draw on lessons learned from the successful experience of Europe. One important difference with the European experience, however, is that the operation of NADBAF does not need to have an aid component. The types of long-term investments that are needed should be socially profitable, and the government must capture enough of the returns to ensure repayment.

Although regional development and adjustment institutions in the European and North American context have the same ultimate goal of rising productivity and real wages in the poorer as well as the richer regions, another set of institutional proposals concentrates on the need to directly harmonize worker rights across countries as a means of raising wages and working conditions of the poorer country to the standards of the richer. Drusilla Brown, J. William Gould, and John Cavanaugh call for the adoption of a "Social and Environmental Charter for North America" that would include some common minimum standards as well as recommendations for regional governments, whose implementation would "take into account different levels of national economic development but that will improve steadily with gains in productivity."[49] Another set of proposals concentrates on the lack of human and labor rights within the United States for immigrant workers, calling for the extension of legal protection to all workers as an essential part of integration.[50] An important area of needed research concerns the interplay of regional economic activity and the method of introducing new standards and institutions.

Conclusion

A number of lessons can be learned from the rather extensive body of modeling work regarding the employment and wage implications of the formation of NAFTA.

Most analysts agree that the impact of NAFTA will be much greater on Mexico than on the United States. At the aggregate level, the effect on wages, profits, employment, and investment in the United States will be tiny, much smaller than the year-to-year fluctuations typically observed historically.

Trade theory predicts that, even without international factor mobility, there should be movement toward wage convergence after the creation of NAFTA, with Mexican unskilled wages rising and U.S. unskilled wages falling. Model results indicate that, on the U.S. side, this result is not empirically robust. The effects on the U.S. side are small, and existing distortions create a second-best environment in which the theoretical predictions become ambiguous. All the CGE models generated plausible scenarios in which wages rise in both the United States and Mexico. Models with imperfect competition and scale economies find procompetitive effects from trade liberalization that easily dominate Stolper-Samuelson effects, generating larger increases in wages in both countries.

Although macroeconomic effects in the United States resulting from the creation of NAFTA are tiny, important sectoral effects exist. There are certainly sectoral winners and losers, and the CGE models work well in identifying them. As one disaggregates sectors and factors, and moves toward assuming sector-specific factors (both capital and labor), the CGE models find significant changes in factor incomes arising from NAFTA. Such observations are certainly consistent with trade theory and are also consistent with the observation that political opposition to changes in trade policy tend to be organized by sector rather than by aggregate factors (that is, steel and automobiles, rather than labor).

International factor mobility is an important part of NAFTA, even though labor migration is not part of the negotiations. Models with international labor migration and investment generate much larger changes in wages and capital rental rates than do models that examine only changes in commodity trade. The CGE models find that, empirically, changes in factor mobility have a much greater impact on factor returns in the two countries than do changes in the volume and composition of commodity trade.

The models that focus on migration issues all indicate a policy tradeoff for trade negotiators. Complete liberalization in Mexican agriculture will greatly increase the speed of out-migration from rural areas. These migrants show up in both Mexican urban and U.S. labor markets, causing adjustment problems and social strains on both sides of the border. Liberalization, however, is good for U.S. agriculture, which greatly increases its exports to Mexico. The model results make a strong argument for having a long transition period for Mexican agriculture, to allow time to make needed infrastructure investments in rural areas and to smooth the process of labor absorption in the Mexican industrial sector.

When seen as an important component of Mexico's attempt to shift development strategy and open its economy, NAFTA may result in large benefits for Mexico. If Mexico succeeds in shifting development strategy and achieving rapid growth, the expansion of trade with the United States will benefit U.S. exporters significantly. Models that examine this "success scenario," with more rapid growth in Mexico, project all incomes (including wages) to rise significantly in both countries.

The creation of NAFTA, while potentially benefiting all three countries, will also create strains, especially in Mexico. The benefits from trade liberalization are gleaned only by changing the sectoral structure of trade, production, and factor employment. CGE models tend to understate the adjustment problems, focusing on medium- to long-run changes in structure without considering the adjustment process necessary to reach the new equilibrium. Policymakers can use such models to indicate where the countries are heading, but they also must consider the political and institutional problems of facilitating adjustment and compensating those who are displaced during the process.

Comment by Anne O. Krueger

I have little to add to the masterful survey that Hinojosa and Robinson have undertaken. It provides an invaluable reader's guide to the various models that have been developed to estimate the effects of a free trade agreement on labor, including not only a description of results but also sufficient information about each model so that the reader can judge its relevance.

Instead, in this comment I consider what the models to date have accomplished, and what they have not covered. As a starting point, I draw a distinction between two issues: on one hand, there is opposition to a potential U.S.-Mexican FTA because of American labor's concerns about the impact of the FTA on wages and employment for American workers; on the other hand, there is, or should be, an effort to pinpoint those issues critical for policy that will in fact determine the probable success of an FTA.

As regards the first issue, the models to date show that concern over the impact of an FTA on American labor is greatly exaggerated. Only one model—that of Leamer—shows a negative impact at all. Once it is recognized that the alternative to more employment and increasing productivity for Mexican workers is certainly more migration to the United States, it is likely that American labor will realize that its true interest lies in the success of the FTA, because (1) the United States is likely to run a trade and current account surplus, thus stimulating exports, (2) more rapid Mexican growth will provide a stimulus to U.S. economic activity, and (3) migratory flows will slow down.

There is one astonishing lacuna in the labor models to date: it would appear that, at most, modelers have considered two classes of labor, skilled and unskilled workers. Arguably, the skills of American "unskilled" labor exceed those of their Mexican counterparts because of greater educational attainments and greater labor force experience. One challenging question that, apparently, has not yet been addressed is, what is the "true" wage gap when adjustments are made to the raw data to account for actual skill differences within broad labor categories? Realistic estimates of the skill differential might allay many of labor's concerns about an FTA and would also inform policy regarding the nominal wage and the nominal exchange rate, as I indicate below.

However, there is ample basis for believing that the determinants of the success of a U.S.-Mexican FTA will be factors other than those that concern American labor. An FTA could flounder in at least two ways, with unfortunate consequences for all participants. First, the United States could become sufficiently protectionist to make the FTA sector-specific and shift it from multilateral to bilateral trading arrangements. Second, Mexican economic policies could be inconsistent with a "genuine" FTA. It is these issues that I address in the remainder of my comment.

As for the first issue, it is very probable that a "GATT-plus" arrangement with Mexico and other countries would be welfare-increasing for all countries. In that circumstance, the Uruguay Round would be successfully concluded, and the North American FTA arrangements would cover integration and removal of barriers even beyond those actions undertaken multilaterally. In that sense, NAFTA would resemble the European Community during the 1950–70 period, when closer integration among the EC countries was accomplished while the height of external tariffs was being greatly reduced. If Europe 1992 proceeds as anticipated, and the Uruguay Round agreement provides for external liberalization of trade and harmonization of other measures, the conclusion of a NAFTA agreement that provided for even further harmonization within the Western Hemisphere would pose few difficulties. One issue would be the conditions under which other countries could access the arrangement, but that is well beyond the scope of this book.

If, instead, NAFTA and Europe 1992 proceed in the context of a failed Uruguay Round, and trade tensions gradually result in increasingly concentrated trade within each region, there will be losses for all. The models that would estimate the effects of such an outcome would be far different from the ones surveyed by Hinojosa and Robinson. Certainly, additional work needs to be done on the potential effects of the emergence of trading blocs.

On the perhaps optimistic assumption that good sense will prevail and the multilateral trading system will remain healthy, a second important issue for the fate of Mexican entry into an FTA with the United States remains: whether Mexico's macroeconomic policies are consistent. For the past several years, Mexico's rate of inflation has been approximately 20 percent, whereas the U.S. rate has been less than 5 percent. Mexican wages have been indexed to the Mexican rate of inflation, while the rate of depreciation of the Mexican peso has been considerably less than the differential in the inflation rate between the two countries. Mexican wages have thus been rising in dollar terms, even though they have been constant in local currency, assuming the Mexican price level index correctly reflects the underlying inflation rate. The recent experience in eastern Germany, where the exchange rate between the ostmark and deutsche mark was set at an unrealistic level, should serve as a warning about the dislocations that can result without policy consistency.

Should these trends in Mexican real wages denominated in dollars continue, the real wage in Mexico may be too high for maintaining reasonably full employment under the FTA. It is in this context that estimates of the true "wage gap" might prove highly valuable. But whatever the gap is or ought to be, it seems improbable, given the rate of growth of the Mexican labor force, that Mexican wages can increase at anything like the rate of the past few years without serious unemployment. An appropriate combination of exchange rate, fiscal, monetary, and wage policy will be essential for the success of an FTA. It would be highly productive to have researchers attempt to analyze the consequences of potential policy mistakes in that dimension, in the expectation that analysis of the consequences could assist in the decisionmaking process.

One final comment is in order: most of the models seem to provide fairly "small" estimates of the gains from tariff reduction and elimination of quantitative restrictions (QRs) under an FTA. Since Mexican and U.S. tariffs are already fairly low and QRs affect a few sectors only, that result is not surprising. There are, however, a number of nontariff barriers to trade. On the U.S. side, these include phytosanitary regulations (which probably are in part protectionist), other agricultural policies, maritime restrictions, and the potential use of antidumping and countervailing duty procedures against Mexican exporters. On the Mexican side, many residual forms of restriction remain from the earlier, import-substitution days. Although these are, in any event, being dismantled, use of tariff rates (or tariff rate equivalents for QRs) only as an estimate of the impact of an FTA probably underestimates what is likely to happen.

To conclude, research to date on labor markets seems to have centered largely on the concerns raised by U.S. labor regarding the effect of a Mexican-U.S. FTA on wages and employment in the United States. Although those concerns seem to have been addressed adequately, many significant policy issues surround the conditions in which an FTA might be effected. Research that increased understanding of those issues would clearly provide a valuable input into the policy process.

Comment by Michael Piore

This paper does a nice job of explaining what is becoming an extensive and complicated literature. Much of that literature rests on CGE models. These models are so complex that it is often difficult to understand what exactly produces the effects they identify, and I cannot offer an independent reading of them. The major points that Hinojosa and Robinson offer are twofold. First, the models do not predict the very large, discontinuous effects from the opening to trade that are associated with the most spectacular success stories in East Asia. The reason is apparently that the models do not incorporate dynamic processes associated with technological and organizational innovation and learning. Even so, the size of the U.S. economy relative to that of Mexico makes it extremely unlikely that the effect of a treaty on the U.S. labor market as a whole will be significant. The treaty could, nonetheless, have an important impact on certain sectors or geographic regions. Second, the models are basically aggregative and comparative statistics, and they provide very limited institutional detail. These characteristics limit their ability to address questions related to how one might alter, or control, the process of integration through policy interventions.

I have made these points a little more sharply, with less qualifications, than the authors, and I have little to add to them substantatively. What I would like to do instead is to sharpen these points further by reference to two specific aspects of adjustment. One concerns migration and the other the clothing industry. These may seem a rather odd assortment but together they illustrate the importance of disaggregation, timing, and institutions in predicting and controlling the impact of the opening to trade.

Migration

The literature on NAFTA suggests that the structural effect in Mexico of the opening to trade, either unilaterally or through a treaty, on agriculture could be substantial and, if so, would probably result in a significant displacement of labor, which could in turn lead to an increase in migration to the United States. This is the one effect on the U.S. economy that could be quantitatively important. But this outcome depends very much on where the displaced agricultural workers migrate. This is one of the areas in which the use of disaggregation is required to arrive at the likely effects. Hinojosa and Robinson attempt to disaggregate migration flows, distinguishing between flows within Mexico and from Mexico to the United States and in both countries between rural-urban migration and interurban migration. But, to predict what actually might happen and to provide insight into how the process might be controlled through policy, it is necessary to put a good deal more structure on the migration process itself. Two aspects of this process require special attention.

First, it is important to distinguish between regions that have already established patterns of out-migration and regions that have not. Established migration streams are very difficult to redirect through public policy, and if agricultural displacement occurs in areas that are already sending people to the United States, out-migration is bound to increase. New out-migration, on the other hand, is more susceptible to policy intervention; it can be directed to expanding areas of the Mexican economy and away from regions that already have a labor surplus.

Another important determinant of migration patterns is land tenure. Regions with small peasant holdings, where migrants can reinvest their earnings abroad in expanding their land or improving it, tend to generate circular migration rather than permanent settlement. The reforms of the *ejidos* in Mexico may thus turn out to be a much more important factor in the impact of agricultural adjustment than trade itself, but the *ejido* reforms are, in fact, the by-product of the trade adjustment.

Clothing Industry

Gordon Hansen, a doctoral student at MIT, has just completed a study of the adjustment in the Mexican clothing industry to the opening of trade. The study is of some significance, since the clothing industry has usually been thought to be one in which Mexico is likely to reap significant gains from freer trade with the United States. Thus far, however, the Mexican industry has been swamped by imports from the United States. The reasons for this are indicative of a variety of dynamic effects that the CGE models do not take into account and illustrate the difficulties of predicting the impact of changes in trading regimes.

The basic problem of the Mexican clothing industry is that, despite the cost advantage, it cannot compete on the basis of quality or fashion even within its own markets. Buyers in Mexico City have, as a result, turned to suppliers in New York and Los Angeles, abandoning Mexican production centers and cutting off Mexican producers from their traditional markets. Domestic producers are struggling to find new markets, but they are handicapped not only by their general ignorance of where the potential markets are but also by a lack of familiarity with the formalities of contracting in international trade. Meanwhile, many of the imports from the United States are coming from Third World countries in Asia. There are Mexican firms along the border with experience in the U.S. market, but they are largely in different segments of the industry and, in any case, show no signs of transferring their experience to producers in the interior. Most of these problems involve information and learning and thus could be overcome with time if the Mexican producers survive, but it is not clear that they will do so. It is, moreover, not a question of individual firms, some of which will last and some of which will not. The clothing industry is composed of regional agglomerations, and the effects of agglomeration will be lost if the transition takes too long.

This particular case study suggests the following general observations:

—Timing is not simply a question of spreading some fixed amount of adjustment over time. The ultimate outcome in terms of what finally survives and what does not may also be affected by the speed with which the new trading regime is introduced. In the clothing sector, a strong case exists for a gradual opening that allows time for learning (but it may also already be too late for this).

—A variety of relatively minor policy interventions that help producers to learn about new markets and adjust to their quality standards and business procedures may speed up the learning process and affect the outcome.

—Rules governing Third World countries could be critical both to the adjustment process and to the nature of the long-run equilibrium. The Mexican industry would probably have done much better if it had simply had to compete with U.S. producers and if reexports from Asia had been excluded initially. American clothing producers seem to fear, not the Mexican industry as it now exists, but the likelihood that Asian firms will provide the capital and expertise to Mexican producers and in this way increase their penetration in the U.S. market.

One final remark: in debates *among* U.S. manufacturers about NAFTA, the most influential argument of its supporters is that the United States is bound to lose markets to low-wage producers, and the central question is one of complementary processes and services that are not themselves so sensitive to labor costs. If the United States loses to Asian producers, the argument goes, these insensitive complements will be lost as well, but if cost-sensitive production moves to Mexico, the complements will remain in the United States. I have not seen any research directed specifically at this proposition.

Notes

1. For a variety of views on this issue, see Jorge Bustamante, Clark Reynolds, and Raúl Hinojosa-Ojeda, eds., *U.S. Mexican Relations: Labor Market Interdependence* (Stanford University Press, forthcoming).

2. Raúl Hinojosa-Ojeda, "Interdependence and Class Relations: A Long Term Perspective on the United States and Latin America," in C. W. Reynolds, S. Krasner, and P. Schmitter, eds., *The Political Economy of Interdependence in the Americas* (forthcoming); and Raúl Hinojosa-Ojeda and Sherman Robinson, "Alternative Scenarios of U.S.-Mexico Integration: A Computable General Equilibrium Approach," Working Paper 609 (University of California, Berkeley, Department of Agricultural and Resource Economics, 1991).

3. "U.S. security without a prosperous and peaceful Mexico is inconceivable. For the U.S., only the Soviet Union compares in importance." W. D. Rogers, "Approaching Mexico," *Foreign Policy*, no. 72 (Fall 1988), p. 196.

4. Raúl Hinojosa-Ojeda, Martin Carnoy, and Huge Daley, "An Even Greater 'U-Turn': Latinos and the New Inequality," in Edwin Melendez and others, *Hispanics in the Labor Force* (New York: Plenum Press, 1991).

5.Turkey, which faced a debt crisis in 1978 and also shifted development strategies, provides an interesting comparator. While Mexico's debt overhang is far larger by any measure, Mexico is an oil exporter and Turkey is an oil importer.

6. For a discussion of the requirements for an open development strategy to be successful, including the need for rapid productivity growth, see Hollis B. Chenery, Sherman Robinson, and Moshe Syrquin, *Industrialization and Growth: A Comparative Study* (Oxford University Press, 1986).

7. Lawrence A. Cardoso, *Mexican Emigration to the United States, 1897–1931* (University of Arizona Press, 1980). The United States played a similar role for Europe during the nineteenth century with the United States actually absorbing a much larger percentage of some countries' populations than has ever migrated out of Mexico. Douglass S. Massey, "Economic Development and International Migration in Comparative Perspective," *Population and Development Review*, 14 (September 1988), pp. 383–413.

8. See, for example, Clark Reynolds, "Will a Free Trade Agreement Lead to Wage Convergence? Implications for Mexico and the United States," in Bustamante, Reynolds, and Hinojosa, eds., *U.S. Mexican Relations*; Wayne Cornelius, "From Sojourners to Settlers: The Changing Profile of Mexican Immigration to the United States," in ibid.; Raúl Hinojosa and Robert McCleery, "U.S.-Mexico Interdependence, Social Pacts and Policy Perspectives: A Computable General Equilibrium Approach," ibid.; Raúl Hinojosa and Rebecca Morales, "International Restructuring and Labor Market Interdependence: The Automobile Industry in Mexico and the United States," in ibid.; Francisco Alba, "Migrant Labor Supply and Demand in Mexico and the United States: A Global Perspective, ibid.; and Philip Martin and J. Edward Taylor, "NAFTA and Mexican Migration to the U.S.," paper presented at a conference on North American Free Trade Agreement: Implications for California Agriculture, sponsored by the UC Agricultural Issues Center and the Giannini Foundation of Agricultural Economics, March 5, 1992, in Los Angeles, Calif.

9. William B. Johnson, *Workforce 2000: Work and Workers for the 21st Century*, report to the U.S. Department of Labor (Indianapolis: Hudson Institute, 1987).

10. Saul Trejo Reyes, "Mexican-American Employment Relations: The Mexican Context," in Bustamante, Reynolds, and Hinojosa, eds., *U.S. Mexican Relations*.

11. Richard Mines and Jeffrey Avina, "Immigrants and Labor Standards: The Case of California Janitors," in Bustamante, Reynolds, and Hinojosa, eds., *U.S. Mexican Relations*; Douglas Massey and others, *Return to Aztlan: The Social Process of International Migration from Western Mexico* (University of California Press, 1987); and Rafael Alarcón, "Norteñización: Self-Perpetuating Migration from a Mexican Town," in Bustamante, Reynolds, and Hinojosa, eds., *U.S. Mexican Relations*.

12. Reynolds, "Will a Free Trade Agreement Lead to Wage Convergence?"

13. Alba, "Migrant Labor Supply."

14. Trejo Reyes, "Mexican-American Employment Relations."

15. Gary Hufbauer and Jeffrey Schott, *North American Free Trade: Issues and Recommendations* (Washington: Institute for International Economics, 1992).

16. Demetris Papageorgiou, Michael Michaely, and Armeane M. Choksi, *Liberalizing Foreign Trade*, vols. 1–7 (Washington: World Bank, 1991).

17. "The multiple of six is roughly based on the 1988 differential between US

and Mexican hourly compensation in manufacturing. This works out to 87,000 new Mexican jobs per additional billion dollars of 'net' exports.'' Hufbauer and Schott, *North American Free Trade*, p. 56.

18. Clyde V. Prestowitz, Jr., and others, *The New North American Order: A Win-Win Strategy for U.S.-Mexican Trade* (Washington: Economic Strategy Institute, 1991), chap. 3.

19. Ibid., p. 47.

20. Ibid., p. 48.

21. Timothy Koechlin and others, "Estimates of the Impact of the Free Trade Agreement on Direct U.S. Investment in Mexico: Summary of Testimony to the U.S. Trade Representative Public Hearings on NAFTA," Washington, 1991; and Koechlin and others, "The Effect of the North American Free Trade Agreement on Investment, Employment, and Wages in Mexico and the U.S.," University of Massachusetts, Amherst, Department of Economics, 1992. Jeff Faux and William Spriggs, *U.S. Jobs and the Mexico Trade Proposal*, Economic Policy Institute briefing paper, Washington, 1991; and William E. Spriggs, "Potential Effects of Direct Foreign Investment Shifts Due to the Proposed U.S.-Mexican Free Trade Agreement," Washington, Economic Policy Institute, 1991.

22. In their testimony Koechlin and others, "Estimates of the Impact," estimated a loss of 260,000 to 439,000 U.S. jobs.

23. Koechlin and others, ibid., note that Ireland and Spain experienced increased direct foreign investment after EC accession and use that data to estimate how much increased investment Mexico might expect. They neglect, however, to point out that overall direct foreign investment into the rich EC countries also rose.

24. Edward Leamer, "Wage Effects of a U.S.-Mexican Free Trade Agreement," paper presented at the Conference on the Mexico-U.S. Free Trade Agreement, Brown University, Providence, October 17–19, 1991.

25. Ibid., p. 52.

26. Ibid., p. 56.

27. Ibid., p. 55. In particular, one might question the Stolper-Samuelson links. For example, using a thirty-sector CGE model of the United States, Hanson, Robinson, and Tokarick found virtually no change in relative factor returns in the United States after the imposition of across-the-board tariffs of 50 percent. Kenneth Hanson, Sherman Robinson, and Stephen Tokarick, "U.S. Adjustment in the 1990's: A CGE Analysis of Alternative Trade Strategies," Staff report AGES9031 (U.S. Department of Agriculture, Economic Research Service, 1990). Once averaged through input-output linkages, sectoral factor proportions appear not to differ enough to generate significant Stolper-Samuelson effects. This result appears again in a variety of CGE models of Mexico and the United States discussed below.

28. INFORUM, "Industrial Effects of a Free Trade Agreement Between Mexico and the USA," report prepared for the Department of Labor (University of Maryland, 1990).

29. Ibid., p. 3.

30. For discussions of trade-focused CGE models in the context of neoclassical trade theory, see John Shoven and John Whalley, "Applied General Equilibrium Models of Taxation and Trade: An Introduction and Survey," *Journal of Economic*

Literature, vol. 22 (September 1984), pp. 1007–51; Drusilla K. Brown, "Tariffs, the Terms of Trade, and Natural Product Differentiation," *Journal of Policy Modeling*, Autumn 1987, pp. 503–26; Drusilla K. Brown, "Properties of Computable General Equilibrium Trade Models with Monopolistic Competition and Foreign Direct Investment," paper prepared for the NAFTA Economy-wide Modeling Conference, sponsored by the U.S. International Trade Commission, Washington, February 24–25, 1992; Sherman Robinson and others, "Agricultural Policies and Migration in a U.S.-Mexico Free Trade Area: A Computable General Equilibrium Analysis," Working Paper 617 (University of California, Berkeley, Department of Agricultural and Resource Economics, 1991); Jean-Marc Burniaux and others, "WALRAS—A Multi-Sector, Multi-Country Applied General Equilibrium Model for Quantifying the Economy-Wide Effects of Agricultural Policies," *OECD Development Studies*, no. 13 (Winter 1989–90, pp. 69–102; Jaime de Melo and Sherman Robinson, "Product Differentiation and the Treatment of Foreign Trade in Computable General Equilibrium Models of Small Economics," *Journal of International Economics*, vol. 27 (August 1989), pp. 47–67; and Shantayanan Devarajan, Jeffrey D. Lewis, and Sherman Robinson, "Policy Lessons and Trade-Focused, Two-Sector Models," *Journal of Policy Modeling*, vol. 12, no. 4 (1990), pp. 1–33. The latter two articles focus on the appropriate role and definition of the real exchange rate in these models.

31. The theoretical properties of models incorporating "semitradables" have recently been thoroughly studied. See the references cited above. One model differentiates products by producer rather than by country of origin. See Drusilla K. Brown, Alan V. Deardorff, and Robert M. Stern, "A North American Free Trade Agreement: Analytical Issues and a Computational Assessment," *World Economy*, vol. 15 (January 1992), pp. 11–30.

32. Horacio E. Sobarzo, "A General Equilibrium Analysis of the Gains from Trade for the Mexican Economy of a North American Free Trade Agreement," *World Economy*, vol. 15 (January 1992), pp. 83–100.

33. Santiago Levy and Sweder van Wijnbergen, "Agriculture in the Mexico-USA Free Trade Agreement," World Bank, Washington, April 1991 (rev. version); and Levy and van Wijnbergen, "Labor Markets, Migration and Welfare: Agriculture in the Mexico-USA Free Trade Agreement," World Bank, June 1991.

34. Their dynamic model has two components. A nine-year transition period is followed by an infinite-horizon, steady-state growth path that the economy is assumed to reach at the end of the transition period. All policy changes take place during the transition period. Santiago Levy and Sweder van Wijnbergen, "Transition Problems in Economic Reform: Agriculture in the Mexico-USA Free Trade Agreement," World Bank, December 1991.

35. Hinojosa and Robinson, "Alternative Scenarios"; and Robinson and others, "Agricultural Policies and Migration in a U.S.-Mexico Free Trade Area: A Computable General Equilibrium Analysis," Working Paper 617 (University of California, Berkeley, Department of Agricultural and Resource Economics, 1991).

36. Such a differential could be achieved in about ten years, assuming a growth differential of about 2.5 percent a year.

37. Hinojosa and McCleery, "U.S.-Mexico Interdependence."

38. Robert McCleery and Clark Reynolds, "A Study of the Impact of a U.S.-Mexico Free Trade Agreement on Medium-Term Employment, Wages, and Production

in the United States: Are New Labor Market Policies Needed?'' paper presented at the CSIS conference session on North American Free Trade: Economic and Political Implications, Washington, June 27–28, 1991.

39. Krueger, for example, argues for expanding labor-intensive exports from Mexico, and Shaiken discusses high technology and capital intensity in automobile exports from Mexico. Anne O. Krueger, *Trade and Employment in Developing Countries*, vol. 2 (University of Chicago Press for the National Bureau of Economic Research, 1983); and Harley Shaiken, *Mexico in the Global Economy: High Technology and Work Organization in Export Industries* (University of California, San Diego, Center for U.S.–Mexican Studies, 1990).

40. U.S. International Trade Commission, "Economy-Wide Modeling of the Economic Implications of a FTA with Mexico and a NAFTA with Canada and Mexico," Preliminary Report on Investigation 332-317 under Section 332 of the Tariff Act of 1930, Washington, February, 1992. The ITC model is not fully documented in this report, and no technical description is available. The description here and in table 1 is based on the sketchy published description, with some additional deduction.

41. Hinojosa and Robinson, "Alternative Scenarios."

42. KPMG Peat Marwick, "The Effects of a Free Trade Agreement between the U.S. and Mexico," paper prepared for the U.S. Council of the Mexico-U.S. Business Committee, 1991.

43. David Roland-Holst, Kenneth A. Reinert, and Clinton R. Shiells, "North American Trade Liberalization and the Role of Nontariff Barriers," paper prepared for the NAFTA Economy-wide Modeling Conference, sponsored by the U.S. International Trade Commission, Washington, February 24–25, 1992.

44. Brown and others, "A North American Free Trade Agreement: Analytical Issues and a Computational Assessment."

45. Koechlin and others, "Effect of the North American Free Trade Agreement."

46. Koechlin and others' specification captures the typical operation of labor markets in developing countries, in which the urban informal sector acts as a labor sink. In the formal sector in Mexico, however, this is a misspecification of the operation of the labor market. Although there is no government unemployment insurance, employers are required to make a substantial severance payment to any worker who is laid off.

47. Hinojosa and McCleery, "U.S. Mexico Interdependence."

48. Albert Fishlow, Sherman Robinson, and Raúl Hinojosa-Ojeda, "Proposal for a North American Regional Development Bank and Adjustment Fund," in Federal Reserve Bank of Dallas, *North American Free Trade: Proceedings of a Conference* (1991).

49. George E. Brown, J. William Goold, and John Cavanagh, "Making Trade Fair: A Social and Environmental Charter for North America," *World Policy Journal*, vol. 9 (Spring 1992), p. 326.

50. Peter A. Schey, "Free Trade and the Human Rights of Migrant Workers," *Immigration Law Bulletin*, vol. 10, no. 1 (1992), pp. 1–7; and Linda S. Bosniak, "Human Rights, State Sovereignty and the Protection of Undocumented Migrants Under the International Migrant Workers Convention," *International Migration Review* (Winter 1991), pp. 737–70.

Modeling the Industrial Effects of NAFTA

Sidney Weintraub

CUSTOMS union theory was developed primarily by examining merchandise trade. Trade creation-trade diversion, the Viner concept to assess the welfare effect of a customs union, the potential for economies of scale, and, more recently, the literature on learning by doing deal essentially with manufacturing. Trade in agricultural products has its own dynamic and has been difficult to incorporate in practice in customs unions and free trade areas because of the constraints imposed by domestic policies. This difficulty is evident in the effective omission of agriculture in the European Free Trade Association and the Canadian-U.S. Free Trade Agreement, and in agriculture's incorporation in the European Community in a way that reduces world welfare because of the inherent trade diversion of the common agricultural policy.

The Canadian-U.S. agreement, apart from its general provisions on the elimination of barriers to imports and on such functional issues as investment and rules of origin, contains separate chapters on three industries: wine and distilled spirits, energy, and automotive goods. The chapter on rules of origin touches on many other industries: minerals, chemical products, rubber products, skins and leather, wood products, textiles and textile articles, footwear, machinery, aircraft, optical equipment, and a catchall for other manufactured products. The separate chapters and provisions reveal a sensitivity in trade in these industries. A comparable sensitivity exists in the NAFTA negotiations. These specific industry provisions often involve derogations from free trade, or contain onerous provisions under which what is euphemistically called free trade can take place. That is particularly true in the automotive sector, by far the most important in Canadian-U.S. and in Mexican-U.S. industrial trade.

Although a customs union or free trade area can be formed even if agricultural investment and trade are effectively excluded, no rationale for such a grouping would exist without the effective inclusion of investment and trade in manufactures. Measurement of the industrial effect of a free trade grouping such as NAFTA is made particularly complex because it is hard to factor in all the derogations that will surely be part of any final agreement. The formal econometric and simulation models deal with free trade—free of tariffs or free of quantitative restrictions, or both—across a number of sectors, but do not fully capture the limits of freedom. The specific sectoral models can more readily incorporate some of these limitations—such as whether free trade in automotive products is for producers or consumers—but not all of them. The more descriptive sectoral analyses are better able to deal with institutional arrangements, such as cross-national affiliations of producers and wholesalers, but at the expense of the precision, or apparent precision, of the more rigorous models.

There is a place for all three types of models, and what follows discusses the conclusions reached for a number of important industries under the three methodologies.

Studies Covered

The studies discussed in this paper are summarized in tables 1–3. Table 1 shows the overall and industrial aspects of general models. Most are computable general equilibrium (CGE) models and static in nature. Table 2 lists two CGE models that focus specifically on three sensitive industrial sectors: automobiles, textiles and apparel, and steel. Table 3 contains what are essentially nonquantitative analyses; they are nonquantitative in that they are not CGE models and, for the most part, use little econometric analysis. Some of these studies are highly industry-specific and others are more general. Most attention is given to the following products: automotive, steel, textiles, apparel, energy, chemicals, machinery, glass, cement, and electronic equipment.

Industrial Implications of General Models

At the broadest level, the CGE models project overall gains in income and employment for all three countries (table 1). The greatest gains are projected for Mexico, more modest gains for the United States, and more indeterminacy for Canada. The dynamic models project considerably greater benefits for Mexico than do the static models. The historical approach of the model by Gary C. Hufbauer and Jeffrey J. Schott—that is, projecting outcomes based on lessons learned from other economic integration experiences and adapting these to the Mexican economy—shows much more

Table 1. Industrial Implications of General Models

Author(s)	Key conclusions	Industries discussed
INFORUM	U.S. exports rise more than Mexican; effects on GDP negligible in both countries	74 to 78 sectors. Employment gains and losses small in both countries
Boyd, Krutilla, and McKinney	Bilateral U.S.-Mexican trade increases, but little overall effect on U.S. GDP or income distribution	12 producing sectors, with differential effects
Brown, Deardorff, and Stern	Positive effects in all three countries, with few necessary intersectoral factor reallocations	29 sectors. Modest labor effects in United States, but also more sectoral specialization in Mexico
Cox and Harris	Canada suffers little loss from Mexico's tariff-free access to United States and gains from competitive effect on Canadian industry	19 industry sectors, based on 1981 input-output matrices and 1989 trade flows
Hinojosa and Robinson	Small effect of free trade by itself, but larger effect if accompanied by open Mexican development strategy; both countries gain, Mexico more than United States	7 broad sectors and 7 comparative statics scenarios; sectoral results highly sensitive to changes in relative prices and real exchange rate
Hufbauer and Schott	Uses "historical" and not CGE approach; concludes high Mexico GDP and employment growth from free trade, but also modest U.S. employment growth	Part of book that covers key sectors in U.S.-Mexican trade; trade results of free trade estimated for 30 sectors
Kehoe	Dynamic CGE model projects large welfare gains for Mexico based largely on learning by doing	Expects specialization in production of final goods; model on a highly aggregated level

(continued)

Table 1 (*continued*)

Author(s)	Key conclusions	Industries discussed
KPMG Peat Marwick	Negligible rise in U.S. income and employment and modest deterioration in U.S. trade balance with Mexico; more substantial increase in real income and employment in Mexico, based almost exclusively on capital inflows	44 sectors in each economy, with differential effects on income and employment
Sobarzo	Large static GDP gain to Mexico from NAFTA of at least 9 percent and 14 percent in real wages	27 production activities, of which 21 are tradable. Incorporates economies of scale and imperfect competition
USITC	Not a CGE model; modest gains for U.S. economy in short term, with little overall effect on U.S. employment; regional impacts in United States vary	15 industries and services discussed separately, with differential outcomes
Young and Romero	Dynamic CGE model that shows substantial GDP gains to Mexico; results highly sensitive to level of real interest rate in Mexico	10 consumption goods sectors and 2 capital goods sectors; rigorous treatment of investment

Sources: Author's interpretation of studies. See text notes for complete sources for models.

substantial gains to Mexican trade, income, and employment than do the static CGE models.[1] This model, as the authors admit, does not lend itself to sectoral detail.

BROWN, DEARDORFF, AND STERN. The most valuable of the static CGE models, in my judgment, is that of Drusilla K. Brown, Alan V. Deardorff, and Robert M. Stern.[2] The overall conclusion of this study is that all three countries would benefit from NAFTA. Wages would rise in Mexico and the United States, but more rapidly in Mexico, thereby reducing the wage gap. There would be beneficial scale effects in all three countries. Capital, primarily coming from outside the North American region, would stimulate new capital formation in Mexico. Little intersectoral relocation of factors would be necessary in the United States from free trade. This study contradicts some of the others that will be cited, particularly the nonquantitative studies, which project much labor displacement from imports made with low-wage Mexican labor. The negative welfare effects on the rest of the world would be relatively small.

The model projections for the industrial sector show substantial increases of Mexican exports of leather products, glass products, electrical machinery, textiles, and apparel. In most instances, the model's conclusion is that the absolute increase in U.S. imports of these products would be quite small because of the small share Mexico enjoys in the U.S. market. Many of the more institutional approaches to sectoral trade challenge the logic of this last conclusion in that it omits increases in investment that would most likely follow in the wake of NAFTA, especially in a relatively footloose industry like apparel. The model also shows considerable increases in U.S. exports to Mexico in textile, clothing, glass products, chemicals and nonelectrical machinery, among others. The bilateral changes in imports generally indicate considerable growth in intraindustry trade.

Brown, Deardorff, and Stern note that the analysis must be deepened, for example by endogenizing investment decisions in the model and adding dynamic effects, such as the effect of learning by doing on productivity. Other CGE models listed in table 1 incorporate these elements. Investment, in this as in other models, sort of drops in like manna from heaven. If it does not come, then Mexico's small current share of the U.S. market in particular sectors can be extrapolated more or less indefinitely into the future, even in such labor-intensive industries as the manufacture of apparel or shoes. If productive investment grows because of the potential of the larger, more or less barrier-free market, then simple extrapolation loses much of its validity. A major shortcoming of the model from the viewpoint of sectoral analysis is that sectors are disaggregated only to the three-digit level and trade, like the devil, is in the details. This shortcoming is true, as a rule, for all the CGE models listed in table 1.

INFORUM. One of the earliest and still much cited of the CGE models is that of INFORUM.[3] The overall conclusion of the study is that NAFTA unequivocally would strengthen the economy of the United States and increase employment, whereas Mexico would face greater adjustment problems. In any event, a free trade agreement is unlikely to make much difference very quickly. As modeled, this study shows a greater trade effect from tariff removal than from the elimination of nontariff barriers. This is not the conclusion of other studies, particularly those that specifically modeled effects in sectors in which the United States has import quotas—textiles, apparel, and steel. Mexico's nontariff barriers are still significant in the automotive sector.

At the sectoral level, this study projects the following winners and losers (their words) in employment. Winners for the United States: chemicals, rubber and plastic products, metal products, and machinery. Losers for the United States: apparel and furniture. Winners for Mexico: apparel, textiles, footwear, and glass. Losers for Mexico: machinery. In all cases, employment effects in the short term are small, amounting to gains and losses in the hundreds of jobs. The study projects the loss of 6,000 jobs in the U.S. apparel industry by 1995, about 1 percent of that industry's employment.

This study is not the last word on the subject of Mexican-U.S. free trade, as the authors admit. I believe it is the first important CGE word. Its contribution is its rigorous pioneering effort. Its weakness is the inadequacy of data, particularly for analysis at a meaningful, disaggregated sectoral level.

KPMG PEAT MARWICK. Another early static CGE study is that of KPMG Peat Marwick.[4] The analysis in this study offers two separate outcomes, one in which no additional capital stock would enter either country and a second in which only Mexico would receive additional investment capital. Under the first, with no additional capital coming into either country, real income, real wages, and real return on capital would increase marginally in the United States. No conclusion is reached on the employment effect in the United States because, by assumption, an increase in labor demand would lead to higher real wages. The U.S. trade balance with Mexico would deteriorate, while that with the rest of the world would improve. In Mexico, increased demand for labor from free trade would result in greater employment rather than higher real wages. Other variables, such as real income, real rate of return on capital, and the Mexican trade balance would all improve modestly. This scenario, as is stated in the study itself, is undoubtedly unrealistic because of its failure to incorporate additional capital entering Mexico. The results are also trivial. The changes are small enough to be swamped by the noise in the model. Many assumptions are clearly arbitrary, such as whether increased demand for labor shows up as an increase in real wages or in employment.

The second scenario assumes enough additional capital flows into Mexico to reduce the real rate of return on capital to its pre–free trade level. The amount of capital required to accomplish this is assumed to be $25 billion. Under this scenario the U.S. trade balance with Mexico would deteriorate sharply, and the other variables would be modestly more favorable for the United States than without additional capital in Mexico. For Mexico, however, the real income and employment increases would be substantial, 4.6 percent and 6.6 percent, respectively, and Mexico's trade balance, both with the United States and the rest of the world, would improve sharply. The real benefits of free trade would come from an exogenous increase in capital. One would expect an increase in investment in Mexico. That, in essence, is the main reason Mexico seeks free trade. But the model merely imposes this result. For that reason, it is not very convincing.

The sectoral outcomes depend heavily on the degree of pre–free trade protection—too heavily, in my opinion, compared with the trade effects of income changes. Thus highly protected U.S. sectors, such as apparel and household appliances, would show output declines. The gains to the more protected sectors in Mexico would also be constrained. These sectors include motor vehicles, machinery and equipment, and transportation equipment. Although total employment in the United States would be unchanged, some sectors, such as motor vehicles, machinery and equipment, and chemicals, would gain at the expense of other sectors, such as textiles, apparel, glass, furniture, computing equipment, and electronic components. The biggest employment gains in Mexico come in the production of apparel, electronic components, motor vehicle parts, household appliances, steel, textiles, glass, and chemicals.

HINOJOSA AND ROBINSON. The model of Raúl Hinojosa-Ojeda and Sherman Robinson adopts many of the same assumptions as the KPMG Peat Marwick model but is technically more sophisticated.[5] Its main conclusion is that Mexican-U.S. free trade, by itself, would have little effect on income, real wages, migration, exports, imports, capital stock, and the exchange rate of either country. If there were effects, they would be modestly more favorable for Mexico than for the United States. In both cases, however, the noise would overwhelm the percentage changes. The model then contains further experiments building on the simple free trade scenario. If free trade is augmented by an open development policy in Mexico, trade between the two countries will expand significantly to the benefit of both. The model also concludes that Mexico will face potentially difficult transitional problems, particularly if capital inflows lead to exchange rate appreciation affecting highly traded products.

The model, in a way, posits the results of "additional" policies that already exist. The authors themselves note that Mexico is already one of the most open economies of the world. Mexico's exchange rate has been appreciating for several years as a consequence of the anti-inflation program. The annual nominal depreciation now permitted in the official rate is about 2 percent a year, despite an inflation differential with the United

States of closer to 15 percentage points. This may partly explain the declining trade surplus in Mexico, although regression analysis designed to understand Mexico's trade outturn explains recent trade performance more in terms of its growing GDP.[6]

One feature of the model absent from other CGE efforts is the incorporation of migration flows, which are assumed to be a function of wage differentials. This feature is an advance, because these flows are an important part of the integration of Mexico and the United States, but the assumptions then required are highly simplified. One such assumption is that equilibrium international migration levels are based on a specified ratio of real wages for rural and urban unskilled labor in the two countries. We know, however, from studies of other countries that high wage differentials do not always stimulate migration, and much lower differentials than exist between Mexico and the United States have stimulated migration.[7]

Like the KPMG model, this model assumes that aggregate employment would remain unchanged but that shifts would occur in sectoral employment. Also, like the KPMG model, this exercise reports the results of many comparative statics and then "shocks" the model by changing exogenous variables to determine the changed equilibrium. One such exogenous imposition is the same $25 billion capital increase in Mexico borrowed from the KPMG model. Another is the introduction of increases in sectoral productivity in Mexico.

Sectors in this model are highly aggregated and perhaps useful for the "big" picture but not for precise industry analysis. The biggest gains seen for Mexico would come in light manufacturing and consumer durables, with smaller benefits in capital goods. Mexico would retain a surplus in bilateral trade with the United States over the medium term in all sectors except capital goods.

BOYD, KRUTILLA, AND MCKINNEY. Roy C. Boyd, Kerry Krutilla, and Joseph A. McKinney estimate the effects on the U.S. economy of the complete removal of all import tariffs on trade between Mexico and the United States. Their main conclusion is that "the impact on the U.S economy of a bilateral U.S.-Mexico trade liberalization may be significantly less than the extensive public debate about the issue would lead one to believe."[8] Their analysis indicates that while tariff removal would significantly increase bilateral trade, it would have an insignificant impact on the level of economic activity, factor prices, or wealth distribution in the United States. This model is static; it includes only tariff removal; it does not measure the effect of including Canada in NAFTA; and it omits any analysis of third-party effects. The sectoral breakdown is highly aggregated. The analysis projects equal percentage increases in U.S. imports and exports of manufactures generally in trade with Mexico.

SOBARZO. Horacio E. Sobarzo's model is designed to measure the effects of NAFTA on the Mexican economy.[9] The special feature of this static model is its incorporation of economies of scale in measuring the Mexican economy and the presence of imperfect competition in Mexican industry. The model thus has two types of industries: competitive, where constant returns to scale are assumed, and noncompetitive, which have long-run declining average cost curves. The sensitive industrial sectors (other than petroleum, which has unique sensitivity in Mexico) fall into the noncompetitive category. The basic assumption is that all tariffs would be removed within NAFTA. The model has three scenarios, depending on assumptions about the distribution of returns in the labor market between increasing employment or increasing the real wage, how much adjustment is permitted in the real exchange rate to determine trade outcomes, and the quantity, and hence the price, of capital available. In all three versions, there would be increases in gross domestic product in Mexico, large increases either in real wages or the level of employment, depending on which is held fixed, and sharper increases in imports than in exports and a deterioration in the trade balance (except in that version in which this is assumed to be zero through exchange-rate adjustment). This model, like others of its type, is highly sensitive to the value of a parameter measuring the response of domestic prices to import competition. The greater the domestic response, the greater the increase in Mexican GDP from industrial rationalization. The version of the model that shows the greatest increase in GDP assumes full employment—that is, the market is cleared through wages—and mobile capital among sectors and countries. The increase in GDP in this model is 8 percent; the increase is much lower, between 1.7 and 2.1 percent, using other assumptions.

Hufbauer and Schott, in explaining why they rejected using such a CGE model, despite its elegance, make the point that this type of model is greatly sensitive to the assumptions made, some of which are not clear to the reader and possibly not even to the modelers themselves. Ironically, so too is the Hufbauer-Schott model sensitive to the assumptions they make.

The sectoral effects differ also in the three versions of the Sobarzo model. Mexican exports to the United States and Canada would increase in all the versions for textiles, apparel, leather, iron and steel, chemicals, electrical and nonelectrical machinery, and transport equipment. Imports from the United States and Canada would increase even more in at least one version for chemicals, iron and steel, electrical and nonelectrical machinery, and transport equipment.

COX AND HARRIS. The model of David Cox and Richard G. Harris is the Canadian counterpart to the Sobarzo Mexican model.[10] Indeed, Sobarzo borrowed much from earlier work by Harris on general equilibrium trade modeling. Among the main conclusions of this study is the projection that Canada would experience little loss from Mexico's tariff-free access to the United States and that, as trade patterns shifted, Mexico would probably gain market share in the U.S. market at the expense of non–North American suppliers. Cox and Harris conclude that what they call a North American trade bloc would form a regional grouping with high barriers against third countries—which would not benefit Canada even if its share of the North American market increased. The main benefit to Canada, they conclude, would come from the rationalization of industry forced by price competition from Mexico. This could raise real income by 1 percent and real wages in Canada by 1.3 percent.

YOUNG AND ROMERO. Two dynamic CGE models are included in table 1, the first of which is the model of Leslie Young and José Romero.[11] They are critical of static models. Their criticism is sharpest of the aggregated treatment of inputs, which they believe will miss gains that result from more efficient use of inputs. Young and Romero also strongly criticize the failure of static models to determine endogenously the changes in investment that would be induced by a free trade agreement. Moreover, they believe static models cannot take account of a fall in the Mexican interest rate that, they think, would accompany the operation of NAFTA. Their conclusions are highly sensitive to interest rate changes.

The Young-Romero model projects a long-run increase in Mexican net domestic product of 6.5 percent at the real interest rate of 15 percent in existence in mid-1991, and much higher increases as the real interest rate falls. If the real rate falls to 10 percent (and, indeed, real interest rates in Mexico have been coming down), they project a long-run increase in the net domestic product of 9 percent. The early versions of this model had highly aggregated output sectors.

KEHOE. The second, still tentative, effort at dynamic modeling is that of Timothy J. Kehoe.[12] Like Young and Romero, Kehoe believes that static modeling does not capture the full growth potential inherent in changes in public policies. He argues that the capital-output ratio, which plays a large role in explaining the growth effect in static modeling, while important, cannot fully explain the relatively low output per worker in

Mexico. On this, I believe he is on firm theoretical ground. Kehoe focuses instead on endogenous technical change—that economic growth is stimulated by the development of new products and learning by doing. Increased openness permits greater specialization in outputs and greater choice in the use of inputs, a point stressed also by Young and Romero. He joins with Young and Romero as well in stressing the role that capital flows can play in lowering Mexican interest rates and thereby increasing the capital-labor in Mexico. Kehoe does not seek to examine free trade in isolation from openness of the Mexican economy, as Hinojosa and Robinson do in one of their exercises; rather, he treats the two as inextricably linked.

Kehoe estimates that if NAFTA allowed Mexico to increase its level of specialization in manufacturing and permitted the import of specialized inputs, then output per worker in manufacturing could rise by some 1.6 percent a year. This is beyond the growth that would exist without NAFTA. Kehoe recognizes that further disaggregation is needed to compute productivity gains in manufacturing, but his paper does not do that.

USITC. Two final contributions included in table 1 contain both general models and substantial sector analysis. Their main contribution, in my view, is not the overall outcomes they project from free trade, but is precisely in the detailed sector-by-sector discussions. The first of these published was by the U.S. International Trade Commission (ITC).[13] Because this study appeared early in the consideration of free trade with Mexico, and even more because it was the first comprehensive discussion of sensitive industrial sectors, it received much attention among scholars and policymakers. Its major general conclusion is that a free trade agreement would benefit the U.S. economy overall, but only marginally in the near to medium term because of the relatively small size of the Mexican economy and because tariff and nontariff barriers are already mostly low in the trade between the two countries. The study concludes that the Mexican economy is likely to grow rapidly in the coming years as a result of economic reforms already adopted, but that free trade would probably augment this growth. Over time, as Mexico grew, so too would U.S. exports and investment in Mexico. These general conclusions are probably the consensus of economists who have studied the Mexican economy and its relationship to the U.S. economy.

For this reason, other aspects of the study drew more attention. One is the conclusion that free trade would have little impact on U.S. employment levels but could cause shifts among sectors. The study also concludes that free trade would have differential effects on U.S. regions, with overall benefits in the southwest and greater uncertainty in other areas.

Summary estimates of the ITC of the effects in the U.S. industries studied are the following:

—Automotive products: uncertainty. The ITC is unsure of the extent of liberalization by Mexico in this sector, what the foreign investment response would be, how thoroughly the Mexican and the U.S. industries would be integrated with benefit to both, how Canada's auto industry would fare, and how much displacement of European and Asian products might occur in North America.

—Cement: negligible. The largest Mexican cement company already maintains extensive operations in the United States. If anything, the ITC expects some increases in U.S. exports to Mexico because of the regional nature of the cement market.

—Chemicals: increase in U.S. exports to Mexico. U.S. tariffs in this industry are already low, averaging 4 percent, and the ITC therefore expects a negligible increase in imports from Mexico from free trade but does expect significant increases in U.S. intermediate chemical exports not produced in Mexico. The report makes a point that merits stress— that the elimination of Mexico's high import duties, now averaging 15 percent, would not by itself lead to substantial U.S. exports, because of long-standing supplier-customer relationships in this industry. It is precisely this judgmental type of conclusion, based on institutional knowledge of an industry, that is not captured in CGE models.

—Electronic equipment: negligible increase in U.S. imports and moderate increase in U.S. exports. Because of the combination of the *maquiladora* program and the U.S. general system of preferences (GSP), effective trade-weighted U.S. import duties on Mexican electronic products now average 2 percent, despite nominal duties that are much higher.

—Energy products: duties are a minor consideration in this trade. The provisions on foreign investment in Mexico's energy sector in NAFTA would be much more significant.

—Glass: greater growth in Mexican than in U.S. exports. Although most U.S. glass imports from Mexico enter duty free under GSP, the U.S. tariff on household glassware averages 22 percent, and removal of this duty could lead to significant import increases. The Mexican duties on all glass products average 20 percent, but the ITC expects Mexico's dominant producer to retain most of the market even as the tariff is eliminated. This, once again, represents an institutional judgment.

—Machinery and equipment: moderate increase in U.S. exports and negligible increase in U.S. imports. The U.S. export increase would come both from the elimination of Mexican duties, which average 10 to 20 percent, and from the capital investment Mexico must make to improve its prospects for economic growth. Trade-weighted U.S. import duties in this field average 3.35 percent.

—Steel: moderate increase in exports by both countries. U.S. tariffs now range from 0.5 to 11.6 percent and Mexican duties from 10 to 15 percent. Their elimination on both sides should have some trade-stimulation effect. The analysis is clouded by uncertainty over the future of U.S. quota restrictions (technically a Mexican voluntary export restraint). The respective increases in exports would be in different steel products. The increased U.S. imports should have a negligible effect on the U.S. industry.

—Textiles and apparel: increased U.S. imports, but little overall effect on U.S. industry because the amount of Mexican exports would be small compared with U.S. production. This is obviously a short-term outlook in that it does not take into account the investment flows that might ensue under free trade. Much will also depend on what happens to the multiplier arrangement in the GATT and its systems of quotas. The trade-weighted U.S. import duty on these products, because of the treatment of exports from the *maquiladora*, is 6 percent, whereas Mexican duties average from 12 to 18 percent for textiles and 20 percent for apparel.

The last detail is provided because it was the target for labor unions and producers who disagreed with the ITC conclusions, and the rock on which many supporters of free trade rested their cases.

HUFBAUER AND SCHOTT. The second study with both overall analysis and sectoral detail is that of Hufbauer and Schott. Their overall conclusions are based on the continuation of the Mexican economic policy adopted in recent years—openness and fiscal and monetary restraint—plus stepped up oil production (which, the authors admit, is controversial). Their projections start from 1989 and extend to 1995, or at the outside, 1997. The historical approach, as Hufbauer and Schott call it, is based heavily on the experiences of other countries that undertook the kind of trade liberalization in which Mexico is engaged. Their calculations show greater growth in U.S. and Mexican exports to each other, in employment in the two countries, and in the Mexican wage rate than do the static CGE models summarized in this paper. The implication of their historical analysis, though in the study this is labeled speculation rather than projection, is that per capita GDP growth in Mexico could be 4 percent a year, which would mean that Mexican living standards in 2023 would surpass the level reached in the United States in 1988.

The Hufbauer-Schott book contains separate chapters on the following manufacturing sectors: energy, automotive products, steel, and textiles and apparel. Their sectoral conclusions are the following:

—Energy: the same conclusion that is reached in the ITC study is reached here, namely, the key question in the energy sector is Mexican treatment of foreign investment. Hufbauer and Schott argue that liberalization of this sector in Mexico could provide large gains for the Mexican economy and the U.S. consumer.

—Automotive: under an integrated automotive market, Hufbauer and Schott expect four features by the late 1990s: Mexican assembly plants will concentrate on entry-level cars and light trucks; Mexico will increase its production of parts; compared with what now exists, an integrated North American market will, on balance, preserve U.S. jobs because it will improve the competitive position of U.S. producers; and both Canada and the United States will experience a decline in unionized jobs in the auto industry.

—Steel: the study makes no projections of what would ensue in either country. Instead, Hufbauer and Schott make recommendations for the elimination of subsidies on steel in the NAFTA countries and the abolition of preferential procurement by government at all levels.

—Textiles and apparel: Hufbauer and Schott expect textile and apparel exports from Mexico to the United States to surge as quotas and duties are eliminated. They also expect U.S. exports of unfinished goods to rise, but by much less. They suggest that Mexican exports of textiles and apparel will reach $3 billion to $5 billion in ten years. They base this conclusion on the export experience of Spain and Portugal after they entered the European Community. The authors state that by end of the 1990s, the United States could well have a textile and apparel trade deficit with Mexico of $1 billion to $2 billion a year.

The CGE models have inherent problems similar to those in forecasting long-range outcomes in the U.S. economy. The models involve both explicit and implicit assumptions. Assumptions on major items are usually explicit, but those on details are usually implicit. The goal of all assumptions is to simplify, despite the complexity of the models themselves. Generally, there are no assumptions on institutional matters, even though these may be crucial in certain industries. All assumptions draw on economic theory, which is not always a settled matter, as is evident in the use of capital-output ratios as the main determinant of productivity comparisons. The data are often quite old. Thus Brown, Deardorff, and Stern use coefficients for production from the 1977 U.S. input-output table, the 1980 Mexican table, and the 1976 Canadian table. Brown and her colleagues are not alone in the use of relationships that may have altered quite radically over the years. When investment is not endogenous, as it is not in the principal static models, the outcomes do not incorporate the key stimulus to economic and production growth that Mexico would expect from NAFTA. Instead, the investment is inserted in the model as an afterthought. Why is $25 billion inserted in the model as is postulated in KPMG and Hinojosa and Robinson? Why not $10 billion, or $50 billion? How do we know how much capital inflow would equalize the return to capital in Mexico and the United States?

The CGE models represent the state of the art in elegant analysis of outcomes of NAFTA. They are clearly more valuable than seat-of-the-pants judgments in that they require precision and not just interested opinion. But they should not be taken at face value. The difference in outcomes between the static and dynamic models is one indication of how far off one or the other, or both, can be in projections. The difference in projected outcomes between the Hufbauer-Schott historical model and the static CGE models must also leave the nontechnical observer, including policymakers, in something of a quandary. Nevertheless, the CGE models do permit informed quandary.

Quantitative Sectoral Models

The following studies look at three sectors—automotive, textiles and apparel, and steel—within the framework of CGE models.

HUNTER, MARKUSEN, AND RUTHERFORD. The automotive sector is the most important in North American industrial trade. It is modeled in the study by Linda Hunter, James R. Markusen, and Thomas F. Rutherford cited in table 2.[14] Their model deals only with finished autos. The two main questions they ask are how the production of finished autos might be reallocated in North America under Mexican-U.S. free trade, and to what extent Mexican production might divert imports from outside North America. The short answers from the model are (1) that Mexican auto production and exports would increase by 22 percent and 52 percent, respectively, from Mexican-U.S. free trade, but that production losses in

Table 2. Quantitative Industrial Sector Models

Author(s)	Industry	Key conclusions
Hunter, Markusen, and Rutherford	Automobiles	Covers only finished autos, not parts; uses 80 simultaneous, nonlinear inequalities; main conclusion, although differs in degree depending on scenarios, is that free trade in autos will benefit Mexico with little or no cost to United States and Canada
Trela and Whalley	Textiles and steel	Quota removal in both sectors would benefit Mexico, largely at expense of third countries; U.S. welfare would benefit from rent reduction; model covers various options on reduction and/or elimination of quotas and tariffs under free trade

Sources: Author's interpretation of studies. See text notes for complete sources for models.

the United States and Canada would be small, less than 1 percent, leading to negligible welfare losses in these two countries; and (2) that increased U.S. imports from Mexico would be more at the expense of third countries than of U.S. and Canadian production. The general conclusion of the study is that free trade in autos, when it is limited to producers, as is the case in the Canadian-U.S. Free Trade Agreement, would give significant benefit to Mexico but is a matter of indifference to Canada and the United States.

The choice to model only finished autos was made because it permitted rigorous, numerical general equilibrium analysis. It thus misses the microeconomic detail, as the authors acknowledge. It also misses the deep policy concern of U.S. workers and their representatives about the potential shift of auto parts production from the United States to Mexico. The model also omits any discussion of plant-level rationalization in the number of parts or models produced in any given plant.

The model contains three scenarios. The first is free trade for producers only, which shows significant gains for Mexico, negligible production and welfare losses for the United States and Canada, and considerable diversion of auto trade from the rest of the world. The second scenario is similar to the first except for the inclusion of Canada in free trade in autos. The outcomes are roughly the same as in the first scenario. The third case permits trilateral free trade for consumers, which would prevent price discrimination among North American markets. In this scenario, markups would drop in Mexico and rise slightly in the United States.

TRELA AND WHALLEY. The second study cited in table 2 is that of Irene Trela and John Whalley, which uses general equilibrium modeling to examine the textile and apparel and steel industries.[15] Mexican exports to the United States in both sectors would benefit both Mexico and the United States, particularly Mexico. Mexican gains in production and consumption would more than offset losses from forgone rents as U.S. quotas and tariffs are removed. The U.S. gain would come from lower prices. These lower prices would adversely affect third countries, against which quotas presumably would continue, by lowering rent transfers to them. These third-country effects would apply to Canada. Lower steel prices in the United States would also lead to increased production and employment in steel-consuming industries. The effects in the United States, when expressed as a percentage of GDP, would be a fraction of 1 percent; the gains in both sectors would exceed 1 percent of GDP for Mexico. When the Mexican gains are expressed as a percentage of domestic use of product, the gains to Mexico would be much greater: 38 percent for textiles and apparel and 125 percent for domestic use of steel.

Mexican use of allowable quotas in the two sectors has been volatile, but has generally been less than 100 percent overall or in subcategories. The model assumes, however, that bilateral quotas would be binding. The model also estimates the effects of variants of the bilateral arrangements involving the complete elimination of tariffs and quotas. If the United States removes quotas and retains tariffs, its gains will be larger because of the more advantageous terms of trade. If only tariffs are removed, the effects will be small, suggesting that the main benefits come from quota removal. Trilateral agreement involving Canada as well would not significantly change the base case results.

Both models cited in table 2 are sophisticated. In my view, they are particularly useful in giving some indication of the nature of benefits from free trade and the direction of change that would occur, though not the precise degree of change. The authors admit as much. The sectoral focus permits detailed attention that is more pinpointed than in the sectoral discussions in the CGE models cited in table 1. These two sectoral analyses are based on general equilibrium analyses and the comments made earlier on the limitations of such modeling apply here as well. The Trela-Whalley model does not capture the production and trade implications of new organizational and institutional arrangements in the apparel industry, such as quick response to style changes. Most Mexican apparel exports now come from *maquiladora* plants, which are heavy users of inputs from the U.S. textile and apparel industry, and the changing role of the *maquiladoras* under free trade is not captured in the model. Trela and Whalley carefully analyze a variety of liberalizing scenarios, but they are unable to assess the implications of a NAFTA that puts other kinds of limitations on textile and apparel trade, such as the definition of rules of origin. The sectoral concentration in these models, like CGE models generally, are valuable starting points or inputs for analysis but not the complete story for making policy.

Nonquantitative Industry Analyses

The two studies listed in table 3 that are most useful from the viewpoint of analyzing sectoral outcomes of free trade are the one by M. Delal Baer and Guy F. Erb, and the one by Sidney Weintraub, Luis Rubio, and Alan D. Jones. The other studies listed discuss sectoral issues, but essentially in the context of overall outcomes, or they antedate the free trade discussions and are thus not directed to assessing the effects of free trade.

BAER AND ERB. This study covers two sectors, autos and electronics.[16] James P. Womack's thesis is that the emerging pattern is for motor vehicle trade to move toward integrated production systems serving regional markets, such as North America.[17] This would be facilitated by a free trade agreement that did not have excessive derogations sapping the spirit of free trade. Womack divides the Mexican motor industry into three segments: *maquiladora* components plants, which would be little affected by free trade because they are already integrated with U.S. production; export-oriented plants, such as world-scale engine plants; and the import-substitution industry supplying the protected domestic market. He makes two major recommendations for an integrated North American market, to shift the production of entry-level small cars and trucks to Mexico, and to locate new component investment as near as possible to the point of final assembly. The outcomes of these changes, he believes, would be a growing Mexican trade surplus in North American trade, but a neutral or even positive outcome for the United States and Canada as larger flows from Mexico displaced imports from Europe and East Asia.

Susan Walsh Sanderson and Ricardo Zermeño-Gonzáles make two recommendations for the electronics industry, that the transition to free trade not be abrupt but that the end of the process be one of open competition.[18] The discussion, which is mostly descriptive, with much lecturing on the

Table 3. Nonquantitative Industry Analyses

Author(s)	Nature of study	Industries discussed
Baer and Erb	Discusses overall U.S.-Mexican relationship and 2 sector studies	Autos (Womack): free trade provides gains for the three countries. Electronics (Sanderson and Zermeño-González): expect gains to Mexico and United States under free trade, but anticipate transition costs
Faux and Rothstein	Seeks to evaluate wage and investment outcomes from free trade between high and low wage countries	No industries discussed as such; industries mentioned are apparel, electronics, and autos and auto parts; study concludes that standard of living will decline in both Mexico and the United States from free trade
Morici	Stress on differences, especially of wages but also productivity, between Mexico and other two countries; advocates structuring agreement to take differences into account	Sensitive industries, such as autos, textiles, apparel, electronics, energy, and industrial machinery, are discussed, but analysis is focused more on functional issues, such as subsidies, investment, and the environment
Prestowitz and Cohen	Proposes structuring agreement so that U.S. investments in Mexico use low-cost labor to foster U.S. and Mexican exports to third countries and not worsen U.S. trade deficit	Autos and parts, textiles, and apparel, electronics, pharmaceuticals, energy, and agriculture are discussed, as are functional issues; focus is on preferential U.S. access to Mexico
Thorup	This is a pre–free trade publication and focus is on using technology to create comparative advantages	Specific industries discussed are motor vehicles, electronics, food, and pharmaceuticals

(continued)

Table 3 (*continued*)

Author(s)	Nature of study	Industries discussed
Weintraub	This is also a pre–free trade publication looking at aspects of conflict and cooperation between Mexico and the United States in industrial activities	Specific industries discussed are petrochemicals, iron and steel, and motor vehicles, and *maquiladoras*
Weintraub, Rubio, and Jones	Industry discussions by experts from within the industries in Mexico and the United States; question asked is potential for integration in each industry	Specific industries covered are autos and auto parts, petrochemicals, pharmaceuticals, textiles and apparel, computers, and food

Sources: Author's interpretation of studies. See text notes for complete sources for models.

need for better education and a stable macroeconomic environment, focuses on three segments of the Mexican industry: computers, telecommunications equipment, and the *maquiladora* output. Their projection is similar to Womack's, even if it is in a different industry, that a regional market in North American is displacing purely national markets and that both Mexico and the United States could benefit from this change.

WEINTRAUB, RUBIO, AND JONES. The special feature on the industry chapters in the Weintraub, Rubio, and Jones book is that most of them were written by practitioners from within the industries themselves.[19] The industries covered are automobiles, petrochemicals, pharmaceuticals, textiles and apparel, computers, and food. Each author, usually one each from Mexico and the United States, looks at the prospects for further industrial integration as seen from the vantage of his or her own country. The chapters, therefore, contain a blend of description and prescription.

The two authors covering the automotive sector are close in their recommendations about the future. Marc E. Maartens concludes that the North American industry would be more efficient if it were consolidated into a single world competitive level and argues that this process should not be delayed until the conclusion of a formal free trade agreement.[20] Florencio López-de-Silanes argues that while integration in this industry would cause some painful reallocation of production, the end-process should be more efficient North American industry and net employment gains in both Mexico and the United States.[21]

There is less agreement between the two perspectives in the petrochemical industry. Benito Bucay, giving the Mexican perspective, states that the excess U.S. supply of basic products, the Mexican shortfall in most basics but a surplus in secondary products, proximity of the two industries along the Gulf Coast, and the proximity of pipeline networks, are tailor-made for a bilateral agreement, within NAFTA, if it comes to pass, or separately if need be.[22] Rina Quijada, giving the U.S. perspective, is far more cautious.[23] After lecturing the Mexican government on the need to seek foreign investment in those parts of the petrochemical industry permitted by the constitution (that is, all but what Mexico refers to as basic products) and in marketing, she concludes that commercial cooperation could take many forms and would not necessarily require free trade. The reading of her text makes clear that she is at best lukewarm to free trade in this sector.

The two perspectives in the pharmaceutical sector are quite different. Robert M. Sherwood stresses the need for greater protection of intellectual property in Mexico.[24] Much of that has since been accomplished in new Mexican legislation. Beyond this, Sherwood sees little of interest in binational integration in this industry. Enrique Gruner Kronheim, in giving the Mexican perspective, sees little future in an isolated Mexican industry and therefore advocates the gradual integration of production processes with U.S. firms.[25]

The analysis of the Mexican textile and apparel industry by Ovidio Botella, Enrique García, and José Giral is particularly interesting in the detail it provides on the competitive and noncompetitive segments of the industry.[26] Two major recommendations are that the industry should focus in the future on clothing exports, particularly from its large installations of spinning and weaving equipment not now fully used, and that dependency on the *maquiladora* segment should be challenged because of the low value added to textile products even as quotas are used up. Stephen L. Lande, writing from the U.S. perspective, also provides rich detail on the textile and apparel trade between the two countries, and he makes a strong recommendation for the integration of the industry in the two countries.[27] He advocates strict rules of origin to prevent Asian countries from using Mexico as a platform for export of Asian components and sewn products to the United States.

In the single paper on computers, Donald R. Lyman notes that Mexico's computer industry is already highly integrated with that of the United States as a result of Mexico's sectoral program, but if the compulsion of this program to invest in Mexico disappears, integration will either decrease or take a different form.[28] Lyman's recommendations are not directed toward integration. Instead, they focus on gradual deregulation of the Mexican industry (which is happening, indeed more rapidly than anticipated in this study) and development of an educational and exchange program to help Mexico upgrade its own industry.

Finally, the studies on the food industry differ on the prospect of future integration of the industry. Lloyd E. Slater, providing the U.S. perspective, sees integration between the large and diverse U.S. food industry and the relatively primitive Mexican one as an illusion.[29] The Mexican authors, José Carlos Alvarez and Herbert Weinstein, expect the industry to become more specialized, with Mexico possibly able to partially prepare foods that require much labor for later sale in the United States.[30]

FAUX AND ROTHSTEIN. The remaining publications shown in table 3 can be covered briefly. The piece by Jeff Faux and Richard Rothstein is an argument against approval of the fast-track process for the U.S.-Mexican negotiations.[31] They argue that the economic costs of free trade would vastly outweigh the benefits by leading to a substantial shift of production to Mexico to take advantage of low wages and result in a net loss of income and employment in the United States. Studies cited earlier here, such as that of the ITC, argued that increased imports from Mexico in such wage-sensitive sectors as apparel would have only a small effect on U.S. production because of the low level of Mexican production. Faux and Rothstein expect U.S. industry to flee to Mexico and augment production levels in such industries. They argue that this would take place in the auto industry as well because Mexico now contains plants as technologically advanced as any in the world. In sum, the expectation is that shifting investment would be costly to U.S. welfare.

PRESTOWITZ AND COHEN. The study by Clyde V. Prestowitz and Robert B. Cohen is not anti-free trade as such, but argues that an agreement with Mexico should be structured so that a large proportion of Mexico's exports are directed away from the United States, and those increased Mexican exports to the United States that do occur should displace third-country exports.[32] All the mechanisms for accomplishing this are not spelled out in the study, but they presumably imply constant monitoring to ensure that the proportion of Mexican exports going to the United States declines as total Mexican exports increase. The study recommends strict rules of origin to prevent third countries from diluting the preferences for Mexico and the United States.

Though placed in table 3 among what I call nonquantitative studies, the Prestowitz-Cohen model includes many calculations. It is not a CGE model, nor does it have precise projections of future trade. The focus, instead, is on the structure of a free trade agreement in its functional areas and in key manufacturing sectors, including autos and parts, electronics, pharmaceuticals, and textiles and apparel. A formula is provided in the textile and apparel discussion to compute the level of duty-free imports that would be permitted from Mexico based on a base level plus a growth component. Though not free trade, such a system would be no more onerous than the current U.S. system of textile and apparel imports. In the automotive, electronic, and pharmaceutical sectors, the study calls for provisions that provide preferences to firms that have already invested in Mexico.

MORICI. Although Peter Morici sees many benefits from NAFTA, particularly the ability for North American specialization using the combination of U.S. and Canadian capital and technology and inexpensive Mexican labor, he also expresses deep concerns that workers will be hurt in such industries as apparel, electrical and telecommunications equipment, and automotive products.[33] He therefore proposes several measures to cushion the transition process for semiskilled labor in the United States and Canada and workers in traditional Mexican industries. The sectoral discussion in the book is limited essentially to the management of adjustments in what he believes are sensitive industries in the United States.

One of the safeguards Morici proposes is a controlled list of industries, presumably those in which some predetermination is made that there would be labor displacement from free trade, in which net duty-free imports into the United States and Canada would be permitted to grow only by some predetermined percentage each year. Imports greater than that would be subject to higher tariffs determined by the difference between U.S. and Mexican wages.[34]

WEINTRAUB AND THORUP. The final two studies in table 3 are pre-free trade efforts that examined industrial integration between Mexico and the United States. The Weintraub study contains chapters examining the Mexican petrochemical and steel industries, the U.S. motor vehicle industry, and the relationship between the steel industries in the two countries.[35] The purpose of the examination is to analyze areas of cooperation and conflict between the two countries in these industries. The study by Cathryn L. Thorup deals primarily with U.S.-Mexican cooperation in the use of new technologies in the motor vehicle, biotechnology and food, and pharmaceutical industries.[36]

Conclusion

The CGE models, without exception, project gains in income, welfare, and employment for the participants in NAFTA. The CGE studies listed in table 1 may cover one, two, or three countries, but none projects welfare or employment losses for the countries included. Each anticipates efficiency gains from economies of scale. Each of the CGE models anticipates that there would be only modest adjustment costs from the phasing in of NAFTA. None anticipates the need for significant intersectoral factor shifts. Each anticipates that those labor shifts that would take place would be small and certainly less than the overall gain in employment by the participating nations.

The gains to the United States and Canada projected over the short term in the static CGE models would be modest. They would be more substantial for Mexico, but still quite small compared with the income gains projected in the dynamic CGE models. The gains for Mexico in the dynamic models would be impressive.

The CGE modelers who produced the studies described here are all mainstream economists, those who believe welfare gains will flow from free as opposed to protected markets. This belief is embedded in the models and their equations. Economists who do not necessarily subscribe to this mainstream view have reached different conclusions, particularly Faux and Rothstein. Their conclusions are precisely the opposite of those of the CGE modelers for the United States, namely, that U.S. income and particularly employment would decline if there were free trade with Mexico. Prestowitz and Cohen and Morici are concerned that free trade, if taken to the limit, would be costly to the United States, either by adversely affecting U.S. production and worsening the trade balance (Prestowitz-Cohen) or bringing labor-adjustment problems (Morici).

Which group is correct? Though my own bias is with the conclusions of the CGE modelers, no definite answer is possible.

The sectoral conclusions also vary depending on who is doing the analysis. The CGE modelers' conclusions of mostly beneficial sectoral outcomes are not surprising given that sectors are key building blocks in their models. There are disagreements among experts in a few sectors. Womack expects a positive outcome for all countries of North America from an integrated automotive market, although Mexico would receive the most benefit. Hunter, Markusen, and Rutherford expect free trade in finished automobiles to benefit Mexico at no cost to the United States or Canada. Hufbauer and Schott believe that, on balance, integrated North

American auto production would save jobs compared with the status quo. Faux and Rothstein anticipate significant job losses from free trade in the automotive sector. The ITC is uncertain about the effect of free trade in autos.

The one industrial sector in which most projections anticipate job losses in the United States from free trade is apparel. But even here, the extent of job losses is uncertain. Much depends on whether increased U.S. imports from Mexico would displace imports from Asia. Trela and Whalley believe there would be gains to U.S. consumers from rent and price reductions.

We know a good deal about the structure of most industries in North America from the studies stimulated by the free trade discussions. I am much more disposed to put my trust in those studies that seek to quantify outcomes, whatever the shortcomings of the models, than in those that make nonquantifiable assertions. The numbers in CGE, econometric, or other models should be accepted not as precise predictions but rather as approximations of outcomes. The quantification then provides a basis for informed judgment of the type incorporated in the non-CGE models. It is useful to have both types of studies, those involving detailed quantification coupled with others based on expert knowledge of the industries and the countries, as the basis for policy. I am also much more disposed to put my confidence in those who seek to eliminate barriers to international trade than in those who wish to keep or increase barriers, or who propound "free" trade circumscribed by many restrictions.

Comment by Robert W. Crandall

Sidney Weintraub provides a useful, comprehensive interpretative survey of the burgeoning literature on the prospective effects of NAFTA on individual sectors and industries. I share Weintraub's unease in using these diverse studies to predict the precise effects of liberalization, but I also agree that quantitative models, however imperfect, are likely to be better than informed guesses.

It is interesting that much of the discussion in the United States has focused on industries in which there might be substantial employment shifts from the United States to Mexico. The main problem, of course, is found in the apparel industry—an industry that has enjoyed decades of trade protection. Fortunately, most of the other industries that the United States protects, such as steel, motor vehicles, machine tools, and semi-conductors, are not likely to be much affected by NAFTA.

Unfortunately, little attention has been given to the industries in which the United States might actually *gain* employment, such as machinery, electronics, and tobacco. These are industries traditionally protected by high Mexican tariffs. If NAFTA and other policies induce a Mexican boom, U.S. capital-goods industries could become major beneficiaries of the Mexican importation of capital. Thus, the U.S. machinery industries may be doubly blessed by NAFTA.

Many of the studies that Weintraub reviews involve estimation of CGE models to assess the effects of NAFTA on individual sectors. These models must be calibrated to reflect consumption and production elasticities in the United States, Mexico, and Canada. Yet there is little information on the transformation function in Mexico because of decades of Mexican government interference with markets. Thus, the CGE models are even more prone to prediction errors for Mexican-U.S. trade and industrial specialization than one would normally expect.

Indeed, it would hardly be surprising if the effects of NAFTA are not swamped by other commendable policies now being implemented in Mexico. These include the massive privatization of the telephone industry, the steel industry, and the financial sector; the lowering of barriers to direct foreign investment; the elimination of a variety of mindless industrial policies; a major new initiative to provide protection of intellectual property; and the introduction of greater monetary-fiscal stability. The combined effect of these policies will be difficult to separate from the effect of NAFTA unless NAFTA is delayed for a decade or more.

Much attention has been devoted to the effects of NAFTA on two heavily unionized, protected U.S. industries—steel and motor vehicles. In fact, several of the studies that Weintraub cites suggest substantial gains for Mexico in these two industries. Unfortunately, the Mexican government has had a heavy hand in both of these industries over the past two or three decades.

In the case of steel, Mexican intervention has been devastating. The privatized remnants of the Mexican steel industry are simply no match for the more efficient U.S. steel producers—especially the U.S. minimills. It is unlikely that new owners—investing foreign capital and technology—will be able to revive these formerly nationalized firms in the next few years even with NAFTA. Indeed, the recent U.S. relaxation of quotas on Mexican steel resulted in little increase in the export of finished steel products to the United States. Virtually all the increase was in low-value semifinished products. I would expect NAFTA and Mexican economic reforms to result in a surge of U.S. exports of steel or steel-bearing machinery to Mexico.

It is much more difficult to predict the impact of NAFTA on the North American motor vehicle industry. U.S. producers are now being buffeted by Japanese products from North American transplants and Japan. As U.S. firms, particularly General Motors and Chrysler, lose market share, they are caught in a dilemma. If they move production to Mexico to reduce labor costs, they incur major direct costs in the form of unemployment and early-retirement benefits for their displaced U.S. workers. If they remain in the United States, they face the continuing problems of high wages, an aging work force, and low worker morale.

Nor is it clear that the Japanese will avail themselves of the lower wages available in Mexico as they expand North American vehicle production. The Japanese supplier base is increasingly in the United States. If they wish to avoid further restrictions on their sales of vehicles in the United States, they will find it necessary to expand production north of the Rio Grande. And the Mexican labor-cost advantage is much lower for the Japanese, given their U.S. plant locations and young work forces.

Weintraub's review shows that the CGE models generally predict substantial gains for Mexico and more modest gains for the United States, a commonsense result given the relative importance of U.S.-Mexican trade to each country. Whether the magnitudes of these effects are correctly estimated is less clear, but NAFTA will probably be more important to Mexican industries on average than to their U.S. counterparts. The adjustment costs from other aspects of recent Mexican economic policy may prove to be quite large. If NAFTA can help to propel Mexico through this difficult and potentially fragile period, it would be unfortunate indeed for the United States to squander this opportunity to save a few thousand jobs in the apparel industry.

Comment by Jaime Ros

Sidney Weintraub's survey is very useful in covering the major studies and the more influential modeling work. There is inevitably a good deal of overlap with Drusilla Brown's survey, a fact reflected in my comment.

Table 4. Reclassification of Studies Surveyed by Weintraub and Brown

Study	No capital mobility	Capital mobility
CGE-CRS[a]	<1	4.6–6.4
CGE-IRS and dynamic[b]	1.6–2.6	5–8.1
Macroeconomic interindustry models[c]	Small employment losses	. . .

a. KPMG Peat Marwick, "Effects of a Free Trade Agreement"; Hinojosa and Robinson, "Alternative Scenarios"; and David Roland-Holst, Kenneth A. Reinert, and Clinton R. Shiells, "North American Trade Liberalization and the Role of Nontariff Barriers," Mills College, April 1992.

b. Brown, Deardorff, and Stern, "A North American Free Trade Agreement"; Sobarzo, "A General Equilibrium Analysis"; and Young and Romero, "A Dynamic Dual Model."

c. INFORUM, "Industrial Effects of a Free Trade Agreement between Mexico and the USA" report prepared for the U.S. Department of Labor (University of Maryland, 1990).

I emphasize what can be learned from comparing the results of different approaches and also complement this comparison by introducing another strand of research; that is, what can be learned about the potential effects of NAFTA from Mexico's experience with trade and investment liberalization since the mid-1980s. The point has been made that the likely effect of NAFTA is an incremental one, over and above what has already happened in Mexico with respect to development policy.

With the help of Brown's paper, I reclassify the studies surveyed in a three-by-two matrix (table 4). The matrix has two columns, one for the studies (or scenarios within a study) that assume no capital mobility—in other words, no additional investment flows to Mexico—and the other for the studies assuming capital mobility, either exogenous flows or additional investment endogenously determined by the model used. Of the three rows of the matrix, the first two are for computable general equilibrium (CGE) models—constant returns to scale (CRS), and increasing returns to scale (IRS) and dynamic models following Brown's classification; the third is for macroeconomic models. Each entry in the matrix can then be seen as referring to different types of gains. For example, in the first column the first entry focuses on classical gains from interindustry trade and specialization, the second on "new trade theory" effects from economies of scale and intraindustry trade (IRS models) as well as investment effects through lower prices of capital goods (dynamic models), and the third on dynamic macroeconomic effects.

There are two major lacunae to consider. First, how important are the endogenous productivity growth effects from dynamic models (especially when interacting with capital flows)? The occurrence of these effects is known not only from "new growth theory" but from the older insights of Allyn Young and Nicholas Kaidor, among others. Second, no research has been conducted on macroeconomic dynamics with endogenous capital inflows. The only macroeconomic model in the matrix (the INFORUM Report model) has no additional investment flows as a result of NAFTA.

By looking across rows in the first column, one can draw the following conclusions about the effects of NAFTA (I focus on Mexico; the gains for the United States are much smaller and, as a percent of its GDP, are roughly ten times less than those for Mexico):

—very small trade gains from resource reallocation and specialization in foreign trade (well below 1 percent of Mexico's GDP);

—larger but still small gains from economies of scale, industry rationalization, and lower prices of investment goods (1.6 to 2.6 percent of GDP, in the Brown, Deardorff, and Stern, Sobarzo, and Young and Romero scenarios without capital mobility);

—small but negative macroeconomic adjustment effects in Mexico (reflected in a fall of employment levels of less than 1 percent over the base scenario in the INFORUM Report).

I find these results hardly surprising and, except for a few shortcomings to be mentioned later, largely consistent with Mexico's recent experience with trade liberalization: small (indeed surprisingly small) resource reallocation among industrial sectors—under even more drastic trade policy changes than those involved in NAFTA; more significant technical efficiency and scale-efficiency effects (although not always positive) associated with processes of industry rationalization;[37] and, indeed, negative macroeconomic effects—which are hidden so far, however, by the turnaround of the capital account since 1989. This experience also partially explains one of the major lacunae noted (endogenous productivity effects): essentially, that virtuous circles between exports, investment, and productivity growth have so far largely been absent. In fact, the only spectacular change that took place in Mexican industry in the 1980s was the export and investment boom in the auto industry, which, however, had little to do with trade liberalization. This Mexican boom is a process that started in the late 1970s, when American multinational corporations decided to relocate in Mexico, that continued in precisely one of the few industries with a protected domestic market throughout the 1980s, and that is likely to continue with or without a free trade agreement.

The examination of trade reform in Mexico also helps to illustrate two shortcomings of the studies surveyed. First, the very different industrial organization features, including the degree of international capital mobility across industries, that explain why the auto industry rather than, say, the garment industry has been expanding in recent years, also explain why the actual resource reallocation effects may differ substantially from what one would expect from a neoclassical CGE model (a point related to Brown's comment on multinationals at the end of her paper). Second, most of the change is occurring at the intraindustry level, and thus the question of "winners" and "losers" needs to be examined at a much more disaggregated level than it has been so far.

By looking across rows of the matrix when the same models are simulated with additional capital flows, one can see the gains from NAFTA multiplied by at least a factor of four: in the Brown, Deardorff, and Stern, Sobarzo, and Young and Romero studies, for example, one moves from the 1.5–2 percent to the 5–8 percent range. And increased capital mobility is, of course, what both the public and trade negotiators have in mind when talking about NAFTA.

The difficulty here, however, is that one also moves onto shaky ground. The specific effects of NAFTA are those incremental capital flows that will result from reduced uncertainty (the effects of locking in current policies) and the ensuing reduction of risk differentials between Mexico and the United States. And this by its nature is difficult to measure. The important issue here, in my view, is not whether one models investment flows as exogenous or endogenous, because in the second case one still has to make an "exogenous" assumption about how much interest rates and risk differentials are likely to fall (let alone about how investment will respond to these reductions in a completely new situation).[38] And that assumption is the real problem.

Besides simply saying that one does not know (perhaps the most sensible answer at this stage), one can address the problem in two ways. One would be to interview corporate executives of multinational corporations about their investment plans under NAFTA. I don't know of any attempt in this direction, nor am I sure of its fruitfulness. The other is to speculate on the basis of other countries' experiences as well as of Mexico's own recent experience with investment liberalization (the "historical method" favored by Hufbauer and Schott).[39]

In this context, the analogy with Spain's recent experience of massive capital inflows is often used. I find this analogy unconvincing for at least two reasons. I share, first, the reservations of the authors of the INFORUM Report: "In Spain, the low wage country was *soon to gain access* to the well-protected markets of Europe. Moreover, with the prospect of 'Fortress Europe' after 1992, many American firms were eager to get a toe-hold inside the Community. By contrast, Mexico *has long had* virtually unrestricted access to the U.S. markets outside the Apparel, Textile, and Steel industries. Foreign investment in Mexico for producing for export has been almost unrestricted since 1972. Further, there is no prospect of a 'Fortress USA' looming ahead. An FTA would remove, at most, the prohibitions on majority foreign ownership for firms investing in Mexico to sell in Mexico. In fact, there seem to have been important exceptions to the present prohibitions. For example, all of the six major automobile companies operating in Mexico have over 90 percent foreign ownership. While an FTA would, we believe, improve the atmosphere for foreign capital in Mexico, there seems little reason to believe that the inflow would be massive.''[40]

Nevertheless, it could be argued that recent capital inflows in Mexico are comparable in size to those of Spain. But there is a second difference. A large fraction of these flows (capital repatriation and foreign portfolio investment) are of a one-time nature. And they are mostly related not to investment liberalization—foreign direct investment performance has, in fact, been disappointing—but to privatization. The time pattern of capital inflows and privatization revenues, slowly increasing in 1989 and 1990 and accelerating sharply in 1991, clearly suggests this conclusion. Privatization revenues started declining in 1992 (down to about $7 billion from about $12 billion in 1991) and, on current plans, will almost disappear by 1993–94. Paradoxically, even though NAFTA is likely to improve Mexico's capital account surplus (compared with what would otherwise happen), a free trade agreement, if reached some time in 1993, will probably be followed by a decline rather than an increase in capital inflows to Mexico.

Even if a free trade agreement brings about substantial additional foreign investments, some other neglected issues need to be examined. What would be the temporal pattern of these flows and the associated macroeconomic dynamics? Would these inflows come at a steady rate of, say, an additional $5 billion a year, or even better at a gradually increasing rate year after year? Or would foreign capital come in massively in the initial stages, say an additional $30 billion in three years, followed by a sharp slowdown? And if that is the case, would the capital inflows lead to a strong appreciation of the peso, causing severe damage to whole parts of Mexican industry—followed by a period of acute balance-of-payments difficulties as capital inflows sharply decline? Or on the contrary, would they put a more gentle pressure on the exchange rate, which, combined with the abundance of investment finance, would give a kick to the technical modernization of Mexican industry?

These unanswered questions lead me to conclude by emphasizing our lack of knowledge and uncertainty as regards the two major lacunae mentioned earlier. This uncertainty exists because the interactions between endogenous productivity effects and macroeconomic dynamics can cut both ways and broaden enormously the range of possible outcomes. For this reason, macroeconomic management is very important, as are, more generally, social institutions. These noneconomic issues have to be brought into the equation to overcome the indeterminacy of economic analysis. One should also start thinking not of a single NAFTA scenario compared with a base scenario but rather of a range of NAFTA scenarios, each having different macroeconomic dynamics. To strengthen this point, I quote from a recent book on the future of the southern European countries in the new European Community: "It was difficult to foresee which of the two divergent paths the new members would take. The double shock of accession and 1992 might drive their economies into depression or accelerate their modernization. Unfortunately, economic principles do not point to a pre-determined outcome. In fact, the degree of undeterminacy is so great that the outcomes may range between brilliant achievement and big difficulties."[41] Although my intuition tells me that Mexico will not follow any of these two extreme paths, I thought it appropriate to conclude with such a healthy note of agnosticism.[42]

Notes

1. Gary C. Hufbauer and Jeffrey J. Schott, *Prospects for North American Free Trade* (Washington: Institute for International Economics, 1992). The overall model is in chapter 3; other chapters deal with sectoral analyses.

2. Drusilla K. Brown, Alan V. Deardorff, and Robert M. Stern, "A North American Free Trade Agreement: Analytical Issues and a Computational Assessment," paper presented at conference on North American free trade sponsored by the Fraser Institute, the Center for Strategic and International Studies, the University of Toronto Centre for International Studies, and Stanford University American Program, Washington, June 27–28, 1991. The other two papers by Brown, Deardorff, and Stern listed in table 1 are "Some Estimates of a North American Free Trade Agreement," Discussion Paper 288, and "A North American Free Trade Agreement: Analytical Issues and a Computational Assessment," Discussion Paper 289, both from the Institute of Public Policy Studies, University of Michigan, October 1991.

3. INFORUM, "Industrial Effects of a Free Trade Agreement Between Mexico and the USA," report prepared for the U.S. Department of Labor (University of Maryland, 1990).

4. KPMG Peat Marwick, "The Effects of a Free Trade Agreement Between the

U.S. and Mexico," paper prepared for the U.S. Council of the Mexico-U.S. Business Committee, 1991.

5. Raúl Hinojosa-Ojeda and Sherman Robinson, "Alternative Scenarios of U.S.-Mexico Integration: A Computable General Equilibrium Approach," Working Paper 609 (University of California, Berkeley, Department of Agricultural and Resource Economics, April 1991).

6. Carlos E. Z. Cabeza Reséndez, "The Theory and Practice of Trade Liberalization: The Mexican Case," Ph.D. dissertation, University of Texas at Austin, 1991.

7. Peter Gregory, "The Determinants of International Migration and Policy Options for Influencing the Size of Population Flows," in Sergio Díaz-Briquets and Sidney Weintraub, eds., *Determinants of Emigration from Mexico, Central Mexico, and the Caribbean* (Boulder, Colo.: Westview Press, 1991), pp. 49–73.

8. Roy G. Boyd, Kerry Krutilla, and Joseph A. McKinney, "The Impact of Tariff Liberalization Between the United States and Mexico: A General Equilibrium Analysis," working paper, Hankamer School of Business, Baylor University, Waco, Texas, 1991, p. 1.

9. Horacio E. Sobarzo, "A General Equilibrium Analysis of the Gains from Trade for the Mexican Economy of a North American Free Trade Agreement," El Colegio de México, 1991.

10. David Cox and Richard G. Harris, "North American Free Trade and Its Implications for Canada," paper presented at conference on North American free trade, June 27–28, 1991 (see note 2).

11. Leslie Young and Jose Romero, "A Dynamic Dual Model of the Free Trade Agreement," University of Texas at Austin and El Colegio de México, 1991.

12. Timothy J. Kehoe, "Modeling the Dynamic Impact of North American Free Trade," Working Paper 491 (Federal Reserve Bank of Minneapolis, March 1992).

13. U.S. International Trade Commission, *The Likely Impact on the United States of a Free Trade Agreement with Mexico*, Pub. 2353 (Washington, 1991).

14. Linda Hunter, James R. Markusen, and Thomas F. Rutherford, "U.S.-Mexico Free Trade and the North American Auto Industry: Effects on the Spatial Organization of Production of Finished Autos," paper presented at conference on North American free trade, June 27–28, 1991 (see note 2).

15. Irene Trela and John Whalley, "Bilateral Trade Liberalization in Quota Restricted Items: U.S. and Mexico in Textiles and Steel," paper presented at conference on North American free trade, June 27–28, 1991 (see note 2).

16. M. Delal Baer and Guy F. Erb, eds., *Strategic Sectors in Mexican-U.S. Free Trade* (Washington: Center for Strategic and International Studies, 1991).

17. James P. Womack, "A Positive Sum Solution: Free Trade in the North American Motor Vehicle Sector," in ibid., pp. 31–65.

18. Susan Walsh Sanderson and Ricardo Zermeño-Gonzáles, "Trade Liberalization in Mexico's Electronics Industry," in ibid., pp. 66–125.

19. Sidney Weintraub, Luis Rubio F., and Alan D. Jones, *U.S.-Mexican Industrial Integration: The Road to Free Trade* (Boulder, Colo.: Westview Press, 1991).

20. Marc E. Maartens, "Automobiles: U.S. Perspective," in ibid., pp. 73–87.

21. Florencio López-de-Silanes, "Automobiles: Mexican Perspective," in ibid., pp. 88–116.

22. Benito Bucay F., "Petrochemicals: Mexican Perspective," in ibid., pp. 119–36.

23. Rina Quijada, "Petrochemicals: The U.S. Perspective, in ibid., pp. 137–57.

24. Robert M. Sherwood, "Pharmaceuticals: The U.S. Perspective," in ibid., pp. 161–79.

25. Enrique Gruner Kronheim, "Pharmaceuticals: The Mexican Perspective," in ibid., pp. 180–89.

26. Ovidio Botella C., Enrique García C., and José Giral B., "Textiles: Mexican Perspective," in ibid., pp. 193–220.

27. Stephen L. Lande, "Textiles: U.S. Perspective," in ibid., pp. 221–45.

28. Donald R. Lyman, "Computers: The U.S.-Mexican Relationship," in ibid., pp. 249–57.

29. Lloyd E. Slater, "Food: U.S. Perspective," in ibid., pp. 261–90.

30. José Carlos Alvarez Rivero and Herbert Weinstein, "Food: Mexican Perspective," in ibid., pp. 291–300.

31. Jeff Faux and Richard Rothstein, "Fast Track, Fast Shuffle: The Economic Consequences of the Administration's Proposed Trade Agreement with Mexico," Economic Policy Institute, Washington, 1991.

32. Clyde V. Prestowitz and Robert B. Cohen, *The New North American Order: A Win-Win Strategy for U.S.-Mexican Trade* (Washington: Economic Strategy Institute and University Press of America, 1991).

33. Peter Morici, *Trade Talks with Mexico: A Time for Realism* (Washington: National Planning Association, 1991).

34. This is the source of the formula for permitted textile and apparel growth noted in the Prestowitz-Cohen study, to which Morici contributed.

35. Sidney Weintraub, ed., *Industrial Strategy and Planning in Mexico and the United States* (Boulder, Colo.: Westview Press, 1986).

36. Cathryn L. Thorup, ed., *The United States and Mexico: Face to Face with New Technology* (New Brunswick, N.J.: Transaction Books for the Overseas Development Council, 1987).

37. Jaime Ros, "Mexico's Trade and Industrialization Experience since 1960: A Reconsideration of Past Policies and Assessment of Current Reforms," paper prepared for the United Nations University—*WIDER* project on Trade and Industrialization Reconsidered, Helsinki, 1992; and James Tybout and D. Westbrook, "Trade Liberalization and the Structure of Production in Mexican Industries," Working Paper 92-03 (Georgetown University, Department of Economics, April 1992).

38. Actually, it may be far more sensible to make an "exogenous" guess at additional inflows rather than try to model them, since, unless the different degree of international capital mobility across industries are fully taken into account, this procedure can lead to very misleading results.

39. Hufbauer and Schott, *Prospects for North American Free Trade*.

40. INFORUM "*Industrial Effects*."

41. Christopher Bliss and Jorge Braga de Macedo, eds., *Unity with Diversity in the European Economy: The Community's Southern Frontier* (Cambridge University Press, 1990); quoted by Garry Helleiner, "Consideraciones sobre un área de libre comercio entre Estados Unidos y México," in Gustavo Vega, ed., *México ante el*

libre comercio con América de Notre (Mexico City: El Colegio de México y Universidad Tecnológica de Mexico, 1991).

42. In his oral reply at the conference, Weintraub interpreted my comment as a quarrel with economic liberalization in general. That is not correct and in fact is totally misguided. Nor am I quarreling with the results, even the most optimistic ones, of CGE models. I believe these models give sensible answers *to the questions they ask*. My quarrel, if any, is that much of recent research has neglected some other important questions—issues of macroeconomic dynamics in particular—that CGE models are poorly equipped to deal with.

NAFTA and Agriculture: A Review of the Economic Impacts

Tim Josling

ALL commentators seem to agree that agriculture poses problems for the negotiators seeking to complete a North American Free Trade Agreement (NAFTA). The extent of government involvement in agricultural markets ensures that negotiations to remove barriers to trade will be complex. Free trade and agriculture rarely coexist comfortably, and the issues facing the negotiators are indeed politically contentious. But how significant will the economic impacts on agricultural producers in the United States, Mexico, and Canada be if NAFTA is consummated? The evidence from economic studies in the public domain is neither clear nor unequivocal. The purpose of this paper is to explore both the direction and size of the economic impacts that might result from the agricultural component of NAFTA and to define a consensus position.

The decision by President Salinas to seek a free trade agreement with the United States took many people by surprise. Included among those unprepared were agricultural trade and policy analysts in the United States (and Canada), who had become preoccupied with the issues surrounding domestic policy reform and the GATT negotiations. Mexico was rarely studied and not often included in multicountry trade models. There had been some interest in Mexican agricultural policies a decade ago, when the ill-fated SAM (Sistema Alimentario Mejicano) program attracted attention as an example of developing-country food policy gone wrong.[1] Mexican specialists were, of course, aware of the dramatic domestic policy changes taking place since 1985, but these developments were not considered of direct relevance to U.S. agricultural trade policy.

As a result of this benign neglect, economists have been slow to respond to the request for quantitative studies on the impact of NAFTA on agriculture.[2] Most papers and reports have attempted no more than a qualitative evaluation, based on a priori reasoning and readily available statistics. The qualitative assessments of the impact of NAFTA on agriculture include the following:

—the 1991 U.S. International Trade Commission report on the likely effect on the United States of a free trade agreement with Mexico;[3]

—the 1991 reports of the General Accounting Office on the effect of liberalization in the agricultural sector on U.S.-Mexican trade;[4]

—the 1991 report from the Library of Congress by Charles Hanrahan;[5]

—the 1991 paper by Stephen Haley and Parr Rosson;[6]

—the chapter by Gary Hufbauer and Jeffrey Schott in a book for the Institute of International Economics;[7]

—two 1991 commissioned papers for the International Agricultural Trade Research Consortium, by Thomas Grennes and others and by Richard Barichello and others, both of which include some of the other work mentioned here;[8] and

—the 1991 report from the Americas Program at Stanford University, sponsored by the Fraser Institute, which was summarized in Josling (1991) and presented more fully in Tim Josling and others (1991).[9]

Notable exceptions to this preponderance of qualitative papers are a small number of studies that use explicit economic models to predict outcomes from policy changes arising from NAFTA. These include the following:

—the results from the use of the SWOPSIM model by economists in the Economic Research Service (ERS) of the U.S. Department of Agriculture (USDA), as presented in Barry Krissoff and others (1991) and Krissoff, Liana Neff, and Jerry Sharples (1992);[10]

—the results from the adaptation of a computable general equilibrium (CGE) model, developed by Sherman Robinson and his colleagues as reported in Raúl Hinojosa-Ojeda and Sherman Robinson (1991), Robinson and others (1991), and Mary Burfisher, Robinson, and Karen Thierfelder (1992);[11]

—the work on Mexican agricultural policy undertaken by Santiago Levy and Sweder van Wijnbergen in connection with a World Bank project, as discussed in Levy and van Wijnbergen (1991, 1992);[12] and

—the collection of studies by a group of economists under the auspices of the American Farm Bureau Federation, which was published in a series of volumes in 1992.[13]

Though not an exhaustive listing, these studies represent the bulk of academic and institutional output on the subject and will consequently provide the raw material for the review in this paper.

The organization of this review takes the following form. The first section examines the complexities surrounding the NAFTA negotiations on agriculture and explains the difficulty that authors have had defining the expected changes. The second section considers the broad effects of NAFTA as given by the qualitative papers listed and distinguishes between points of consensus and places of divergence. The third section looks closely at the quantitative evidence to see whether the authors of these studies agree on possible magnitudes of economic impacts and explores the reason for any disagreements. The final section attempts a reconciliation and conclusion.

What Is the Agricultural Component of NAFTA?

The first problem confronting any economist addressing the impact of NAFTA on agriculture is to define the agricultural component in NAFTA in isolation from the changes in government policy now taking place. Though no doubt a problem in other NAFTA areas, this definition of components is particularly troublesome in agriculture. The NAFTA talks are but one of three sets of policy discussions, each with its own dynamic. Although connected by subject matter, the processes themselves are quasi-independent. A brief look at these three processes is essential to understanding why different authors have come up with different specifications for the agricultural part of NAFTA.

NAFTA and Mexican Policy Changes

The most dramatic set of policy changes is that underway in Mexican agricultural policy. A bold decision to include the agricultural sector fully in the economic restructuring has led to an abrupt reversal of traditional policy. This reversal is seen in three areas: the change in trade policy subsequent to Mexico's decision to join GATT, which led to a removal of much of the network of import controls and licenses and to a reduction in tariffs; the change in internal market policy, involving the encouragement of private trading and less government intervention; and the revision of the constitutional constraints on land tenure and their consequent impediments to investment. These three elements amount to a potential transformation of Mexican agriculture and markets to an extent rarely experienced in any country. Any attempt to model such changes must be very tentative indeed.

These Mexican policy changes should be separated from the NAFTA talks. Negotiations on market access are, of course, designed to lock in the unilateral changes in the Mexican import regime and to lead to the removal of tariffs and quantitative restrictions on intra-NAFTA trade. But the process of change in Mexican policy has been much more rapid than that likely to be demanded by NAFTA. The issue is, therefore, not whether the Mexican market can be opened up by NAFTA, but "to whom" and "under what conditions" the Mexicans will choose to grant market access. NAFTA secures some (perhaps transitory) preference for the United States and Canada and provides guarantees beyond the GATT bindings. No one has attempted to quantify (or even describe fully) this true "NAFTA" effect. Instead, most authors combine the NAFTA preference impact with the Mexican trade liberalization effect. Though politically related, these two policy changes are clearly separable.

A similar confusion attends the internal market changes in Mexico. Privatization, along with the removal of many costly domestic subsidies, is transforming the Mexican agricultural economy in advance of NAFTA. The key issue in this regard is the domestic regime for maize, or corn, the key product from the small-farm sector and a staple in rural and urban food consumption. The policy until recently emphasized high producer prices and lower consumer prices, maintained through the monopoly position of a parastatal, CONASUPO (Comision Popular de Subsistencias Populares). Much of CONASUPO's role in marketing, in crops other than maize and dry beans, has been transferred to the private sector, and new marketing institutions are emerging in response. Consumer subsidies have been greatly reduced and targeted toward lower-income households. At issue is how to maintain incomes in those sectors of Mexican agriculture dependent upon sales of maize. It is likely that some combination of border protection (through a tariff) and targeted domestic producer subsidy will be chosen, allowing internal markets to develop.

How much of this internal development is a "NAFTA" effect is debatable. Negotiators for the United States (and Canada) are presumably pushing for more domestic market liberalization. But there seems little doubt that accommodation in this area will come only to the extent that the Mexican government sees it as useful to link the two processes. In terms of quantitative estimates of a "NAFTA effect," this distinction is critical: the changes in Mexican producer and consumer prices for corn are among the key economic variables identified by all the studies. But how much NAFTA will change those prices is rarely discussed.

This feeling that more important policy changes are occurring outside of the NAFTA talks is even more true for the changes in land tenure. It would be politically unwise and analytically unsound to attribute changes in the Mexican Constitution to NAFTA pressures. No one has made that connection. But in Mexican terms, the reform of the "ejido" system of collective farms, granting ownership, allowing rental arrangements, and encouraging investment by individuals, corporations, and foreigners, together with the security given to private landholders, offers a new beginning to two-thirds of the agricultural sector. What effect NAFTA will have on Mexican trade and farm incomes depends crucially upon how far and fast the structural reforms are pursued.

NAFTA and the GATT

The second parallel set of policy discussions that have complicated the NAFTA process is the Uruguay Round of GATT trade negotiations. A complex symbiosis has developed between the GATT Round and the NAFTA talks, as it did between the GATT Round and the U.S.-Canadian talks five years ago. The main agricultural connections can be grouped under two headings: an agenda overlap and a timing issue.

The agenda for the agricultural component of NAFTA is similar to that under consideration in the GATT for the last six years. Domestic support policies that cause problems among NAFTA members are also those that are under fire in the GATT. Mexican import restrictions of a nontariff kind (for example, quotas on corn imports) would be removed over time under a GATT pact, as would Canadian import quotas for poultry and dairy products and U.S. tariff quotas on sugar.[14] A GATT agreement would therefore remove an array of issues from the NAFTA agenda. In the absence of such an agreement, the NAFTA talks take on an additional burden, to negotiate reductions in nontariff barriers and changes in domestic price supports away from those that distort intrabloc trade.

The GATT Round has staggered under the ambitious objectives of reforming the rules under which agricultural trade takes place and defining the set of permitted policies for domestic agriculture. In addition to resolving some of the internal NAFTA trade conflicts (as discussed above), a completed GATT Round would change the trading regulations for countries. This has a direct effect on the amount of preference conferred by NAFTA. It also changes the nature of the world market into which the United States and Canada sell and hence the terms of trade for Mexico.

The timing issue complicates the matter further. The GATT Round has missed several deadlines since it was scheduled to end in December 1990, and it could well drag on through 1992. Both trade agreements need to go to Congress early in 1993 for approval. A NAFTA package that is advanced quickly and presented to Congress before the GATT package would necessarily have less agricultural content and represent little more than a tariff-cutting exercise. A NAFTA accord following a successful GATT agreement could be somewhat more ambitious, as the agenda links mentioned above are exploited. A NAFTA deal following a rejected GATT package, or in the aftermath of a failure to agree on such a package, would face a very different climate in Congress. Though some might attempt to push the trilateral talks as an alternative to a failed multilateral round, the chance that any new regional initiative in agriculture could replace the prospect of global trade reform is remote.

These complexities illustrate the difficulty in identifying the effect of NAFTA from among the many other policy changes under way. Many authors link Mexican trade and domestic reforms to NAFTA, though few include changes arising from the completion of the GATT Round. Domestic sectoral interests may not care what combination of circumstances brings about changes in their market, but politicians voting on individual trade measures need to make such distinctions. In the case of agriculture, a more careful identification of the true NAFTA effect is needed.

Broad Effects of NAFTA on Agriculture

With such a range of different interpretations of the agricultural component of NAFTA, some disagreement on the effect on agriculture is inevitable. In fact, a broad consensus in qualitative terms emerges from the studies cited above. This consensus is discussed before the key differences in the studies are identified. This section is focused on the descriptive studies; evidence from the economic models is reviewed in the next section.

The starting point for the qualitative evaluations is the status quo levels of trade and protection in North American agriculture. The broad consensus, based on descriptive statistics (usually from USDA sources), is as follows:

—Trade between the United States and Mexico is dominated by grains, oilseeds, and livestock products flowing south and horticultural products coming north. Some intermediate trade flows occur (Mexican cattle moving up to feedlots in the United States, and Mexican sugar moving to the United States for refining and reexport) to complicate the picture. Agricultural trade between Mexico and Canada is small and is made up largely of grains going to Mexico and beer exported to Canada.

—Mexico has higher levels of protection for agricultural products, in particular for grains, oilseeds, and livestock, than do Canada and the United States. Mexican protection is (or was) by means of import licensing, sometimes on top of significant tariffs set when Mexico joined the GATT. The United States protects its fruit and vegetable markets through tariffs, often varying on a seasonal basis, in a way that restricts Mexican exports. The United States also uses marketing orders to control quantities entering particular fruit and vegetable markets at certain times of the year. Insofar as these marketing orders can discriminate against imports from Mexico, they represent a trade barrier.

—The "winners" from a NAFTA that lowers trade barriers would include U.S. producers of grain, particularly corn, and of livestock products; and fruit and vegetable producers in the north of Mexico, already geared up for selling to the United States, who would find expanded markets. The "losers" would be Mexican grain farmers, in particular if domestic prices were greatly reduced, and those U.S. fruit and vegetable producers who would face greater import competition. The consensus is that Florida growers, including citrus producers, would feel the effect more than growers in California and Arizona. Additional Mexican imports would compete in the winter vegetable market, currently supplied in large part by Florida.

—Most authors point to the effect of lower Mexican grain prices and production on labor use in rural Mexico, rural-urban internal migration, and Mexico-U.S. labor flows.[15] Capital is assumed to flow into Mexico to set up businesses to take advantage of new trade opportunities. Labor freed from the less profitable parts of Mexican agriculture would move to urban jobs in Mexico or venture north to seek employment in the United States. Processing activities will also tend to migrate south to find lower wage costs and to be close to raw material supplies. Some parts of the Canadian horticultural industry might shift south to Mexico.

—The qualitative consensus also emphasizes the importance of environmental regulations in influencing trade patterns. Generally, more lax enforcement of Mexican domestic regulations, along with different lists of acceptable farm chemicals, are said to give a cost advantage to Mexican growers. Prohibitions on the importation of certain farm products from Mexico, such as avocados (into California) or poultry (because of Newcastle disease), raise questions about whether sanitary and phytosanitary regulations are being used as trade barriers.[16]

Quantitative Evidence of NAFTA Effects

With so much consensus on the broad issues, disagreements on the direction of change are hard to find. But does the broad consensus from the qualitative studies still survive when authors try to put numbers on the magnitude of the changes? In this section, the results from the rather small number of empirical studies are reported. Due regard is paid to differences in model structure, data and assumptions, and to the various interpretations of what changes in policies are implied by NAFTA. The studies are first discussed individually, to bring out their most significant results, and then are compared by commodity group to bring out any differences.

General Equilibrium Studies

Establishing a free trade area among the three North American economies is likely to have significant cross-sectoral implications, as factors shift to take advantage of new trade opportunities. This argues a priori for a general equilibrium approach to modeling the effects of NAFTA. Indeed, NAFTA seems to have been subjected to more CGE analyses than any other trade negotiations.[17] For the exploration of the agricultural effect of NAFTA, the CGE approach poses a dilemma. The complexity of individual commodity programs and the disparate nature of the agricultural sector make any use of aggregated models problematic. The problem is not that aggregated results, such as the effect on farm incomes, are uninteresting, but that measuring such effects requires detailed knowledge of the program changes, production response, market potential, and input use of each sector. For these reasons, the results of many of these CGE studies of NAFTA are difficult to interpret.

Despite this difficulty, Grennes and his colleagues have attempted to compare the agricultural results from the CGE models of Drusilla Brown, Alan Deardorff, and Robert Stern; INFORUM; KPMG Peat Marwick; and Hinojosa and Robinson.[18] A variant of this last paper is discussed in detail below. With respect to the other three models, Grennes and his colleagues point to the inconsistency of the results as to the overall effect on U.S. agriculture, the INFORUM study finds significant gains, while the studies of Brown and others and KPMG Peat Marwick expect some net loss to agricultural output.[19] INFORUM's optimistic results seem to stem from an assumption that U.S. exports to Mexico would expand by 10 to 20 percent a year from 1989 levels as a result of the elimination of nontariff barriers. No such gains are apparent when only tariffs are reduced. The Brown, Deardorff, and Stern paper treats agriculture as a single sector, asserted to be protected more highly in the United States than in Mexico. Free trade, therefore, results in an increase in imports and a contraction of U.S. farm production. The disaggregation of the agricultural sector in the KPMG Peat Marwick study, to include animal products, field crops, fruits and vegetables, and "other" agriculture, does not seem to rescue the situation: all except the animal products sector suffer loses. However, the authors point out that the field crops sector could receive a stimulus.

Among the more recent CGE studies of the effects of NAFTA, some have attempted to introduce economies of scale into the models. One of these is the 1992 study by David Roland-Holst, Kenneth A. Reinert, and Clinton R. Shiells (cited in note 19). In their model, agriculture is treated as one sector, with somewhat low levels of initial protection. One would expect the usual rather modest results. But as a sector that is assumed not to enjoy scale economies, agriculture has to bid for factors against sectors that do reap such benefits. Thus Mexican agriculture is disadvantaged not so much by the removal of a 1 percent tariff and a 10 percent "sectoral import distortion" but by its having to compete with an expanding non-agricultural economy. The result is a contraction of nearly 10 percent under each of two alternative imperfect competition assumptions (Cournot and contestable pricing). It is small consolation that Canadian agriculture also is forced to contract, by 3 to 6 percent, as a result of a 5 percent increase in average costs. Whether agriculture is really so passive a sector is doubtful. Given the present poor structure of much of Mexican agriculture, one could imagine gains in efficiency comparable to those in industry as a result of changes in the economic incentives to the sector.

The CGE studies that come closest to capturing both the detail of the agricultural sector and the general equilibrium intersector effects are those based on the CGE model developed by Sherman Robinson in conjunction with economists at the Economic Research Service of USDA.[20] This model has been modified to include Mexico, and the results are reported in various places and forms.[21] This discussion focuses on the results presented in December 1991, in Robinson and others, and on the preliminary results of an expanded version of the model reported in Burfisher, Robinson, and Thierfelder (see note 11). The model of Robinson and others contains eleven sectors, of which four represent the farming industry and one the food-processing industry. Corn for human consumption is modeled specifically as a separate activity, with feed corn, food grains, soybeans, and cotton grouped together as "program crops." Fruits and vegetables make

Table 1. Impact of Including Agricultural Trade Liberalization in NAFTA
Percent increase relative to base model

Item	United States	Mexico
Real GDP		
Industrial liberalization only	0.1	0.0
Industrial liberalization and agricultural tariffs	0.1	0.1
Full trade liberalization[a]	0.2	0.2
Exports to partners		
Industrial trade liberalization	8.0	4.2
Industrial trade liberalization and agricultural tariffs	9.0	5.0
Full trade liberalization[a]	10.5	5.4

Source: Mary Burfisher, Sherman Robinson, and Karen Thierfelder, "Agricultural and Food Policies in a U.S.-Mexico Free Trade Area," unpublished paper, 1992, pp. 30, 31.
a. Includes the removal of nontariff barriers in agriculture.

up another sector, including the staple dry bean crop in Mexico, and "other agriculture" includes livestock, poultry, forestry, and fisheries.[22] The Burfisher, Robinson, and Thierfelder version is expanded to twenty-eight sectors, of which ten are agricultural and ten are food-processing activities. In this version, food grains and feed corn are modeled separately, as is the forestry and fisheries sector. Farm programs are modeled as a combination of fixed and endogenous price wedges (gaps between traded prices and domestic prices) and income transfers. Deficiency payments (in the United States) are endogenous, as are the domestic price of goods subject to import quotas and the levels of domestic subsidy to Mexican agriculture. The main income transfer program is the tortilla subsidy to low-income Mexican households.

In both versions of the model discussed here, several different scenarios are reported. The first two scenarios in Robinson and others assume liberalization of industrial border measures and all border measures, respectively. Burfisher, Robinson, and Thierfelder run an additional model that keeps agricultural nontariff measures out of the liberalization process. These models provide useful benchmarks against which to look at the effect of agricultural trade in NAFTA.[23] Table 1 compares the impact on gross domestic product (GDP) and bilateral trade of these three scenarios. For the United States the removal of agricultural tariff barriers alone does not imply any significant benefits in terms of GDP, whereas removing the nontariff barriers in agriculture raises the projected impact on the U.S. GDP to about two-tenths of 1 percent. For Mexico, including the liberalization of tariff and nontariff barriers in agriculture raises the GDP effect

Table 2. Sector Results of Alternative NAFTA Scenarios
Percent change from base model

Item	Scenario[a]			
	3	4	5	6
United States				
Food grain output	0.7	1.5	1.2	0.1
Food grain exports	80.8	130.6	140.7	86.9
Food corn output	7.5	8.8	9.1	4.4
Food corn exports	192.9	209.3	222.8	118.4
Feed grain output	0.9	1.6	1.5	0.5
Feed grain exports	52.1	71.4	74.1	55.6
Fruit and vegetable output	0.3	1.1	0.9	−0.1
Fruit and vegetable exports	14.8	14.7	15.0	16.2
Oilseeds output	1.3	2.7	2.5	0.6
Oilseeds exports	8.0	16.4	18.3	9.9
Mexico				
Food grain output	−6.5	−16.4	−14.1	−7.4
Food corn output	−15.2	−21.7	−20.2	−1.4
Feed grain output	−3.2	−5.6	−5.0	−3.7
Fruit and vegetable output	10.3	10.1	9.6	8.2
Fruit and vegetable exports	25.8	25.6	25.3	24.7
Oilseed output	−4.7	−45.6	−46.5	−13.9

Source: Burfisher, Robinson, and Thierfelder, "Agricultural and Food Policies," pp. 34–35, 49–50.

a. 3 = Trade liberalization—remove tariffs and quotas from all sectors
   4 = Trade liberalization and Mexican agriculture liberalization—eliminate all Mexican agricultural support policies
   5 = Trade liberalization and partial Mexican agriculture liberalization—eliminate Mexican input subsidies but not processor subsidies
   6 = Trade liberalization and Mexican deficiency payments—deficiency payment for corn

from zero to about two-tenths of a percentage point. Bilateral exports are also boosted by full trade liberalization—by about two and a half percentage points for the United States and one percentage point for Mexico. On these figures, the negotiators should at the least pay attention to the beneficial impact of the agricultural aspects of NAFTA, even if the promise is not dramatic.

In addition to free trade, the authors choose several other scenarios as a way of handling the ambiguities mentioned regarding the link between NAFTA and Mexican domestic policy change. In the Burfisher, Robinson, and Thierfelder version, scenario 3 adds total Mexican liberalization to NAFTA, while scenario 4 assumes the removal of input subsidies but not price supports to processors, along with NAFTA. Scenario 5 assumes that Mexico switches to deficiency payments on maize. The specific sector results from the Burfisher, Robinson, and Thierfelder study are shown in table 2. The results accord well with a priori reasoning: U.S. cereal exports to Mexico, such as wheat, food, and feed corn, increase significantly.

But so do oilseeds exports, as well as sales to Mexico of U.S. fruits and vegetables. Smaller increases are indicated for livestock products and various processed foodstuffs. No agricultural sector is hurt by free trade with Mexico under these results, though they are not, of course, differentiated by region.

Mexican agriculture is less fortunate, as corn and other crop output drops significantly. Fruit and vegetable exports respond to the better access to the U.S. market, as expected, but maize output is estimated to decrease by 15 percent with trade policy liberalization implied by NAFTA (table 2). If domestic liberalization is added, the reduction could reach 22 percent. Coupled with a drop of wheat and oilseeds production, the outcome is indeed one of major adjustments to the rural economy. Maintaining domestic maize prices with a deficiency payment, as in scenario 6, keeps maize output unchanged and restricts the cut in other field crops to more modest levels. This internal stability is purchased at the cost of a reduced, though still positive, benefit to U.S. cereal exporters.

The recent work by Santiago Levy and Sweder van Wijnbergen brings the apparatus of a CGE model to bear on the particular policy issue illustrated by these results. The issue, crucial to Mexican agriculture and central to NAFTA discussions, is the pace of liberalization of the maize market. As Levy and van Wijnbergen point out, maize policy "is Mexico's de facto rural employment and anti-poverty program."[24] To remove that policy too rapidly could cause social and political problems: to hold on to a distorting policy too long denies the Mexican economy the full benefits of restructuring. The CGE model developed by Levy and van Wijnbergen contains five rural goods sectors and two urban sectors, seven factors (distinguishing between rural and urban labor and irrigated and nonirrigated land), and six types of households, including landless rural workers and subsistence farmers. Results are reported as efficiency gains (discounted to the present), real wages, land values, and irrigation flows. The main outcome is severe initial adjustments imposed on rural households as a result of a fall in the maize price, involving lower land prices (by perhaps 25 percent), and lower wages (by 13 percent) for the most affected groups. Allowing labor to move between sectors cushions much of this effect but threatens to send 700,000 more migrants to the cities. The Levy and van Wijnbergen paper fully discusses the various options for spreading these adjustments out over a period of years, and the complementary investment programs that could be introduced, particularly investment in irrigation. In this context, the only specific NAFTA component of the Mexican CGE model is the assumption made in some model runs that the

United States removes its 5 percent tariff on its fruit and vegetable imports from Mexico. This has the effect of reducing migration pressure by 200,000 persons and benefiting particularly the owners of irrigated land. Further comparison of the effect on the agricultural markets in Mexico with other studies is hampered by lack of reported information on output and consumption levels and on the change in product prices.

Partial Equilibrium Multimarket Studies

The most significant partial equilibrium model used to evaluate the agricultural effects of NAFTA is the USDA/ERS SWOPSIM model, developed under the general tutelage of Vernon Roningen and Praveen Dixit. This model formed the basis for ERS staff work on a number of trade issues, including that of multilateral trade liberalization. The SWOPSIM model is a multicountry partial equilibrium model comprising individual supply and demand relationships and world market closure. Welfare calculations and market balances are generated by manipulating policy parameters, largely of the price wedge kind. Countries can be aggregated into the "rest of world" category to allow any group of countries to be studied. In the version discussed here, Armington-type assumptions are used in the trade model, implying less-than-perfect substitution among sources of import supply. Bilateral trade flows can therefore be identified in the solution.[25]

Early results from a three-commodity U.S.-Mexico SWOPSIM model were reported in Krissoff and others (cited in note 10). The model was subsequently expanded to twenty-nine commodities, covering 75 percent of the farm trade between the United States and Mexico. The base solution for this model represents the 1988 set of policies and trade flows.

Three scenarios are reported in Krissoff, Neff, and Sharples (cited in note 10). Scenario 1 assumes free bilateral trade (that is, no tariffs and nontariff border measures); scenario 2 assumes that Mexico removes all border protection (on goods from all countries); scenario 3 combines these two assumptions. The overall results are shown in table 3. U.S. exports of agricultural products to Mexico increase by more than $480 million, under a preferential trade agreement, with some reduction in exports to the rest of the world. But much the same effect ($440 million) is noticed if Mexico continues its present path of trade liberalization. In that case, getting preferential access to the Mexican market is of no additional value—as one would expect. Mexican exports are increased by about $170 million if the United States agrees to give preferential access. Understandably,

Table 3. Impact on Agricultural Trade and Sectoral Welfare, Alternative NAFTA Scenarios
Millions of dollars

Item	Scenario[a]		
	1	2	3
U.S. agricultural exports	423	389	394
To Mexico	482	435	438
Mexican agricultural exports	171	49	178
To United States	166	25	160
U.S. agricultural imports	169	41	160
Mexican agricultural imports	443	465	469
U.S. producer welfare	225	279	222
Consumer welfare	− 122	− 232	− 126
Government cost	207	201	199
Net	310	248	295
Mexican producer welfare	− 438	− 503	− 457
Consumer welfare	978	1,068	1,035
Government cost	− 440	− 500	− 462
Net	100	65	116

Source: Barry Krissoff, Liana Neff, and Jerry Sharples, "Estimated Impacts of a Potential U.S.-Mexico Preferential Trading Agreement for the Agricultural Sector," U.S. Department of Agriculture, Economic Research Service, Washington, January 1992.

a. 1 = Preferential Trade Agreement (PTA)
   2 = Unilateral Mexican trade liberalization
   3 = PTA and Mexican trade liberalization

Mexican trade liberalization does not by itself generate that kind of response.

The effect on sectoral welfare is of interest. U.S. farm welfare (producer surplus) rises by $200 million under NAFTA, whether or not there is Mexican trade liberalization: the increase is greatest when Mexico unilaterally liberalizes—as this generates export growth without allowing greater access to the U.S. market. Consumers pay somewhat higher prices in all three cases, and the U.S. government saves some program costs. On balance, the U.S. economy gains most from NAFTA, about $310 million, though gains are almost as much if NAFTA is accompanied by Mexican tariff removal with the outside world.

Prospects for Mexican farmers appear less rosy—at least in terms of aggregate income. Table 3 shows a possible decline of $440 million in producer surplus arising from NAFTA, jumping to $500 million if Mexico unilaterally opens its border to imports. Despite significant gains to consumers through lower prices, net benefits to Mexico are smaller than for the United States, ranging from $65 million with unilateral liberalization to $116 million with both NAFTA and open markets (with preferential

Table 4. Impact of NAFTA on U.S. and Mexican Commodity Exports
Millions of dollars

Product group	United States	Mexico
Grains and oilseeds	369	11
Livestock, meats, and dairy	49	57
Horticulture	3	98
Other agriculture	2	5
Total	423	171

Source: Krissoff, Neff, and Sharples, "Estimated Impacts," p. 41.

access into the United States but no Mexican border protection). The overall picture is, therefore, much the same as projected in the Robinson and others CGE model: both the United States and Mexico gain from the mutual reduction in trade barriers, but Mexican farmers would be adversely affected and U.S. farmers would stand to benefit.

The commodity gains and losses also accord with the direction given in the CGE study. Table 4 shows the commodity composition of the export expansion.[26] Preferential access to each other's markets would boost U.S. grain and oilseed exports by $50 million. Mexican horticultural exports would expand by about $100 million, and livestock exports by nearly $60 million. The model foresees a significant increase (of 26 percent) in feeder cattle sales from Mexico to the United States. Table 5 gives the Krissoff, Neff, and Sharples welfare impacts by commodity group, confirming the gains to U.S. grain and oilseed farmers of about $340 million, and the loss to their counterparts in Mexico of $390 million. The considerable gain to Mexican livestock income is presumably a result of the expanded market for feeder cattle in the United States (see below) and the consequent higher cattle prices in Mexico (up by 16 percent). However, as the Mexican beef price actually falls, it appears that the losers are not consumers but the buyers in Mexico of Mexican feeder cattle. Moreover, the magnitude of this effect is worrisome. The model appears to say that an expansion of sales of feeder cattle to the United States is worth over three times as much as the loss to Mexican farmers of freeing up grain imports. On a priori grounds this looks doubtful.

One strength of the partial equilibrium analysis is its ability to handle detail in many products (without the need to construct a full-blown sector for, say, green peppers). Table 6 compiles some of this commodity detail from the results given by Krissoff, Neff, and Sharples. The main message of these results seems to be that Mexican cereal output would decline, but by no means be eliminated, with freer trade (though presumably the decline would be greater with Mexican liberalization) and that Mexican

Table 5. Impact of NAFTA on Sectoral Welfare, by Commodity Group
Millions of dollars

Item	United States	Mexico
Producer welfare		
Grains and oilseeds	338	− 392
Livestock, meats, and dairy	− 88	1,472
Horticulture	− 31	32
Consumer welfare		
Grains and oilseeds	− 260	835
Livestock, meats, and dairy	72	− 1,345
Horticulture	72	− 12
Government costs		
Grains and oilseeds	− 279	27
Livestock, meats, and dairy	17	87
Horticulture	52	0
Net welfare		
Grains and oilseeds	357	28
Livestock, meats, and dairy	− 35	40
Horticulture	− 12	19

Source: Krissoff, Neff, and Sharples, "Estimated Impacts," pp. 44, 45, 48.

fruits and vegetables would expand in output. The regional and labor force implications of this switch are clearly significant, as recognized in the CGE analyses.

Commodity-Specific Studies

As both the qualitative assessments and the models described above point to very different implications for particular commodity sectors in U.S. and Mexican agriculture, it is appropriate to see whether these results are confirmed by commodity-specific studies in which analysts have combined knowledge of commodity particularities with quantitative models. A major report from the American Farm Bureau Federation (cited in note 13) includes several such studies, undertaken by academic economists conversant in particular commodity areas. The studies discussed here (identified by senior author) are

—Wesley Peterson, on grains and oilseeds;

—Parr Rosson, on livestock and meat;

—Emily McClain, on dairy;

—Roberta Cook, on fruits and vegetables; and

—Thomas Spreen, on citrus.

Table 6. Impact on Mexican Production, Mexican Consumption, and Trade, by Commodity

Percent change

Item	Mexican production	Mexican consumption of Mexican products	Mexican consumption of U.S. products	U.S. consumption of Mexican products
Corn	−7.3	−7.3	64.0	. . .
Coarse grains	−10.9	−13.9	50.1	. . .
Cattle	0.2	−0.5	11.2	26.0
Beef	−0.2	−0.2	15.0	. . .
Pork	0.5	0.5	25.3	. . .
Poultry	2.1	2.1	23.9	. . .
Eggs	2.5	2.5	4.8	. . .
Melons	2.4	−0.6	. . .	10.8
Frozen orange juice	18.6	−13.4	. . .	32.1
Cucumbers	6.6	−1.3	. . .	10.8
Onions	3.8	−0.7	. . .	13.7
Green peppers	1.6	−0.2	. . .	10.2
Tomatoes	1.6	−0.4	. . .	10.2

Source: Krissoff, Neff, and Sharples, "Estimated Impacts," pp. 42, 46, 47.

Peterson's study on the effect of NAFTA on the cereal and oilseed sector concentrates on the effect on Mexico. A "simple model of the key grain and oilseed industries in Mexico is used to analyze the implications of forming a NAFTA for U.S.-Mexico trade in these commodities."[27] The model uses elasticities from USDA economists (presumably similar to those in the SWOPSIM model). Price changes resulting from trade liberalization are applied to the baseline model to give new market balances.[28]

The study reports two NAFTA scenarios. NAFTA I assumes full liberalization of Mexican markets, implying "real prices received by Mexican producers and paid by Mexican consumers gradually become equal to the lower, real U.S. border price."[29] NAFTA II, considered by the author more realistic, involves incomplete liberalization. Real prices for corn do not change under this scenario, and only one-half of the protection is removed from grains and soybeans in the first five years of the agreement. Consumer prices are, however, reduced, implying a series of deficiency payments replacing current policies. Projections are given for five years, 1991–95, by which time it is assumed that the policy changes will have been completed.

The main results of the Peterson model are summarized in table 7: Mexican corn production drops by 2.2 million (21 percent) and con-

Table 7. Impact of NAFTA Alternative Scenarios on Mexican Cereal and Oilseed Balance
Thousands of metric tons

			1995	
Projections for Mexico	1991	Baseline	NAFTA I[a]	NAFTA II[b]
Corn production	10,088	10,088	7,927	10,286
Corn consumption	14,238	15,576	17,336	17,335
Corn imports	4,150	5,488	9,409	7,049
Wheat production	3,829	4,027	3,467	3,652
Wheat consumption	4,445	4,841	4,867	4,867
Wheat imports	616	814	1,400	1,215
Sorghum production	3,821	4,043	3,011	3,286
Sorghum consumption	5,789	6,024	6,629	6,273
Sorghum imports	1,968	1,981	3,618	2,987
Soybeans production	662	726	585	626
Soybeans consumption	2,333	2,540	2,940	2,712
Soybeans imports	1,671	1,814	2,355	2,086

Source: Wesley Peterson, in American Farm Bureau Federation, *NAFTA: Effects on Agriculture*, vol. 3 (Park Ridge, Ill., 1992), pp. 35–37.
a. NAFTA I = Complete liberalization of production and consumption prices, equal to U.S. border price.
b. NAFTA II = Real corn prices stay at base level, 50 percent of protection on other crops removed. All consumer prices drop to border price levels.

sumption increases by 1.8 million tons (11 percent) as a result of full liberalization. Much smaller effects are projected if the deficiency payment system is introduced (NAFTA II), along with retention of one-half of Mexican protection. Corn production would actually increase (as other crops lost competitiveness), but the consumption increase would still take place, leading to more than 7 million tons of imported corn (presumably from the United States) relative to 5.5 million tons in the baseline projection. The extra 1.5 million tons presumably might be worth $150 million in U.S. export earnings, and represents a 71 percent increase in Mexican corn imports, not far from the 64 percent increase in the Krissoff, Neff, and Sharples study.

The picture for other cereal and oilseed products shows a jump in imports of wheat (72 percent), sorghum (83 percent), and soybeans (30 percent) as a result of complete liberalization of markets in Mexico. However, it should be remembered that the baseline assumption is for protection to stay at about 1989 levels.[30] In fact, considerable liberalization has taken place in the past two years.

Dairy and beef market analyses of NAFTA are less apparent. The Farm Bureau study on livestock by Parr Rosson does not employ a formal model and makes no quantitative estimates on the effect of NAFTA. However,

Table 8. Projections of Mexican Milk Balance under Alternative Growth Assumptions
Millions of metric tons of imports

	Production growth			
	Low (5%)		High (8%)	
Consumption growth	1995	2000	1995	2000
Low (2%)	2.76	2.72	1.32	-1.72
High (4%)	4.59	7.03	3.15	2.59

Source: McClain and Harris, in AFBF, *NAFTA: Effects on Agriculture*, vol. 2, p. 119.

in the absence of such estimates, it is useful to compare the qualitative judgment of Parr Rosson and colleagues with the dramatic conclusion of the SWOPSIM model that feeder cattle exports to the United States would expand rapidly. Rosson states that "the elimination of the Mexican export tax and the low U.S. tariff on cattle would most likely result in stable to moderately higher exports of feeder cattle from Mexico to the United States in the near term,"[31] but that these exports depended upon new investment in Mexico and would fall off as the domestic beef market expanded.

The dairy study, by McClain and Harris, does attempt some projections of Mexican imports, though not strictly qualifying as estimates of a NAFTA effect. McClain and Harris project dairy exports to Mexico under varying assumptions of growth rate for both domestic production and consumption. The results are summarized in table 8. Imports are projected to remain at about 2.7 million metric tons with slow growth in production and consumption and to rise to 3.15 million metric tons by 1995 with high growth assumptions. The authors argue that "the high rate of income and demand growth is viewed as the likely outcome of continued privatization of the economy and the successful conclusion of a FTA. The lower rate is more likely with the abandonment or reversal of economic reforms and the failure of the FTA negotiations"; the higher rate of production is also seen as more consistent with "an expected boost to production from cheaper feed and other input prices and potentially higher demand-driven milk prices under further deregulation and the successful conclusion of an FTA."[32] In the absence of any more detailed single-commodity models, one should probably conclude that dairy imports from the United States will continue and could well increase if investment is not attracted to Mexican production and processing.[33]

The fruit and vegetable sector poses the most difficult problems for analysis. First, the sector is complex, with more than one hundred different products entering world trade. Second, the degree of government regulation in the production and marketing of these products can be extensive, despite their not being, in general, a part of national farm price policy legislation. Third, the regulation is often at a subfederal level, either through state legislation or parastatals operating in particular markets. Finally, the seasonality and climate and soil specificity of production, coupled with the range of different ways to consume the product, make understanding the pattern of prices and protection a complex empirical task. Thus, models that include the fruit and vegetable sector cannot hope to explain the complexity of the market, and adequate models for evaluating policy changes by individual commodity are rare. As a compromise, one can look at a range of different products and hope to pick those in which changes in trade policy are likely to make a difference. This involves both looking at trade barriers per se and at the effect that changes in protection would have on competitiveness.

The Farm Bureau report contains a lengthy examination by Cook and others of the present market position and possible competitiveness of fourteen fresh and processed fruits and vegetables grown in Mexico, Florida, California, Arizona, and Washington state. The report also includes a detailed discussion by Spreen and others of the citrus industry as it might be affected by NAFTA—including the results from a world citrus model that has been modified to take into account Mexican expansion in the market for frozen orange juice.[34]

Cook and her colleagues collected data on farm and processing costs from a number of sites and sources in the United States and Mexico. A summary of the results from fourteen chapters is attempted in table 9. The costs shown in the table are a rough indication of whether Mexican fruit and vegetable production is actually "low-cost" relative to the United States. Competing producers in the United States fear that Mexico can take advantage of low labor wages and less rigorous environmental and labor laws to export cheaply into the United States. Cook and her colleagues point out that (1) low wage rates do not always translate to low labor costs, as productivity of farm workers is generally less in Mexico, (2) high transportation costs and other infrastructural problems in Mexico make it difficult to compete even when labor costs are low, (3) water shortages and rising prices of inputs have limited and will continue to limit Mexican expansion, and (4) any cost advantage from different environmental laws is eroding as Mexico adopts U.S. regulations. The sphere of direct competition is actually rather limited. Mexico (in particular the state of Sinaloa) provides fresh vegetables (such as tomatoes) to the U.S.

Table 9. Comparison of Costs of Production, Selected Horticultural Commodities, United States and Mexico
Costs in dollars

| Product | United States | | Mexico | | Page |
	Region	Cost	Region	Cost	
Asparagus	Imperial Valley (CA)	25.64/carton	Mexicali/ San Luis	16.65/carton 21.65/carton[c]	77
Fresh broccoli	Imperial Valley (CA) San Joaquin Valley (CA)	6.17/carton 5.24/carton	Mexicali/ San Luis	6.06/carton 7.06/carton[c]	126
Avocado	California	20–26,000/acre[a] 3,250–3,550/acre[b]	Michoacan	6,500/acre[a] 1,075–1,375/acre[b]	155 . . .
Strawberries	Plant City (FL) Santa Monica (CA)	7.10/tray 4.65/tray	Baja- California	3.68/tray 5.13/tray[c]	193 194
Tomatoes (processing)	Sacramento (CA) Imperial Valley (CA)	48/ton 54/ton	Sinaloa	61/ton	237
Tomatoes (fresh)	Florida (average)	3.43/unit 6.84/unit[d]	Sinaloa	2.43/unit 6.53/unit[c]	281
Green peppers	Florida (average)	3.54/unit 8.42/unit[d]	Sinaloa	2.43/unit 6.96/unit[c]	306
Cucumbers	Southwest Florida	3.04/unit 7.70/unit[d]	Sinaloa	2.99/unit 8.20/unit[c]	322

Commodity	U.S. location	U.S. cost	Mexican location	Mexican cost	Page
Eggplant	Palm Beach Co. (FL)	3.13/unit 5.55/unit[d]	Sinaloa	3.18/unit 7.24/unit[c]	337
Squash	Dade County (FL)	4.93/unit 9.50/unit[d]	Sinaloa	4.54/unit 9.30/unit[c]	353
Cantaloupe	Imperial Valley (CA) San Joaquin Valley (CA)	5.40/carton 4.45/carton	Mexicali/ San Luis	5.31/carton 7.41/carton[c]	375
Apples	Washington State	691/ton 845/ton[e]	Mexico (medium tech)	583/ton	407
Peaches	California	580/ton 760/ton[e]	Mexico (medium tech)	418/ton	434
Table grapes	California	771/lug	Mexico	11.61/lug	451
Oranges, juice	Florida	4.72/box[f]	Veracruz, *ejido*	3.26/box	518–27
Oranges, navel	California/ Arizona	2.61/carton[f]	Veracruz, private	3.13/box	. . .

Sources: Robert Cook and others, and Thomas Spreen and others, in AFBF, *NAFTA: Effects on Agriculture*, vol. 4.

a. Development costs over three years.
b. Yearly cost for bearing trees.
c. FOB in United States.
d. Including harvest and packing costs.
e. FOB in Mexico.
f. Delivered in cost (prepackaging or processing).

market in the winter period (November to May) at a time when California produce is not harvested. California takes over in the spring, summer, and fall, competing only with Baja California for this seasonal market. Winter produce does, however, conflict with Florida production, which peaks in fall and spring but continues through the winter.

The cost studies assembled by Cook and her colleagues confirm this picture. Mexico appears to be able to ship tomatoes, green peppers, squash, and cucumbers to the United States at prices competitive with Florida's, but the cost difference is not large. For other commodities, asparagus and broccoli in particular, competition with the irrigated agriculture in the California valleys is likely to intensify. Avocado costs appear much lower in Mexico, and if the disease problems can be resolved to the satisfaction of U.S. authorities, a market will open up in this commodity—to the benefit of U.S. consumers. For several other commodities, lost differences seem so small as to lead one to expect little effect from liberalization.

Cook and her colleagues add another dimension to the discussion on fruits and vegetables, arguing that U.S. producers of such crops as apples and peaches could find expanding markets in Mexico. Single-commodity projection models are used to look at potential market size, on assumptions linked to NAFTA.[35] The baseline trend assumes 2 percent growth in Mexican per capita income, which increases to 3 percent with the effect of NAFTA.[36] In addition, a "higher share" of U.S. imports in total supply is assumed as a result of NAFTA. These rosy assumptions lead to projected imports of 129,000 tons of apples and 66,000 tons of peaches—in both cases more than threefold increases over existing sales.

For citrus, the focus is on the ability of Mexico to compete in the market for frozen orange juice now shared between Florida producers and Brazilian imports. Mexico has a small share (about 2 percent) of this market at present, and is far behind Brazil as a supplier to the U.S. market. Spreen and his colleagues use a model of the citrus industry, based on tree ages and replanting decisions, to look at long-term developments in market share. Their results are summarized in table 10, which shows production and "on-tree" revenue (before picking and processing) of oranges for juice. The NAFTA scenario assumes a doubling of the rate of growth of Mexican production, adding another 7 million gallons of orange juice into the market each year, as well as the removal of the tariff of thirty-five cents a gallon levied on imports to the United States.[37] Mexican output would jump under such a set of assumptions to 150 million gallons, from a baseline projection of 60 million gallons. However, the Mexican output would substitute for Brazilian production and not affect

Table 10. Projections of Orange Production for Frozen Orange Juice and On-Tree Revenue, with and without Mexican Expansion, 2000

Area	Orange production (millions of boxes)	On-tree revenue (millions of dollars)
Florida		
Base model	228.0	1,136
Mexican expansion	226.6	1,064
Brazil		
Base model	285.2	598
Mexican expansion	272.3	512
	Orange juice production	
Mexico		
Base model	58.9[a]	35
Mexican expansion	149.0[a]	115

Source: Spreen and others, in AFBF, *NAFTA: Effects on Agriculture*, vol. 4, pp. 536–43.
a. Millions of gallons.

that in Florida. To the extent that inward investment into Mexico could take place without NAFTA, the actual impact of trade liberalization appears on this evidence to be rather small.

Reconciliation

The quantitative studies generally bear out the qualitative assessments of gains to U.S. grain, oilseed, and livestock producers and losses to those that compete with Mexico in fruits and vegetables. The pessimism of the Almon and Brown, Deardorff, and Stern CGE models does not reappear in those with more specific commodity and policy detail. In some cases, the studies even agree on the magnitude of the effects. Peterson sees corn output in Mexico declining by 21 percent if Mexico liberalizes its agricultural markets, and Robinson and others also suggest a 21 percent drop in corn output. Robinson and others show a 7 percent drop in corn output just with trade measures liberalized, and Krissoff, Neff, and Sharples find a 7 percent drop for their "PTA" scenario with no domestic measures changed. As mentioned earlier, Peterson's 71 percent increase in Mexican corn imports matches reasonably with the 64 percent increase expected by Krissoff, Neff, and Sharples.

There appears to be no counterpart, on the other hand, to the large boost in feeder cattle exports from Mexico to the United States in models other than the SWOPSIM, perhaps because such flows of intermediate foods are not easy to capture in economic models.

The vegetable picture is also consistent, although actual comparisons among models are difficult. The Mexican crops expected by Krissoff, Neff, and Sharples to do well in sales to the United States (melons, cucumbers, onions, green peppers, and tomatoes) show up as among those identified by Cook and her colleagues as being produced more cheaply in Mexico. An expansion of over 30 percent in sales of frozen orange juice to the United States is small compared with the almost tripling of output expected by Spreen, and others. But all these studies agree that the aggregate impact on U.S. fruit and vegetable producers is small and is likely to be offset by additional sales to Mexico as incomes rise and barriers fall. Problems of intensified competition will be localized and would, in any case, be phased in over time. Snap backs or other safeguard measures will no doubt be offered to producers in such markets.

The overall picture then is one of rather modest developments in agricultural markets stemming directly from a NAFTA and some quite dramatic changes in Mexico (to the benefit of U.S. exporters) if Mexico continues to liberalize internal markets for agricultural products. NAFTA will probably not put tight constraints on such domestic policy changes, though the GATT could modify policies considerably. From a U.S. agricultural perspective, the NAFTA talks should not present a major problem: much bigger changes are afoot in other negotiations.

Comment by Darryl McLeod

Tim Josling effectively molds a diverse "first round" of research on agriculture under NAFTA into a cautiously optimistic consensus. Given the little that is known about the negotiators' objectives and the diverse methodologies of these studies, this is an achievement in itself. One key point of agreement is that regional agricultural integration offers large potential gains for the United States and Mexico, perhaps the largest of any industry group. The United States and Canada will export more grain and livestock products, while Mexico will produce more fruit and vegetables. This expansion is particularly important for Mexico, since these crops use at least twice as much labor per acre as grain crops.

The second point of consensus is that, despite large potential gains, there are important transitional hazards. In Mexico, too rapid an opening of the grain market could create severe hardship for millions of poor, small, rain-fed corn farmers, perhaps resulting in a new wave of migrants into rural, or urban, or even U.S. labor markets. In the United States and Canada, too rapid an opening of fruit and vegetable markets may create pockets of local but effective political opposition to the accord.[38] The best way to avoid these pitfalls, it is argued, is to proceed slowly with phased reduction of trade barriers in both grains and horticultural crops.

Since this survey charts the common ground so well, I focus on some key differences among these studies. These disagreements center not so much on how agriculture will respond to liberalization but on what a regional trade agreement like NAFTA can or should accomplish. Once these conflicting views of what NAFTA involves are clarified, I think the "go slow" component of the consensus loses much of its rationale.

Since the goals of regional trading areas in general, and of NAFTA in particular, are not well defined, each research team invented its own liberalization scenarios. Three alternate views of NAFTA emerged. One scenario combines tariff reduction with a redesign of Mexico's domestic agricultural policies along American and Canadian lines. This accords with Paul Krugman's argument that regional agreements like Europe 1992 and perhaps NAFTA are "not so much trade agreements as an agreement to coordinate policies that have historically been regarded as domestic."[39] Although no "common agricultural policy" is on the horizon, under this NAFTA II scenario (as the American Farm Bureau Federation calls it) domestic agricultural policies become increasingly similar in three countries.

Under NAFTA II, Mexico replaces its system of price supports and tariff barriers with a combination of direct "deficiency" payments and input subsidies, much as the United States did in the 1960s. Since producer subsidy equivalents for corn are now about the same in both countries, these reforms cause the price of corn to fall to U.S. levels but lead to a relatively small drop in Mexican *corn* production.[40] In other words, *NAFTA II does not lead to major transitional hardship for rain-fed corn farmers.* Mexico eventually phases out its income supports in concert with the United States and Europe, as envisioned in the current GATT round.

For fruits and vegetables policy, coordination mainly involves environmental, phytosanitary, and other quality standards rather than income supports, perhaps under the auspices of U.S.-like marketing orders. These institutional changes and regulations are even more important for encouraging greater interregional trade and investment flows.

The major drawback of the NAFTA II harmonization scenario is that replacing price supports with direct payments increases the "on the books" fiscal cost of these programs (though it reduces the implicit "tax" on grain products). Similarly, considerable government effort and expense may be required to establish and enforce environmental and quality standards.

The second widely analyzed NAFTA scenario focuses mainly on "unilateral" agricultural liberalization by Mexico. *This is the policy strategy that leads to a large reduction of corn production on small rain-fed farms.* In their detailed study of what the Farm Bureau calls "NAFTA I," a World Bank team uses a model and a little data to argue that a slow (five-year) phasing out of tariffs sacrifices very little of the welfare gains from grain liberalization.[41] The main attraction of a unilateral opening is that it allows Mexico to shift the burden of its grain subsidies to U.S. taxpayers. The World Bank team argues that the resulting fiscal dividend should be used to finance new irrigation projects. Building these projects would tighten rural labor markets and help compensate displaced corn farmers.[42]

The problem is that the World Bank analyzes this process more or less independently of NAFTA. In particular, the World Bank assumes the United States and Canada are indifferent toward either a quick or slow opening of Mexico's grain market. But certainly U.S.-Canadian producers would expect some quid pro quo for delays, such as delayed reduction of tariffs in fruits and vegetables or more liberal provisions for the use of "snap-back" tariffs.[43] The strategic implications of changes in grain policy for other sectors and NAFTA are ignored.

The general acceptance of a long (twenty-year) snap-back transition period for fruits and vegetables derives from yet another less explicit view of the NAFTA based largely on the 1989 Canadian-U.S. Free Trade Agreement for agriculture. Elsewhere, Josling termed this agricultural policy a "trade irritant" scenario. Here the agricultural agenda is pared down to include only issues whose omission would delay or prevent progress in other areas. Modest goals make it possible to claim some progress when in fact little has occurred.

The risk is that worries over the high transitional cost of NAFTA I (unilateral liberalization) will lead not to NAFTA II, but to this NAFTA III scenario, where the transition is so long that very little happens in agriculture.[44] That would be especially unfortunate for Mexico, because its agricultural sector has been neglected for so long. Virtually every study notes the long drought of public and private investment in rural Mexico, the region where most of the extremely poor live and work.[45]

In summary, the danger is that a go-slow strategy will discourage new private investment in Mexico's fruit and vegetable sector, which could more than offset the gains to corn farmers from delays. Recent low private investment in agriculture partly reflects ownership restrictions and exchange rate instability, but the imminent threat of tariff retaliation is also a key factor.[46] Twenty-year snap-back provisions, even of the fairly innocuous "price trigger" variety, perpetuate this uncertainty and discourage private investment. Export-oriented agriculture is well positioned to benefit from capital inflows. Many horticultural producers and processors already operate on both sides of the border. A shorter transition period (perhaps five years) with falling tariff ceilings is likely to draw private investment to Mexico. The needed time to invest and gear up for export would provide a natural phase-in period.

NAFTA negotiators now have a set of very useful sectoral studies. What is missing is a set of alternative scenarios that take into account the strategic interaction between sectoral liberalization, private investment, and fiscal outlays in Mexico.[47] These are difficult phenomena to model and were largely irrelevant to the U.S.-Canadian Free Trade Agreement or the GATT, but they are the key to anticipating the impact of a NAFTA on rural Mexico.

Notes

1. See, for instance, James Austin and Gastoro Estera, "SAM Is Dead—Long Live SAM," *Food Policy*, vol. 10 (May 1985), pp. 55–60.

2. There have been some consultancy reports to the governments concerned with evaluating such issues as competitiveness of particular agricultural sectors. These reports are not public, and are not discussed in this paper. Similarly, the negotiating teams have their own technical support staff that undertake evaluations, again outside the public domain.

3. United States International Trade Commission (USITC), *The Likely Impact on the United States of a Free Trade Agreement with Mexico*, USITC Publication 2353, Investigation 332-297 (Washington, February 1991).

4. U.S. General Accounting Office, "U.S.-Mexico Trade: Impact of Liberalization in the Agricultural Sector," GAO/NSIAD 91-155 (Washington, March 1991).

5. Charles E. Hanrahan, "Agriculture in a U.S.-Mexico-Canada Free Trade," Library of Congress, Congressional Research Service, Washington, March 14, 1991.

6. Stephen Haley and Parr Rosson, "U.S.-Mexican Free Trade Agreement: Overview and Implications for U.S. Agriculture," Louisiana State University, Department of Agriculture, January 1991.

7. Gary Hufbauer and Jeffrey J. Schott, "Agriculture," in Hufbauer and Schott,

eds., *Prospects for North American Free Trade* (Washington: Institute for International Economics, October 1991).

8. Krissoff and Sharples were coauthors of the Thomas Grennes and others paper, "An Analysis of a United States-Canada-Mexico Free Trade Agreement," International Agricultural Trade Research Consortium, November 1991, which includes in some detail the results of the study listed as Krissoff, Neff, and Sharples (1992). To avoid confusion the empirical results will be discussed as coming from Krissoff and coauthors.

9. Tim Josling, "Agriculture in the NAFTA: Issues and Options," Stanford University, Food Research Institute, paper presented to Fraser Institute Conference, Washington, June 27–28, 1991; and Tim Josling and others, "Agriculture in the NAFTA: A Consideration of the Issues and Options for Negotiation," Report of the Study Group on Agricultural Trade Issues, U.S.-Mexico Agricultural Project, Americas Program, Stanford University, August 1991.

10. Barry Krissoff and others, "Implications of a U.S.-Mexico Free Trade Pact: Some Preliminary Evidence for Agriculture," U.S. Department of Agriculture, Economic Research Service (ERS), Washington, February 4–6, 1991: and Barry Krissoff, Lina Neff, and Jerry Sharples, "Estimated Impacts of a Potential U.S.-Mexico Preferential Trading Agreement for the Agricultural Sector," U.S. Department of Agriculture, ERS, Washington, January 1992.

11. Raúl Hinojosa-Ojeda and Sherman Robinson, "Alternative Scenarios of U.S.-Mexico Integration: A Computable General Equilibrium Approach," Working Paper 609 (University of California, Berkeley, Department of Agricultural and Resource Economics, April 1991); Sherman Robinson and others, "Agricultural Policies and Migration in a U.S.-Mexico Free Trade Area: A Computable General Equilibrium Analysis," Working Paper 617 (University of California, Berkeley, Department of Agricultural and Resource Economics, December 1991); and Mary Burfisher, Sherman Robinson, and Karen Thierfelder, "Agricultural and Food Policies in a U.S.-Mexico Free Trade Area," unpublished paper, 1991.

12. Santiago Levy and Sweder van Wijnbergen, "Maize and the Mexico-United States Free Trade Agreement," Boston University and World Bank, Washington, January 1991; and Santiago Levy and Sweder van Wijnbergen, "Mexican Agriculture at the Crossroads," unpublished paper, January 1992.

13. American Farm Bureau Federation, *NAFTA: Effects on Agriculture*, 4 vols. (Park Ridge, Ill., 1991). Not all of the papers in this collection have quantitative estimates. Those that do include the chapters by Peterson, Parr Rosson, and others, McClain and Harris, Cook and others, and Spreen and others.

14. This statement assumes that the agreement is based on the "Dunkel Draft" of December 1991.

15. Other papers in this book deal specifically with labor issues, including migration, and consequently the topic is not discussed here in detail.

16. A further link with the Uruguay Round is apparent in this area, where a GATT agreement has been drafted that would make intra-NAFTA issues of this type easier to resolve.

17. Other papers in this book examine these models, both with respect to their macroeconomic results and their labor market implications.

18. Drusilla Brown, Alan Deardorff, and Robert Stern, "A North American Free

Trade Agreement: Analytical Issues and a Computational Assessment," paper presented to Conference on North American Free Trade, Center for Strategic and International Studies, Washington, June 27–28, 1991; INFORUM, "Industrial Effects of a Free Trade Agreement between Mexico and the USA," report prepared for the U.S. Department of Labor, (University of Maryland, 1990); KPMG Peat Marwick, "The Effects of a Free Trade Agreement between the U.S. and Mexico: Executive Summary," Policy Economics Group, Washington, February 27, 1991; and Hinojosa and Robinson, "Alternative Scenarios."

19. Grennes and others, "An Analysis," p. 33. Grennes also discusses the results reported in the USITC paper, but these are apparently from partial equilibrium studies and are reported only in qualitative terms. USITC, "Likely Impact on the United States," p. 4-1. Economists from the USTIC have been involved in a more recent CGE study reported in David Roland-Holst, Kenneth Reinert, and Clinton R. Shiells, "North American Trade Liberalization and the Role of Nontariff Barriers," unpublished paper, February 1992.

20. For a description of these models see Sherman Robinson, Kenneth Hanson, and Maureen Kilkenny, "The USDA/ERS Computable General Equilibrium Model of the United States," U.S. Department of Agriculture, ERS Staff Report AGES 90-49 (Washington, 1990); Maureen Kilkenny, "Computable General Equilibrium Modeling of Agricultural Policies: Documentation of the 30-Sector FPGE GAMS Model of the United States," U.S. Department of Agriculture, ERS, Staff Report AGES 91-25 (Washington, 1991); and Maureen Kilkenny and Sherman Robinson, "Computable General Equilibrium Analysis of Agricultural Liberalization: Factor Mobility and Macro Closure," *Journal of Policy Modeling*, vol. 12 (1991), pp. 527–56.

21. See for instance, Hinojosa and Robinson, "Alternative Scenarios."

22. Robinson and others, "Agricultural Policies," p. 7. Much of the emphasis in this model is on labor markets and migration. These aspects are not reported here.

23. An alternative model would have been to have run the model with only agricultural trade liberalization.

24. Levy and van Wijnbergen, "Maize," p. 3. The paper also contains an analytical discussion, in partial equilibrium mode, of the impact on different types of farms, consumers, and workers of maize price changes. The empirical part of the paper is based on a general equilibrium model.

25. Armington trade models are not universally popular in the agricultural trade literature. For some of the problems see Julian M. Alston and others, "Whither Armington Trade Models?" *American Journal of Agricultural Economics*, vol. 72 (May 1990), pp. 455–67.

26. Results on a commodity basis for the Scenarios 2 and 3 are not presented in Krissoff, Neff, and Sharples, and so cannot be reviewed here.

27. Wesley Peterson and others in AFBF, *NAFTA*, vol. 3, p. 14.

28. Yields are assumed not to change with prices. Production is determined by acreage changes that depend on direct and cross-price elasticities. Cross-elasticities are also included on the demand side. Unlike the SWOPSIM model, U.S. and Mexican corn appear to be perfect substitutes.

29. AFBF, *NAFTA*, vol. 3, p. 17.

30. The price ratios between Mexican and U.S. prices are calculated from USDA

PSE calculations as reported in Myles Mielke, "Government Intervention in the Mexican Crop Sector," U.S. Department of Agriculture, ERS Staff Report AGES 90-49 (Washington, 1989). See Peterson in AFBF, *NAFTA*, vol. 3, p. 67, for a discussion of these price gaps.

31. Parr Rosson and others, in AFBF, *NAFTA*, vol. 2, p. 89.

32. McClain and Harris, in AFBF, *NAFTA*, vol. 4, p. 119.

33. The papers by Rosson and others and McClain and Harris contain much useful detail on the structure of the Mexican livestock and dairy sector. In that sense, they might properly be included as "qualitative" studies in the division used in the paper.

34. Both studies are in AFBF, *NAFTA*, vol. 4.

35. Actually, the same model (and the same elasticities) is used for apples and peaches—an income elasticity of 1.3 and an own-price demand elasticity of 0.5. Population is assumed to increase by 2 percent a year.

36. For apples: Cook and others, *NAFTA*, vol. 4, p. 401; for peaches: ibid., p. 419.

37. Spreen and others ran the orange juice model with just the tariff change, and found the impact on the orange juice market negligible. They argue that investment in Mexican production could follow NAFTA (and reform of the ejidos) and hence boost production over and above the "pure" price effect from removing U.S. protection.

38. While stressing the overall appeal of a NAFTA for U.S. horticultural producers and processors, the American Farm Bureau Federation reminds us never to "underestimate the potential for arcane agricultural interests to sidetrack trade negotiations." AFBF, *NAFTA*, vol. 1, p. 9.

39. Paul Krugman, "The Move toward Free Trade Zones," in Federal Reserve Bank of Kansas, *Policy Implications of Trade and Currency Zones*, a symposium (August 1991).

40. Corn subsidies measured in "producer subsidy equivalents" have been falling recently in both countries from a level of 50 percent in the late 1980s. Krissoff, Neff, and Sharples, "Estimated Impacts," estimate Mexican corn subsidies would have to be reduced from $35 to $31 per metric ton to be commensurate with U.S. levels, or less than 10 percent. For soybeans and other coarse grains, however, subsidies would fall 30–50 percent. American farmers would thus gain market share, but not mainly in corn. The fact that U.S. yellow corn is not a perfect substitute for the white corn preferred by Mexican consumers will also slow corn imports.

41. Levy and Van Wijnbergen, "Mexican Agriculture at Crossroads," argue that deficiency payments would be impractical and vulnerable to diversion in rural Mexico. However, experience in other countries indicates that these programs can be effectively administered locally (in the United States this was done through a network of agricultural extension and Farm Bureau agents who also served as farm and marketing advisers). Apart from tube wells, the benefits of the irrigation projects can also be divested by local officials, as studies of Indian and California irrigation districts demonstrate. In contrast to guarantee prices and tariffs that confer rents on the most efficient (irrigated) farmers, deficiency payments can be capped and directed to particular regions.

42. This is clearly a high-risk, high-gain strategy for a reform-minded and revenue-

strapped government. It is not, however, directly linked to or even implied by NAFTA. The original title of the Levy and van Wijnbergen paper referred to the NAFTA transition. The new title, ''Mexican Agriculture at the Crossroads,'' reflects their shift in emphasis toward internal reform. Linked or not, the ''enclosures'' style displacement of corn farmers with labor migration that they envision has become associated with NAFTA and is now perhaps the main rationale for the go-slow consensus.

43. In their most benign form, ''snap-back'' tariffs are triggered by a fall in prices below some preset minimum. This lowers the expected profits of growers in Mexico and, more important, reduces the losses of growers who do not move to Mexico or switch crops. They also prevent Mexican growers from building market share in a particular crop, something the government may want to see before it commits resources for infrastructure, quality regulation, and the like.

44. Given the high levels of income supports for grain farmers in the United States and Canada, it is hard to imagine a demand for complete liberalization coming from these countries. The bargaining process is difficult to anticipate, but it does seem that the NAFTA II subsidy matching strategy for grains is likely to be more consistent both with existing U.S. trade policy and with a shorter transition period for fruits and vegetables.

45. The World Bank study recognizes the opportunities for profitable investment in agriculture. The study proposes a partly World Bank–financed increase in irrigation investment. But since the most profitable irrigation opportunities are in the United States and Canada, much of this expenditure can only reach poor corn farmers in Mexico indirectly through its effect on rural wages (in Robinson and others, ''Agricultural Policies,'' as an exogenous rise in investment absorbs migrating workers before they reach the border). In some sense, the issue boils down to whether new public investment in Mexico or more rapid liberalization of fruits and vegetable markets will induce more private investment in rural areas.

46. The Farm Bureau commodity studies find surprising low tariffs (5–10 percent) in many fruit and vegetable sectors. Here phytosanitary standards, poor infrastructure, and low yields or product quality are the real barriers. The performance in seasonal tariff free crops where tariff barriers are absent demonstrates that all of these problems can be overcome. Why isn't this investment taking place now? Clearly one reason is that in the past when import penetration occurred, tariffs rose to 20–35 percent, thus penalizing the successful firms and discouraging new investment. The talk of a NAFTA for agriculture has not yet convinced growers on either side of the border that this situation will change in the near future.

47. The study by Robinson and others, ''Agricultural Policies,'' comes close in this regard but lacks strategic and sectoral detail in its modeling of investment, especially with respect to private investment and tariff policy.

NAFTA as the Center of
an Integration Process:
The Nontrade Issues

Robert A. Pastor

IN the spring of 1990, Mexican President Carlos Salinas de Gortari proposed a free trade area with the United States. From the perspective of Mexico, which had tried for most of the twentieth century to keep the United States at arm's length lest Mexican sovereignty be diminished, Salinas's idea was genuinely revolutionary. His goal was to guarantee access for Mexico's goods to U.S. markets and, by doing so, to promote foreign investment to provide jobs and develop his country.

By the time negotiations formally began in June 1991, Canada had joined the United States and Mexico at the bargaining table to negotiate a North American Free Trade Agreement. Salinas, U.S. President George Bush, and Canadian Prime Minister Brian Mulroney all wanted to confine the agenda to trade and investment issues, using as a model the U.S.-Canadian Free Trade Agreement signed in 1988. But NAFTA was not a typical free trade negotiation; it was the first time that industrialized countries were negotiating with a much poorer developing country on the basis of reciprocal access. The accession of Spain and Portugal to the European Community in the late 1980s bore some resemblance to NAFTA, except that the income disparity of northern-to-southern countries was substantially wider in North America than in Europe.[1]

There were misgivings about such a scheme on both sides of the border. Salinas knew it would be difficult to persuade his country and his political party, the Institutional Revolutionary Party (PRI), to cross the great sovereign divide of trade and investment. "The political and cultural elite of Mexico," wrote Lorenzo Meyer, "fear that the resulting intense exposure to North American lifestyles could bring about a loss of national values, of national identity and of the nationalist sentiment that surged so greatly during the revolutionary period."[2] Dismantling the trade and investment

I would like to thank Patrick Lowe for his comments on a draft of this paper.

barriers was a problem that Salinas had anticipated. His surprise was that the United States as a nation had reservations about an agreement with Mexico and insisted on a wider agenda that included noneconomic issues.[3]

Americans shared some of Mexico's fears, albeit for different reasons. Whereas Mexicans were worried about U.S. business and television dominating their country, many Americans were anxious about losing their jobs to Mexico or to Mexican immigrants. Other Americans were concerned that environmental standards would be reduced; still others were apprehensive that the United States would be doing business with a country that played according to different political rules. "The systematic violations of human rights and fraudulent electoral practices in Mexico are nails in the coffin of a Free Trade Agreement," said U.S. Representative Robert Toricelli, chairman of the House Foreign Affairs Subcommittee on Western Hemisphere Affairs. "A North American Free Trade Agreement is, and must be, a democracies only club. . . . We have a right to ensure that . . . [Mexico] obtain[s] a certain level of democratic institutions" before concluding NAFTA.[4]

These concerns were shared by a large number of representatives and senators, and during the debate on whether to grant the president authority to negotiate NAFTA, Representative Richard Gephardt, House Majority Leader, wrote President Bush and asked him "not [to] limit the talks to what used to be traditionally known as 'trade issues.'" Gephardt refused to support an agreement that did not address "issues like transition measures, wage disparity, environmental protection and worker rights." Had the president been unresponsive, Congress probably would not have passed the legislation giving him the authority to negotiate NAFTA on a "fast track," which means that Congress would have to approve the agreement without amendment within ninety days. On May 1, 1991, Bush sent identical letters to Gephardt and to the chairmen of the Senate Finance and House Ways and Means Committees, promising not to weaken U.S. health, safety, or environmental laws or standards and insisting he would maintain the right to "prohibit entry of goods that do not meet our" standards. Bush also pledged "expanded programs of cooperation on labor and the environment."[5] On the basis of these assurances, Gephardt assembled a majority to approve the fast-track authority.

The broader agenda that Congress wanted addressed was unorthodox for a trade negotiation, but it was a sign that NAFTA was only one part of a wider social and political process of integration. NAFTA was the first decision by the United States and Mexico to manage systematically the integration of the two countries that really began in the early 1960s when Mexicans began journeying north to the United States legally and illegally in very large numbers.

This migration has been the most momentous social movement within the Americas since the Bering Strait was walkable. More than 2.5 million Mexicans have legally immigrated to the United States since 1960, and many more have come illegally or have traveled back and forth. In the fall of 1986, a *New York Times* poll in Mexico found that half of those interviewed said they had a close relative who lived in the United States.[6] Based on a representative sample, the survey indicated that about 40 million Mexicans had family in the United States.

Social integration preceded and then coincided with the increase in U.S.-Mexican trade that began to surge in 1980 when Mexico became the United States' third largest trading partner. With the decline in the peso's value in the mid-1980s, the assembly plant, or *maquiladora*, industry on the border boomed. The growing interconnection of the automobile industries in the three North American countries was still another manifestation of a deepening economic integration that was no longer "silent."[7] The next stage in the integration process involved increased transnational and intergovernmental interaction that was accelerated by the decision to negotiate NAFTA.

In retrospect, and considering the growing exchanges between the two countries, Salinas's proposal seems more like a political acknowledgment of the social and economic process of integration that had already begun to transform Mexico and the United States. But this idea understates the pivotal character of NAFTA and the extent it could reshape the relationship.

The NAFTA negotiations are three-sided, but the center of the debate is between Mexico and the United States. The negotiations for a U.S.-Mexican free trade area were made trilateral because Canada asked to participate, and both the U.S. and Mexican governments wanted to remain on good terms with Canada. But it is clear that Canada has been less of an *actor* in the negotiations than a *defender* of the interests it acquired in the U.S.-Canadian Free Trade Agreement.

There are other reasons why the U.S.-Mexican side of the trilateral talks are the most salient. The United States and Canada share a language, a predominantly northern European, democratic heritage, a similar level of economic development, and a multiethnic immigrant population. Canada and Mexico have very little trade; indeed, the main thing they have in common is the United States. In contrast, the United States and Mexico share a difficult relationship, which stems from deep cultural, historical,

LIBRARY RESOURCES:
INTERNET SUBSCRIPTIONS FOR SCHOLARLY RESEARCH

■ This List is Not for Distribution Outside the NYIT Community.

The NYIT Libraries purchase subscriptions to research services on the Internet to enhance the print collections and provide expanded access to scholarly resources for the NYIT community. Some services may be searched from home in addition to the NYIT campus - please check the following list:

Services Searchable from Off-Campus

➤ **Computer Abstracts** - http://www.anbar.co.uk/compabs/home.htm
   Username: 24compf   Password: fortran
   This British-produced index to computing literature covers articles from 1994 onward. Output is ranked according to a relevancy scale.

➤ **Design Online** - http://www.dsgnonline.com
   Username: NYITSC   Password: DESIGN
   The main section consists of manufacturer catalogs for both residential and contracts furniture and furnishings. Additional links to product catalogs, directories, electronic journals, and professional organizations make this website valuable for architects,

interior designers, dealers in furnishings, and facility managers.

➤ **Education Abstracts Full Text** - http://webspirs.silverplatter.com/cgi-bin/login.cgi
   Username: c122831   Password: be4ukiboow

Education Abstracts Full Text contains abstracting and indexing coverage for all 427 periodicals included in Education Index as well as full text of over 133 periodicals.

➤ **Engineering Village** - http://www.ei.org/village
   User Id: nyit   Password: nyit
   • For off-campus access use "wizard" for both User Id and Password.

This service provides access to a wide range of information services and web sites of interest to engineers, including the Engineering Index from 1980 to the present. there is much to interest non-engineers--news, weather, travel, careers, scholarship information, etc. are among other areas covered.

➤ **MLA Bibliography** - http://webspirs.silverplatter.com/cgi-bin/login.cgi
   Username: c122831   Password: be4ukiboow

Published by the Modern Language Association, this is the prime index for research in the areas of modern literatures, languages, folklore, and linguistics. This citation database dates from the early 1960's to the present.

economic, and political differences. This paper focuses on how the non-trade issues relate to the more problematic side of the trilateral negotiations—that between the United States and Mexico.

In the past, the United States and Mexico had been almost impervious to each other's political complaints. A typically unpleasant encounter occurred during the Senate hearings conducted by Jesse Helms in 1985, when he accused the Mexican government of corruption and authoritarianism, and the Mexicans accused him of arrogance and ignorance. This unproductive pattern of interaction was repeated often in U.S.-Mexican relations.[8] Neither side listened to the other, or rather both sides pretended *not* to listen. During the NAFTA negotiations, both countries began to show a responsiveness to the other and to a common agenda which had never occurred before.

Compared with most of the other papers in this book, this one spends less time reviewing the literature on the possible impact of NAFTA. Such a survey is less suited to the subject of nontrade issues because much of the literature is characterized by its advocacy more than by its analysis. In this paper, I first identify and examine the substantive agenda in the nontrade area. Second, I discuss the process by which the debate on these issues within and between the three countries occurs and has become interconnected. Finally, I offer some proposals on ways to ensure that the broader integration process prospers.

The Substantive Debate

A cursory analysis would suggest that the U.S. Congress has been the principal engine behind the nontrade agenda. Congress has articulated an uneasiness found among some U.S. sectors, notably the labor movement, that NAFTA's principal effect will be to encourage the relocation of U.S. industries to Mexico. The AFL-CIO and the United Automobile Workers have viewed NAFTA as "an economic and social disaster for U.S. workers and their communities."[9] After the fast-track authority was approved, the labor movement changed its strategy to try to restrict the number of economic sectors covered by the trade agreement while trying to widen the social and environmental agenda so as to discourage U.S. companies from investing there. Others in Congress recommended including other issues like democracy in Mexico, immigration, drugs, or foreign policy, but the three major nontrade issues on the NAFTA agenda have been the environment, the social agenda, and democracy and human rights.

Although the U.S. Congress has been making most of the noise on these issues, the reality is that Mexican groups have been using the leverage provided by the congressional debate to advance their own agenda. The "Group of 100," a group of intellectuals led by former Mexican Ambassador Homero Aridjis, has been pressing the Mexican government for more than a decade to address the environmental problems of Mexico City, and there have been other groups doing similar work on the border. Mexican unions have advocated the social agenda; human rights groups and the two other major political parties—the National Action Party (PAN) and the Party of the Democratic Revolution (PRD)—have been the main sponsors of the political agenda. President Salinas has tried to be responsive, perhaps because he shares many of their concerns and does not want them to interfere with NAFTA.

The result is a new phenomenon—a two-level debate within and between the two countries on a social and political agenda. One of the possible causes of this new event is the convergence of public attitudes between the two countries and the generally supportive positions by the people of both countries for freer trade.[10] The two-level debates have a concealed and a public dimension, a dynamic that could accelerate integration and one that could inhibit or reverse the process. Some of the groups on each side oppose NAFTA, but few have publicly said so. More typical, the groups have pressed particular interests; those with incremental objectives have been flexible; others, intransigent. The Bush-Salinas strategy of trying to respond to substantive concerns has, thus far, been relatively effective in separating those who want to advance interests in the environment and society from those who want to defeat NAFTA. But the voices who want to limit integration are not history. The newly connected debates give the opponents the chance to advance their cause if the incumbents become insensitive or unresponsive.

Environment

During the last two decades, the environmental movement has grown in power and reach, affecting the calculations of an increasing number of businessmen and government officials throughout the world, but especially in the most developed countries. Some "greens" have come to view the international trading system as a source of the environmental problem due to "competing ideologies." Whereas environmentalists want to restrict and regulate development, advocates of freer trade are devoted to reducing political barriers.[11] Some environmentalists see no possibility of compromise; they see free trade as a new form of colonialism. If free trade regimes like NAFTA and GATT advance, Edward Goldsmith writes, "human, social, and environmental imperatives will be ruthlessly and systematically subordinated to the purely selfish, short-term financial interests of a few transnational corporations." The prescription, according to this view, is "not to increase the freedom of commercial concerns but, on the contrary, to bring those concerns back under control—to limit the size of markets, rather than expand them; to give local people control of their resources, not to hand them over to the transnationals."[12]

It is Mexico's fate that its free-trade proposal has collided with the environmentalists' new preoccupation with trade, but most greens do not take as absolutist a view as Goldsmith and, indeed, they are groping for the right formula and balance between the need to preserve the environment and promote trade and development. That an important U.S. environmental group decided to support the fast-track negotiating authority after President Bush assured them he would take their concerns into account was a sign of such flexibility.[13] The environmental movement is not monolithic.

There are three sets of environmental issues of concern to the United States and Mexico: (1) border issues; (2) the continental question of standards—specifically, whether lower standards or lax enforcement in Mexico will encourage U.S. corporations to flee, thereby having a depressing effect on U.S. jobs and environmental standards; and (3) global concerns related to the destruction of the rain forest, the pollution in Mexico City, the degradation of land, and the loss of plant and animal life.

These last, global concerns were the subject of the U.N. Conference on the Environment and Development in Rio de Janeiro in June 1992. Some of these issues, for example the dolphin, require international negotiations, and progress is being made on dolphin safety and other such issues.[14] Some greens believe the international community should prescribe similar and equal solutions for the problems of all communities, for example grouping Monterrey with Peoria, but Gary C. Hufbauer and Jeffrey J. Schott argue cogently for the need to be tolerant of local priorities based on different needs and requirements.[15] Los Angeles and Mexico City, for example, have a compelling need to limit auto emissions, whereas Montana and Alberta have other ecological needs.

What is the likely effect of NAFTA on the two issues of the border and environmental standards? The environmental problems on the border are primarily the result of an explosion of economic growth in the last decade caused mostly by investments by *maquiladoras*. The assembly plant program began in the mid-1960s and increased gradually until a series of peso devaluations in the 1980s widened the wage disparity between Mexican and U.S. labor. By December 1990, the number of *maquiladoras* soared to 2,000, employing 500,000 workers, about 20 percent of Mexico's total manufacturing work force.[16]

The population on both sides of the border grew at a similar rate. The new industrialization overtaxed a thin infrastructure and generated numerous health hazards stemming from improper or inadequate waste treatment or air or water pollution. The National Wildlife Federation identified the border pollution issue as its highest priority in U.S.-Mexican environmental relations, and the data support that conclusion. At Nuevo Laredo-Laredo, 25 million gallons of raw sewage flow into the Rio Grande every day. Contamination levels are 1,650 times greater than those considered safe for recreational use. In San Elizario, Texas, where a shared aquifer has been contaminated, 35 percent of the children contract hepatitis A by age eight, and 90 percent of adults have had it by the age of thirty-five.[17] Numerous reports confirm the multitude of health and environmental problems in the region.[18]

No one, least of all the people on the border, disputes the seriousness of the environmental problems. The operational questions related to NAFTA are: (1) whether the discrepancy in environmental standards serves as a magnet attracting U.S. companies to Mexico and, by doing so, places a burden on U.S. communities to lower their standards, leaving both countries environmentally worse off than before; (2) what effect NAFTA is likely to have on this equation; and (3) whether the United States can assist Mexico in improving significantly the protection of the border's environment.

Stories of furniture companies in Los Angeles that moved to Mexico to escape tough pollution laws were mentioned several times in the congressional debate as an indication of what would happen if NAFTA were approved.[19] The General Accounting Office therefore conducted a study of this problem and found that between eleven and twenty-eight furniture manufacturers in the Los Angeles area relocated to Mexico between 1988 and 1990, affecting approximately 960 to 2,547 jobs. About 83 percent of these furniture companies mentioned the differences in wages and workers' compensation as the principal motive for relocating; 78 percent also cited stringent environmental controls. Comparing the number of firms that left with the total number of furniture manufacturers in the Los Angeles area, however, one finds that only 1 to 3 percent left, which affected only 2 to 10 percent of the jobs of local furniture workers. The percentages shrink to insignificance if one includes all furniture manufacturers in the United States.[20] The anecdote on furniture firms evidently does not tell the whole story.

Studies of the decisionmaking process of U.S. corporations that invest abroad indicate that environmental considerations have been a negligible or nonexistent factor.[21] Recent studies of the environmental factor found little evidence that pollution abatement costs influence decisions on where industries move. Indeed, Gene Grossman and Alan Krueger found that the costs involved in complying with environmental laws "are small in relation to the other components of total cost that determine whether it is profitable to operate in the United States or Mexico."[22] Mexico's comparative advantage is low wages, not lax environmental regulations. A second, more general study found that the weighted average cost-to-output of pollution abatement and control equipment was less than 1 percent of the cost of doing business, and the highest costs were just over 3 percent. These numbers are simply too low to be considered an incentive for relocation.[23]

With regard to the possible effect of NAFTA on border development and pollution, two studies suggest that the border is likely to grow faster if NAFTA is rejected than if it is approved.[24] The main reason for this apparent paradox is that the *maquiladoras*, which rely on a partial exemption from tariffs, would, theoretically, become obsolete if tariffs were eliminated on trade between the two countries. There are other reasons why future investments in Mexico might go inland rather than stay at the border: the relatively higher cost of labor on the border (the average wages in the *maquiladoras* are "considerably higher than in the interior of the country"[25]); the extremely high turnover of workers, who often just stop on the border on their way to the United States, where they can earn ten times as much for similar work;[26] and the environmental and infrastructural problems that are much more severe on the border. The Mexican government already discourages investment in Mexico City and other urban-congested areas and provides additional incentives to investors to set up plants in "priority zones" that need development. With NAFTA and the increasing attractiveness of investing in Mexico as a whole, one would expect that the incentives to invest away from the border would exceed those to invest in the border area. In brief, NAFTA would reduce the environmental problems on the border.

This discussion assumes that environmental regulations and enforcement on the border and elsewhere in the country would remain the same, but that is already impugned by the rapid changes in the last four years. In 1988, the Mexican government passed the General Law for Ecological

Equilibrium and Environmental Protection, its first environmental law. Modeled on the U.S. Environmental Protection Act of 1970, the law prohibits air, water, and soil pollution and contamination by hazardous wastes, pesticides, and toxic substances. In some ways, Mexico's law went beyond U.S. laws, for example, by requiring an environmental impact statement (EIS) on any investment involving hazardous wastes. The United States requires an EIS only for public-related projects.[27]

The new law, however, was not enforced very actively until Salinas's inauguration, and especially after talks began for NAFTA. Since then, Mexico's environmental efforts have accelerated, particularly in Mexico City and on the border. The number of personnel assigned to enforce the law has increased, and Mexico has closed 980 industrial sites, 82 of them permanently. Most spectacular was the decision by Salinas to close the oil refinery on the outskirts of Mexico City—at a cost of $500 million and 5,000 jobs—on the anniversary of the expropriation of the oil companies. Within Mexico City, the government has gradually replaced public transportation, prohibited private cars from driving in the city one day a week, and required cleaner-burning gasoline. Salinas personally promised that he would not allow new investment that did not meet stringent requirements. Mexico, he promised, would not seek investments that brought pollution.[28]

The pollution problems on the border are not as severe as in the capital, but they have a greater impact on the United States. Although some environmentalists discovered the border's problems during the debate on approving the fast-track authority, the people on the border and the two governments have been working on these problems for a long time. The people on the border have a long history of trying to solve common problems and avoid instructions from their central governments.[29] One institution that has been very effective in working across the border on a range of sensitive problems, including water resource and sanitation issues, is the International Boundary and Water Commission, which was established more than one hundred years ago, and reorganized into its current form in 1944. In addition, the U.S.-Mexico Border Environmental Agreement, signed in 1983 in La Paz, linked the two federal environmental agencies to expedite solutions to the border's pollution problems. The vaguely worded agreement, however, was weak on enforcement, and it did not address the region's growing shortage of fresh water.[30]

On February 12, 1992, after conducting many hearings among groups in both countries and after circulating a draft, the two governments presented a three-year integrated plan for cleaning the border. President Bush pledged nearly $250 million in fiscal year 1993 that included funding for three waste treatment projects. Mexico also promised to spend $640 million during the three years of the plan, to work closely with the Environmental Protection Agency to train border environmental inspectors, and to develop data bases that could be used by both sides.[31] In a comprehensive analysis of the plan, Jan Gilbreath Rich commended it as "the first large-scale attempt to integrate the planning and environmental strategies used by the two federal governments and a first attempt to recognize the direct link between natural resources and trade." The integrated plan dealt with many of the problems that had been overlooked by the La Paz agreement of 1983, but it promised more than its budget and personnel could possibly deliver, and many of the projects lacked specific implementation plans. Rich writes that such a plan was compiled *because of NAFTA*, but, ironically, it deals with today's problems rather than the ones that will be faced after NAFTA. The second irony is that Mexico promised more resources than the United States, and the U.S. federal government promised more state resources (over which it has no control) than federal resources.[32]

John Audley of the Sierra Club also recognized that the integration plan represented real progress, but he thought the environment should be handled as an integral part of NAFTA rather than as an appendage to it. He proposed an agreement in which "environmental protection would no longer be regarded as exceptions to trade rules, but rather legitimate constraints to trade that must be accepted by economic interests. Business activity would not be seen independent from social and environmental goals, but a component of them."[33]

Some environmentalists argue that any growth is damaging to the environment. Grossman and Krueger tested this hypothesis by relating environmental pollution to levels of economic development worldwide, and they concluded that pollution has a worse effect on low-income countries. As a country develops, it passes a certain threshold where it begins to shift resources to clean the environment. Their formula suggests the threshold occurs when a country's per capita gross domestic product reaches $5,000. Since Mexico's income is near that level (in terms of purchasing power), then one could expect new environmental investments.[34] Their argument is a powerful one that contrasts with Mancur Olson's view that interest group resistance to collective action increases as a country develops and then inhibits further growth.[35] Grossman and Krueger suggest that interest group efforts *on behalf of collective choices* increase as an economy develops and the environment becomes polluted and, second, that such public choices improve the prospects for further growth. The increasing power of groups advocating a cleaner environment in Mexico seems to confirm their thesis, and if external resources can be mobilized to supplement Mexico's, then the $5,000 threshold could theoretically be reduced.

The NAFTA negotiations injected life into Mexico's inchoate environmental strategy. Provided that the integrated plan is implemented seriously and effectively, NAFTA might prove to be a boon for environmental concerns in both countries. The decision by Mexico to postpone the building of a large dam in the south because of its implications for the rain forest is also a positive sign,[36] but these issues need continuous monitoring. Betty Ferber de Aridjis, spokesperson for the Group of 100, Mexico's principal environmental group, noted: "Plant closings tapered down dramatically after the U.S. Congress approved fast-track procedures."[37] Nonetheless, when one compares the progress that Mexico has made in the four years since enactment of its environmental law with what the United States accomplished in the two decades since the passage of the EPA, it is hard to avoid the conclusion that NAFTA has already had a profound and positive effect on the environment in Mexico. And if U.S.-Canadian relations offer a guide, then cooperation after NAFTA might actually be better than before. Senator Alan Simpson noted that the acid rain agreement between the United States and Canada was reached after the trade agreement.[38]

Social Agenda

Like the environmental issues, the principal problems on the social agenda stem less from a difference on policy than from a gap in capabilities (political will, resources, personnel) to enforce the laws. There are three sets of issues on the social agenda: labor standards, occupational safety and health, and food health and safety standards.

Although the U.S. and Mexican labor movements have had close relations over many years, they disagree on whether NAFTA should be approved, for the simple reason that U.S. labor believes it will lose jobs to Mexico, and Mexican labor agrees with that. Efforts by U.S. labor leaders to persuade their Mexican counterparts to negotiate a transnational "social charter" have therefore met with lack of interest or silence.

A second reason that the dialogue between the two labor movements has been muted is that they relate to their governments in very different ways. The labor-government relationship in the United States has been at arm's length, sometimes cooperative, but more often adversarial, particularly when Republicans occupy the White House. Although labor is one of the Democratic Party's principal constituent groups, the differences between the party and the unions are much wider than between Mexican labor and the PRI-dominated Mexican state. The enormous Confederation of Mexican Workers (CTM), with about 5 million members and 90 percent of all industrial workers, is ostensibly stronger than U.S. unions, but in fact, the CTM's power is more limited because of the nature of its bargain with the state. The latter has prevented any rival unions from competing with the CTM, which, in turn, has moderated demands for wage hikes and kept strikes to a minimum. Since December 1987, CTM support for the Solidarity Pacts negotiated by the state, labor, and management permitted Mexico to reduce its inflation even while labor sustained a massive cut in real wages.

In terms of labor standards, this relationship has produced a more comprehensive set of legal protections for workers than in most countries of comparable levels of development. "In many respects," writes Tom Barry, "Mexico has one of the most advanced labor laws on the continent, largely as a result of the Mexican Revolution."[39] Indeed, Mexico's social legislation has more in common with Europe's than with the United States'. The labor laws contain elaborate guidelines on collective bargaining, the right to strike, rights regarding dismissal, an eight-hour day, housing benefits, vacations, profit sharing, minimum wage, social security benefits, child care, and health services. A comparison of Mexican, Canadian, and U.S. labor laws suggests that U.S. labor unions would benefit the most from a harmonization of standards. Unlike the governments of Mexico and Canada, the U.S. government does not require paid vacations or maternity leave (Mexico provides six months; Canada, seventeen weeks), and the United States is alone in permitting businesses to hire nonunion replacement workers during a strike.[40] And, in fact, Mexican unions, which are dominated by the state, have begun to lower their standards down to those of the United States. Among the "reforms" being considered by Mexican unions are removing the government's role in protecting workers' rights, converting the daily shift and wage into an hourly measurement, giving preference to nonunion workers, restricting the right to strike, and giving employers more rights to lay off workers.[41]

The major labor problem is that Mexico's minimum wage is roughly one-tenth that of the United States and Canada; Mexican labor laws are rarely enforced, and they have no effect on the army of unemployed (about 20 percent), underemployed (25–40 percent), and the large informal sector. In reviewing Mexico's labor laws, Arturo Alcalde, a labor lawyer, said, "You're in a world of science fiction. The theory is different from the practice."[42]

As part of his pledge to Congress, President Bush instructed the U.S. secretary of labor to sign an agreement with her Mexican counterpart to provide for joint action on the labor-related issues. The memorandum, along with those signed with the Canadians, promises to promote "higher living standards, and a safe and healthy workplace with adequate social security, medical and financial benefits." How this intent is translated into the real world is not clear, and U.S. labor unions are skeptical.

The same pattern applies to occupational safety and health issues, another area that President Bush pledged to improve in his letter to Congress. Ironically, on this issue as well as on labor standards, the conditions are probably better in the *maquiladora* industry and generally in U.S. corporations in Mexico than in most Mexican firms.[43] On the other hand, there are *maquiladoras*, particularly electronic assembly plants, that have been negligent in protecting their workers or the surrounding population from toxic materials in the production process.

One of the obstacles to protecting the safety of the workplace in Mexico is the lack of reliable or comprehensive data on the number or prevalence of work-related injuries or deaths. The International Labour Office (ILO) publishes cross-national statistics, but it has pointed to the paucity and unreliability of much of the Mexican data. Nonetheless, ILO data from the late 1980s suggest that the Mexican rate per million insured worker-hours is 0.12 fatalities, compared with 0.03 for U.S. workers, or roughly four times as high.[44] Unfortunately, the data are not detailed enough to allow one to determine in which industries or at what times these fatalities or injuries are concentrated.

Regarding food health and safety standards, the United States and Mexico are concerned about the problem of trade in contaminated foods, and both have signed the Agreement on Technical Barriers to Trade (the Standards Code). This code obliges its signatories to harmonize and make "transparent" their scientific certification procedures. Between this general principle and the application of equivalent standards and regulations, however, is a shadow that remains to be negotiated in the Uruguay Round. If those GATT negotiations fail, and possibly even if they succeed, the United States, Canada, and Mexico will still have serious problems in finding common standards and procedures for each particular case, harmonizing the accreditation standards, and enforcing these provisions in a nondiscriminatory way.

Liberal groups in the three countries have proposed a "social charter," similar to the European Community's Charter of Fundamental Social Rights for Workers. The EC Charter lists numerous goals, including collective bargaining, equal treatment for men and women, health and safety, and protection of children, the elderly, and the disabled, that would be compatible to laws or norms in all three North American countries.[45] The EC also calls for the free movement of labor, but this characteristic is what makes the EC a common market and NAFTA a free trade area.

The major motivation behind a charter is the fear that integration based on existing disparities between the United States and Mexico will have a downward effect on standards, wages, and working conditions unless specific thresholds are legislated. A study of the relationship between trade and labor standards worldwide suggests that increased trade can improve labor standards, but this improvement rarely occurs immediately, and whether it occurs at all depends on the political framework in the particular country and the governing philosophy of its leaders.[46] The neo-classical philosophy believes the best way to improve labor standards in the long term is not to interfere with the market in the short term by legislating higher wages or working conditions. The neo-institutionalists believe the best way to sustain development is to increase aggregate demand by legislating an improvement in wages and working conditions. The studies and the empirical evidence suggest that both arguments might be true: low wages and bad working conditions are apparently necessary to attract investment and promote early growth, but unless wages improve after a certain period, further development is inhibited.

The concept of linking social improvements abroad with U.S. trade is not new. The U.S. Congress has already conditioned trade benefits and investment guarantees on whether a foreign government provides basic rights to its workers. The Omnibus Trade and Competitiveness Act of 1988, to take a prominent example, makes violation of labor rights an "unfair trade practice." The rights identified in that law are guaranteed by the Mexican and Canadian governments. The only questions regarding NAFTA are whether to incorporate such a charter in NAFTA or in a parallel agreement and, if so, how specifically the provisions should be defined.

Human Rights and Democracy

In the 1970s, the governments of Spain, Portugal, and Greece understood that they could not become members of the European Community until they were fully democratic. That proved to be a powerful incentive, both for joining and for maintaining democratic institutions. The economic and political differences between northern and southern Europe are narrower than those between the United States and Mexico, and, owing to a troubled history, the sensitivity in Mexico to U.S. interference in its internal political affairs is much more acute than any similar concern in the EC.

Nonetheless, the issues of Mexico's democracy and its human rights record are unavoidable in a debate on NAFTA. Senator Daniel Patrick Moynihan explained to his colleagues that the reason he had "the strongest reservations about the free trade agreement with Mexico [was because it would be] the first free trade agreement we are being asked to consider with a country that isn't free."[47] In Mexico, Hector Aguilar Camin, the editor of an influential journal, and probably the intellectual who is closest to President Salinas, noted that the "institutional logic" of opening Mexico's economy and linking it with the United States is that it "ultimately demands transparent and competitive rules in the political marketplace as well." Those rules, he acknowledged, do not yet exist in Mexico. After recounting the undemocratic and unjust flaws in Mexico's political system, he concluded: "Sooner rather than later, I hope, our tolerance for illegality will shrink, and I also hope we will learn that it is better for us to correct our mistakes ourselves, for otherwise, we will be forced to correct them by pressures from outside."[48]

President Salinas has emphasized that NAFTA is an economic agreement, and that his government will never permit the United States to impose political conditions or to interfere in Mexico's internal affairs. Mexico's political sovereignty, Salinas insisted, "is not subject to external evaluation."[49] Cuauhtemoc Cardenas, the leader of the PRD, asserts a more historic, defensive nationalism. However, he has departed from that tradition by taking his case to the United States, encouraging American leaders, albeit indirectly, to use their leverage to compel Salinas to open up the political system in Mexico and invite international groups to observe Mexico's elections.

There is a certain irony in Cardenas's criticism *in the United States* of Salinas in that many in his movement had berated leaders of the conservative PAN for similar behavior a decade before. Regrettably, and with an irony that completes the circle, Salinas, the redefiner of economic sovereignty, used the old arguments to discourage this new attempt to engage the United States directly in debate. At the PRI's National Assembly in September 1990, Salinas denounced "those of the opposition who denigrate the party inside the country and who have no political shame in criticizing the PRI and the government abroad . . . without caring about the damage that this attitude can cause to the country.'' He denounced the Cardenistas as ''those who seek to trample on the national sovereignty.''

This is the old way that nationalism was defined in Mexico to stifle debate, and it is inconsistent with Salinas's own promises of greater democracy. It also betrays his own contribution to the redefinition of sovereignty. ''Historically, nationalism has been the answer to any external challenge,'' Salinas said. ''Now the big challenge is not being left out of the great integrationist efforts and the great exchange of resources.''[50]

Salinas won the presidency in an election widely viewed as rife with fraud. Since then, however, his electoral record represents a decided improvement over those of his predecessors, but it is not one that has attained international democratic standards. In July 1989, for the first time since the revolution, an opposition party won a governorship, which occurred in a border state. At the same time, electoral irregularities impugned the results in several other states. The government's electoral record from that moment through the midterm elections of August 1991 was uneven. The opposition parties won some local elections but charged that others were stolen, and there was some evidence to support that.[51] Salinas negotiated an electoral reform law with the conservative PAN, but Cardenas's supporters and some PANistas opposed it because the government retained control of the new federal electoral institute.

By the midterm elections, Salinas and the PRI had recovered substantial popular support because of the economic recovery and a program—Solidarity—aimed at helping poor communities. At the same time, Cardenas's party fractured, and the PAN lost support. The PRI therefore won an overwhelming victory in August 1991, leaving the opposition demoralized. Again, there were charges of fraud, and these were not without foundation, although they were exaggerated. Because he permitted exit polls in August 1991, and because three PRI governors, who were accused of election irregularities, were replaced, Salinas sent a signal to the PRI cadre that such ''alchemy'' was no longer acceptable. But another signal that he sent was that the ''system'' was still being managed.

There are two significant problems in Mexico's politics. First, there is a lack of confidence in the political system. Before the election in 1991, a survey indicated that only 42 percent of the Mexican people believed their vote would be respected. That was an improvement over 1988 when only 23 percent answered that way, but it still meant that the majority of the Mexican people thought that the government was manipulating the electoral system.[52] Second, as Aguilar noted, the intimacy between the ruling party and the state contributes to the unequal position of those competing against the state.

Salinas has been candid in explaining his efforts to manage the political process gradually so as to assure a stable political transition and continued PRI dominance. "Electoral democracy is not attained through practices that endanger the nation's stability or the continuity of our institutions."[53] He believes that it is essential for economic reforms to be fully implemented before undertaking thorough political liberalization. Gorbachev's mistake, in Salinas's view, was to undertake political reforms first, and as a result, he lost the support he needed to achieve his economic or his political agenda. "I believe in glasnost, *not* glasses that break," he told me.[54] Whether Salinas's glass is half full (and rising), as his supporters claim, or half empty (and dropping), as his critics say, there is no question that the political system remains in an awkward and unstable transition.

The same conclusion can be drawn from a review of the human rights conditions in Mexico and Salinas's response to them. In June 1990, Americas Watch issued a scathing report on human rights abuses in Mexico.[55] The report criticized Mexico's government for torture, disappearances, extrajudicial killings by police and security forces, abuses in the criminal justice system, electoral fraud, rural repression, media censorship, and violence against unions. The fact that Mexico is often overlooked by the human rights community, the report charged, is "more a testament to the Mexican government's cultivation of its pro-human rights image than its care to ensure that individual human rights are respected." The Americas Watch report and charges by other human rights groups stung Salinas, and he established a National Human Rights Commission, under the chairmanship of Supreme Court Justice Jorge Carpizo, and with an advisory council of credible, independent leaders, including Carlos Fuentes and Carlos Payan, editor of the independent *La Jornada*.

Carpizo acknowledges that the federal and local police are the principal sources of human rights violations, a view that the public shares.[56] He structured the commission to act as an "ombudsman" in investigating human rights violations and to use "transparency"—publicity—to embarrass senior officials in the attorney general's office or in local police stations to remove and, when possible, try human rights violators. Most impressive, Carpizo and the commission's executive secretary, Rosario Green, visited several cities in the United States to explain the purposes and plans of the commission. A visit to the United States by a senior group of Mexicans to discuss human rights violations in Mexico would have been unthinkable just two years earlier.

Salinas's predecessors did not control the police, but they were unwilling to acknowledge that fact, fearful that the power of the presidency might be diminished in the public mind if people knew the truth. Yet Salinas created in the commission an institution whose work begins from the dual premises that the police are the most serious human rights problem and that the president does not control them—candid admissions.

In less than two years, many of the human rights groups in Mexico that had been so critical of the government recognized the credibility of the National Human Rights Commission. Carpizo's own integrity and boldness were, to a great degree, responsible. He embarrassed the attorney general by disclosing that conversations in the commission were being electronically intercepted, and the attorney general was replaced. Carpizo confronted a number of high-profile cases against government officials, and Salinas supported him at crucial moments. The problem of government officials or police acting with impunity has not been erased in Mexico, but important steps in the right direction have been taken.

During the debate on the fast-track authority, Congress addressed two sets of questions related to the political issues: first, whether the United States should have a free trade agreement with an undemocratic neighbor; and second, how the United States could facilitate the country's democratization. Some members of Congress proposed tying the agreement to an improvement in human rights and democracy, while others argued that Mexico was far more likely to become democratic if NAFTA were approved than if the United States imposed preconditions and Mexico retreated behind its economic and political walls.[57] The fast-track authority was approved, but the arguments were not resolved, and they are likely to be rejoined when NAFTA is sent to Congress.

Mexico also has legitimate concerns about human rights in the United States, particularly the treatment of undocumented Mexican workers. Americas Watch issued another scathing report, this time denouncing U.S. border patrols for routine "beatings, rough physical treatment, and racially motivated verbal abuse." Moreover, the report found that investigations have been "perfunctory, and the offending agents escape punishment."[58] A second concern that President Salinas has raised is the use of the death penalty—which is prohibited in Mexico and many other countries—against Mexican citizens by U.S. authorities. He personally asked the governor of Texas to stay the execution of a Mexican national, and the issue was only temporararily averted when the presiding judge decided to delay the execution, pending further review. The human rights issues on both sides of the border require a new continental approach. The most egregious political action by the United States was the kidnapping of a Mexican national, Dr. Alvarez Machain, in Mexico by the Drug Enforcement Agency, to bring him to trial in the United States for complicity in the murder of a DEA agent. The U.S. Justice Department asserted a right to kidnap, and it pursued the case despite decisions by two U.S. courts that such an act violated an extradition treaty with Mexico. On June 15, 1992, the Supreme Court ruled in favor of the Justice Department, and Mexicans were enraged by the decision. If the United States wants Mexico to consider U.S. concerns seriously, it will have to find a different way of responding to Mexico's legitimate concerns.

Salinas has made progress in the area of human rights and in opening the Mexican political system, but the journey, as Hector Aguilar Camin noted, is far from complete. No doubt, some in the U.S. Congress will hammer this theme, but their credibility will diminish in direct proportion to the degree that Salinas's credibility increases.

The Political Process of Integration: Connecting the Debates

NAFTA is distinguishable from previous bilateral negotiations between the United States and Mexico in both the nature of the issues and the negotiating process. Traditional diplomatic issues, like conflicts in Central America or the territorial question of the Chamizal, have involved the U.S. and Mexican foreign ministries but few others. The NAFTA negotiations cover domestic and international policies and many domestic agencies and groups. Also, the process by which the two countries have debated NAFTA is very different from the historical way in which the two governments have stiff-armed each other and transformed minor concerns into crises of sovereignty. Today, not only are the issues debated openly in both countries, but groups within each country have built transnational coalitions with counterparts in the other two North American countries to stimulate governmental attention and substantive progress on areas of mutual concern.

The agenda—particularly the nontrade issues—appears to be only a list of U.S. concerns, but Salinas was the one who posed the challenge of a free trade area, and there are many groups in both countries that share the same goals in the environment, labor standards, and democracy. Indeed, it might be more accurate to say that groups in Mexico are using the U.S. debate to enhance their bargaining leverage within Mexico than to say that the United States is using NAFTA to press its agenda on a passive Mexico.

The agenda may reflect a convergence of public attitudes in all three countries. Ronald Inglehart of the United States, Neil Nevitte of Canada, and Miguel Basañez of Mexico conducted surveys in all three countries at the beginning and end of the 1980s. They found that attitudes are not only similar but have been converging in a way that makes further integration more feasible. In all three countries, the basic values are concentrating in support of political liberalization, free market but *not* laissez-faire, economic policy, and a higher priority for autonomy and self-expression in all spheres of life. Even more important was the convergence in values that parents are trying to give to their children. When asked which of seventeen qualities people would like to instill in their children, respondents from all three countries chose the same qualities and even ranked them similarly. The authors believe the main cause of the convergence in value systems is that young people in all three countries are much better educated and more affected by international communications: "A narrow nationalism that had been dominant since the 19th century is gradually giving way to a more cosmopolitan sense of identity."[59]

In a free trade area, any domestic policy that confers a discriminatory advantage on a country's exports or a disadvantage on imports is legitimately a trade issue, and any selective incentive for investment or relocation is an investment issue. Moreover, if a country's laws require that imported products be produced according to certain safety, labor, or environmental standards, then a nontrade item can become a trade issue. Once tariffs and quotas are eliminated, trade-related "distortions" that become eligible for negotiation include a wide swath of policies, such as sales taxes, safety or environmental laws, subsidized oil or gas prices, tax inducements, and access to timber on government lands at below market prices. Labor rights or workers' compensation in one country becomes an issue in the other. As integration proceeds, the line that separates internal and external issues blurs.

As one conceptualizes the integration process in these terms, NAFTA may become a device for smoothing the differences in policies as a way to keep the expanding economic integration as equitable as possible. If the European Community or the U.S.-Canadian agreement is a guide, however, the process of harmonization is likely to be difficult. To keep relations respectful and integration on track, one needs to understand how the political process has thus far handled these issues and how it can be improved.

Of the three North American governments, Mexico has the strongest president, and it required such a strong leader to travel so far so fast. In 1980, Mexico rejected the idea of joining the GATT and repeatedly found itself in positions where relatively minor differences with the United States were magnified and interpreted as major challenges of sovereign rights. In the course of moving from this past "closed" position to one in which virtually all domestic and foreign policies were negotiable, the Mexican political system began to open.

In 1988, the president of Mexico for the first time in history allowed a strong dissident movement within his party to leave and contest the presidency without facing repression. The differences between this dissident group under the leadership of Cuauhtemoc Cardenas and the Salinas administration today constitute the parameters of a debate that will shape Mexico's response to the hundreds of issues that will follow NAFTA. For the sake of simplicity, the Salinas group can be described as "first-world modernizers," who prefer a leaner state that respects the efficiency of the market but tries to compensate where the market fails. Salinas describes this political philosophy as "social liberalism," which involves negotiating hard but pragmatically with the United States.

The Cardenistas or "third-world progressives" have faith in a bigger state and distrust the private sector and the United States. Instead of negotiating directly with the United States, leaders representing this perspective are more inclined to seek alliances with Third World—mostly Latin American—nations in order to bring pressure on the United States and the industrialized world to change the international economic system. The Cardenistas are more likely to strike immovable postures and walk away from the bargaining table with the United States for the sake of national pride than the "first-world modernizers," who are more likely to seek a compromise.

Although Salinas's philosophy is ascendant at this time, the more traditionally nationalistic perspective of the Cardenistas might someday return to power. With that in mind, it is useful to examine the nature of Cardenas's influence on the current debate. Despite misgivings, Cardenas has not rejected NAFTA and has hinted that he would not change it much if it worked.[60] More important, he has legitimized and reinforced efforts by some Americans to press Mexico on the nontrade agenda, particularly on the need for human rights, democracy, a clean environment, and a "social charter." Therefore, if he were to come to power, which in 1992 appears unlikely, he would be hard-pressed to oppose other Mexicans who chose to raise these issues in the United States.

Within the United States, the principal forum for the debate is Congress, although the president initially set the trade agenda. Opponents of NAFTA and those committed to specific concerns—such as human rights and the environment—have joined to insist on expanding Bush's agenda. The nature of the debate within Congress and between the branches of government is such that opponents of NAFTA will use whatever issue they can find to undermine support for the agreement, but they will only succeed if the president fails to respond to legitimate concerns.

During the debate on the fast-track authority, Senator Ernest F. Hollings introduced the issue of Mexico's relations with Cuba, arguing that either Mexico should end its trading relationship with Cuba, or the United States should not accept NAFTA.[61] Despite widespread hostility to Cuba in Congress, this issue gathered little support. It was viewed as peripheral to the central issues of NAFTA. In contrast, House Majority Leader Richard Gephardt raised a number of issues, including the environment, workers' rights, and trade adjustment for American workers in a letter to President Bush. If Bush had stonewalled Gephardt, he probably would have failed to gain congressional approval. Instead, the president responded with a serious and detailed program, which permitted Gephardt to inform his consitutents and Congress: "On many of these issues, they [the Bush Administration] have moved a good distance responding to Congressional pressures."[62] Presidents who have been responsive to legitimate concerns raised by Congress have actually found that they are given more discretion and authority to negotiate than those who have refused to take Congress seriously.[63]

What is new in the case of NAFTA is not the responsiveness of the U.S. president to Congress but of the Mexican president to the nontrade agenda. Salinas understood, as no recent Mexican president has, that the best way to avoid getting boxed in a corner is to define the agenda and preempt U.S. pressure. He employed his strategy first on the drug-trafficking issue, which had been a stumbling block in Mexican-U.S. relations under his predecessor. Salinas understood that the drug issue was a two-sided sovereignty issue—not only was it necessary to keep the United States out of Mexico's affairs but it was essential to keep drug traffickers from taking control of local or state governments. Salinas moved quickly and forcefully against the drug traffickers. Although he did not completely succeed, any more than any government has, no one in the United States or Mexico has questioned his commitment. When problems arose, such as the evident collusion of Mexico's military with drug traffickers, he arrested the general under suspicion. His efforts to preempt other issues, including human rights and the environment, followed the same pattern. Salinas has anticipated rather than reacted to problems; that is often the difference between a leader and a victim.

The role played by transnational coalitions of human rights advocates and environmentalists has also become very important in defining the North American agenda and monitoring and enforcing a common agenda. These groups are at the forefront of an emerging transnational political process in North America.

The Future Policy Agenda

Acceptance of a free trade agreement is not the end of negotiations among the United States, Mexico, and Canada; it is the beginning of a continual process of negotiating issues that had been previously considered wholly domestic. The Salinas proposal, in brief, will set in motion an awkward but healthy process of integration.

Now is the time to devise procedures and mechanisms that will keep the dialogue fruitful and the tensions to a minimum.[64] First, the three North American countries need to develop "early warning systems" to alert decisionmakers to emerging problems. No one wants to wait for a small problem to blow up to the point where it becomes an issue of the "old" sovereignty once again. To the extent that such problems can be identified early, the prospects of resolving them practically through negotiation are greater.

Second, it is important to establish new institutions and mechanisms of consultation to review the domestic and international agenda and suggest ways to harmonize or eliminate impediments to freer trade. The institutions should be of two kinds: those charged with discussing and negotiating new rules, and those that should adjudicate disputes and enforce compliance.

Third, freer trade in North America will benefit all nations, but it will not benefit them equally, and it will not benefit all groups within a nation equally. American workers, for example, will lose jobs to Mexicans, while American industry becomes more competitive. Unfortunately, the loss of jobs because of cheaper imports is more visible and painful than the gains to trade because of increased exports. This asymmetry has obvious political consequences. If new institutions are not established to redistribute the gains of trade to those who lose out and to help those backward regions in all three countries connect with the modern economy, then NAFTA will not endure.[65]

These three proposals are not panaceas, but they are devices to cope with the coming tensions of interdependence. A freer trade regime in the hemisphere will lead to more trade disputes, not fewer, because as trade increases, more businesses and workers will become more dependent on the new flows of goods. Workers who lose their job by a "surge" in imports will find many reasons—some quite justifiable—for why the trade was unfair. To contain and eventually resolve those problems while expanding the boundaries of economic sovereignty requires a number of measures that will give additional confidence to all parties in the system.

Mexico's contribution to the dismantling of trade and investment barriers within the Western Hemisphere is potentially historic, particularly given the country's record. Instead of resisting or ignoring economic integration with the United States, President Salinas decided to manage and intensify economic integration. This decision represents both a definitive break from the past and a hopeful early sign of an emerging hemispheric community. The future success of an economic agenda, however, might well depend on the progress made on the nontrade issues.

Comment by Gustavo Vega-Canovas

Because I agree with so much of what Robert Pastor has written on the substantive issues of the nontrade agenda of NAFTA, my task as a commentator is not an easy one. His presentation is so comprehensive that I have to look into a few corners to find useful additions to his work. On this account, I will concentrate on Pastor's overall interpretation on the meaning of NAFTA and the likely future of North American economic, social, and political relations.

Pastor aptly claims that NAFTA represents a crucial decision to manage an integration process that began in the early 1960s and accelerated in the late 1970s during the oil boom, when Mexico became the third largest trading partner of the United States. Since then the bilateral economic exchange has become more and more important so that at the present time both countries have shown an interest in promoting closer economic relations between one another and with Canada to deal with the variety of trade, debt, immigration, and political problems that affect both countries.

Does the NAFTA negotiation, however, represent the first step toward the wider process of social and political integration analogous to the experience of the European Community (EC)? The title of Pastor's paper and his overall argument seem to suggest that this is the case. I must say that I disagree. I do not think that in North America we are ready to take the European Community road in the near future. Specifically, I do not believe that because Mexico, the United States, and Canada have decided to negotiate a free trade agreement we will see a tendency to move more or less automatically to higher levels of economic integration (a customs union, common market, or economic union).

Economists usually distinguish between a basic, "negative" form of integration, which entails the removal of discrimination and of restrictions on the free movement of goods and factors of production between countries, and a more advanced "positive" form, which requires the development of common institutions and policies to enable the integrated market to function effectively and to promote collective political and economic objectives.[66] Balassa's classic model, for instance, formulates economic integrations as a process in which three cumulative stages of negative or market integration (free trade area, customs union, and common market) are superseded by two stages of positive or policy integration (economic union and total economic integration).[67] In principle, each stage incorporates all features of the preceding one, plus a new element. The question is whether once the process of integration is initiated at the lower level there is a tendency to move more or less automatically from one stage to the next. Political theories of integration that Pastor clearly supports have often asserted such a logic, while pure economic theory remains more skeptical.[68]

Taking the European Community example as Pastor does, one could argue that indeed there is an inexorable logic to economic integration even though the recent decision of the Danish electorate clearly proves that progress beyond the customs union is unlikely to be smooth. However, if one takes other examples like the free trade arrangements forged on an individual basis between the EC and members of the European Free Trade Association (EFTA) (Iceland, Norway, Sweden, Finland, Austria, and Switzerland), one could reasonably argue that preferential trading areas can achieve stable equilibrium at levels that do not entail significant elements of supranationality, that is, that economic integration can be managed and contained at an early stage.[69]

In my opinion, it can easily be demonstrated that in North America we are choosing what I would call the EFTA route rather than the EC route. In effect, all the current proposals for more Mexican, U.S., and Canadian economic integration concern the lower reaches of negative or market integration with a minimum of shared institutions. For instance, no serious proposals have been made for a North American customs union, common market, or full economic and monetary union.[70]

So far I have tried to emphasize that it is important not to accept uncritically the notion of a relentless march from free trade to economic and political union. However, it is equally important to allow that North American integration might take an unprecedented form in which elements of policy integration were instituted before lower levels of integration were complete. In fact, a central message of Pastor's paper is that the issue of free trade with Mexico has become contentious in the United States and Canada. Powerful Canadian and U.S. labor movements and environmental groups that were generally opposed to the Canada-U.S. Free Trade Agreement (CUSFTA) are expressing even stronger concerns about the inclusion of Mexico in a NAFTA. These groups, therefore, suggest that any trilateral agreement with Mexico should contain a social charter based on common standards for labor, social policy, and the environment in order to prevent a lowering of these standards after the completion of NAFTA. Obviously, groups making these proposals think that the EC model should be imitated in North America. Will these groups be powerful enough to force the inclusion of common policies in NAFTA before full liberalization is implemented? Should these ideas be supported?

In principle there is no reason why common standards should be opposed, but there are several issues in practice that should be carefully addressed. For instance, why would such a code be needed to ensure that Canadian and U.S. standards remain high? No such provision exists in the GATT, and yet it is in this context of freer trade under the GATT that Canadian and U.S. standards were elevated. The issue should be how to improve Mexican labor, social, and environmental standards, not simply how to impose common standards.

International distinctions of tolerable levels of environmental risk or of labor and working conditions are created because the weight attached to environmental, labor, and social standards tends to vary with the income levels of different countries. In low income countries, even if environmental and health risks and poor working conditions are acknowledged, income levels do not permit a structure of environmental regulation and labor standards comparable to that in rich countries. Given differences in the levels of economic development and national priorities, it is clear that environmental, labor, and social standards cannot be wholly uniform. Besides, who is to judge what is acceptable? Some mechanism must be found to accommodate differences in national priorities linked to levels of economic development and cultural factors, but a trade agreement is not the best mechanism.

True, the European Community has been a very successful integration arrangement through which less affluent societies have managed to improve their social and labor standard almost to the level of the richer countries. The EC, however, recognized that integration alone cannot guarantee that less affluent countries will grow fast enough to catch up with the more prosperous EC countries. To help incorporate economically diverse members into one community, the EC relies on transition periods and structural assistance for less affluent countries. The Community has more than doubled its regional development fund over the past ten years to 4.7 billion ECUS (roughly U.S. $6.5 billion).[71] Are the more affluent societies of North America prepared to create a similar fund? I think the answer is obviously not.

Moreover, would all three countries be prepared to accept the loss of sovereignty that is associated with the European model? Mexico has clearly stated that it is not willing to sacrifice any more sovereignty than is implied by a free trade agreement. I doubt that the United States and Canada are prepared for such a sacrifice either.

The European Community is a common market attempting to harmonize national economic policies to form an economic union. A common market calls for free movement of goods, services, labor, and capital among member countries, and for common tariffs and harmonization of protected trade policies applied to nonmembers.

The Mexican government rejects a common market or customs union as inappropriate in the North American context for two reasons. A common market requires that a uniform set of trade and commercial policies be applied to all nonmembers. In the past, Mexico has not always wished to follow U.S. initiatives on trade with the outside world; for instance, Mexico maintained trade relations with Cuba and Nicaragua after the United States ceased to do so. If Mexicans are to preserve their autonomy in foreign policy, the Mexican government cannot accept a common market's legal restriction on its capacity for independent action.[72]

Since a common market involves the free movement of both labor and capital among member states, it would require a coordination of other policies besides those concerned with foreign trade. Control over foreign immigration is a basic national policy, and the obvious need for Mexico, the United States, and Canada to maintain control in this field is sufficient reason to rule out a common market. Moreover, in Mexican government views, it will be desirable for Mexico to reserve the right to exercise some control over the movement of U.S. and Canadian capital into Mexico. Such reservations enabling Mexico to deal with specific problems arising from the operations of U.S. and Canadian firms in Mexico would be impermissible under a common market. It is not realistic, therefore, to expect Mexico to sign a social charter guaranteeing equality of wages, as some U.S. and Canadian labor leaders would like. It is difficult for a developing country such as Mexico to attract industry without the incentive of low wages. But after investment comes wages will rise and working conditions will improve.

Wages in the *maquiladora* industry, for instance, are already improving. According to a recent survey carried out by the Colegio de la Frontera Norte the average daily wage of a *maquiladora* employee in Tijuana and Ciudad Juarez was about 60 to 75 percent higher than the salary of an industrial worker in Monterrey in 1990.[73] Furthermore, the nature of the *maquiladora* is changing. In recent years, the *maquiladora* program has attracted more sophisticated forms of production in automobile-related manufacturing and advanced electronics assembly. This "second wave" of *maquiladora* plants has made substantial investments in complex technology; they are also hiring growing numbers of male workers.[74] Overall, the number of men employed in *maquiladora* plants has increased from less than 20 percent ten years ago to about 35 percent today. In some sectors like transportation equipment men now comprise up to 50 percent of the workforce.[75]

These "new" *maquiladoras* are significant because they demonstrate that sophisticated, high quality exports can be produced in Mexican plants using advanced production technologies. Whereas the "old" *maquiladoras* typically are export enclaves that generate employment and foreign exchange, but use few local material inputs and have limited spillover effects on the rest of the country's industrial structure, the new *maquiladoras* enable Mexico to move to a higher level of development by fostering a more highly skilled workforce. This would give Mexico a stronger competitive position in the global economy. Finally, the *maquiladoras* have now furnished Mexican producers with more inputs, and local content in the *maquiladora* has increased from about 1.7 percent to 6.0 percent. In sum, stimulating trade and investment among the three North American economies will foster economic growth, enhance economic competitiveness, and provide more resources allocated for environmental and social purposes.

In conclusion, some people think the EC's example in dealing with labor, social, and environmental issues should be followed by North American economies, but it is important to note the differences between the EC and NAFTA. The EC is not only a customs union, it is also a common market that permits free movement of persons and investment and provides transfers from high income to low income areas. Since neither the United States nor Canada are willing to permit free movement of people, nor are they willing to provide substantial fiscal transfers to Mexico, a different model for regional economic and environmental cooperation must be developed specifically for North America. In my opinion, this model is the free trade agreement technique. A NAFTA in the terms it is being negotiated, apart from offering economic benefits and creating a more stable climate for trade and investment, will become a catalyst to greater environmental, social, and political cooperation, but efforts to foster cooperation must be sensitive to national interests in each of the three societies.

Notes

1. In January 1986, when Spain and Portugal entered the European Community, their per capita GNP was 40 percent and 19 percent, respectively, of that of West Germany. In comparison, Mexico's per capita GDP in 1992 is about 12 percent of that of the United States and Canada. Gary Clyde Hufbauer and Jeffrey J. Schott, *North American Free Trade: Issues and Recommendations* (Washington: Institute for International Economics, 1992), pp. 7–8.

2. Lorenzo Meyer, "The United States and Mexico: The Historical Structure of Their Conflict," *Journal of International Affairs*, vol. 43, no. 2 (1990), pp. 269–70.

3. Author's interviews with Carlos Salinas de Gortari, Mexico City, July 24, 1990, November 30, 1990, and April 24, 1992.

4. *Update on Recent Developments in Mexico*, Hearing before the Subcommittee on Western Hemisphere Affairs of the House Foreign Affairs Committee, 102d Cong. 1 sess. (Government Printing Office, 1991), pp. 2, 54–55.

5. Richard Gephardt's letter to President Bush, March 27, 1991, and President Bush's response, May 1, 1991.

6. William Stockton, "Mexicans, in Poll, Call U.S. a Friend," *New York Times*, November 17, 1986, p. 6.

7. Clark Reynolds used the term "silent integration" and correctly predicted that it was "bound to increase over the next twenty years." Clark Reynolds and Carlos Tello, eds., *U.S.-Mexico Relations: Economic and Social Aspects* (Stanford University Press, 1983), p. 21.

8. For many examples of the difficulty of the relationship and the reasons, see Robert A. Pastor and Jorge G. Castañeda, *Limits to Friendship: The United States and Mexico* (Knopf, 1988).

9. American Federation of Labor and Congress of Industrial Organizations, *U.S.-Mexico Free Trade: Exploiting Both Sides* (Washington, February 1991), p. 1.

10. See Ronald Inglehart, Neil Nevitte, and Miguel Basañez, "Convergence in North America; Closer Economic, Political, and Cultural Ties between the United States, Canada, and Mexico," unpublished manuscript, 1992.

11. For a good discussion of these competing ideologies, see Michael Hart and Sushma Gera, "Trade and the Environment: Dialogue of the Deaf or Scope for Cooperation?" paper prepared for the Canada-U.S. Law Institute Conference on the Law and Economics of Environmental Regulation," Cleveland, Ohio, April 24–26, 1992, pp. 1–10.

12. Special issue of *Ecologist*, vol. 20 (November–December 1990), p. 204.

13. In response to President Bush's commitment to take environmental considerations into account, the National Wildlife Federation announced support of the fast-track authority; the Sierra Club and the Friends of the Earth opposed it; and the National Audubon Society, the Environmental Defense Fund, and the Natural Resources Defense Council adopted low profiles.

14. After the United States restricted imports of tuna from Mexico because of inadequate safeguards for preventing dolphin deaths, Mexico took its complaint to the GATT court and won. Despite that, Mexico agreed to join the United States and eight other nations in negotiations for a new regime to safeguard dolphins. In April 1992, the Inter-American Tropical Tuna Commission announced that the ten nations had reached agreement to cut the killing of dolphins by 80 percent during the 1990s. See two articles by James Brooke in the *New York Times*: "America—Environmental Dictator?" May 3, 1992, p. F7; and "10 Nations Reach Accord on Saving Dolphins," May 12, 1992, p. B9.

15. Hufbauer and Schott, *North American Free Trade*.

16. For data from 1969–83, see Joseph Grunwald and Kenneth Flamm, *The Global Factory: Foreign Assembly in International Trade* (Brookings, 1985), table 4-1, p. 140. For more recent data, see American Embassy, Mexico, *Foreign Investment Climate Report*, (August 1991), p. 28.

17. See Remarks by Stewart Hudson, National Wildlife Federation, "Opening up the Debate: The Free Trade Agreement with Mexico and Environmental Concerns," January 15, 1991.

18. See, for example, National Safe Workplace Institute, *Crisis at Our Doorstep: Occupational and Environmental Health Implications for Mexico-U.S.-Canada Trade Negotiations* (Chicago, February 1991), and the articles by William Langewiesche, "The Border," *Atlantic*, May and June 1992.

19. See, for example, Judy Pasternak, "Firms Find a Haven from U.S. Environmental Rules," *Los Angeles Times*, November 19, 1991, reprinted in *Congressional Record*, November 22, 1991, p. E3967.

20. U.S. General Accounting Office, *U.S.-Mexico Trade: Some U.S. Wood Furniture Firms Relocated from Los Angeles Area to Mexico*, Report to the Chairman, Committee on Energy and Commerce, House of Representatives, GAO/NSIAD-91-191 (April 1991), pp. 1–4.

21. See, for example, C. Fred Bergsten, Thomas Horst, and Theodore H. Moran, *American Multinational Corporations and American Interests* (Brookings, 1978); Raymond Vernon, *Sovereignty at Bay* (Basic Books, 1971); and Richard J. Barnett and Ronald E. Muller, *Global Reach: The Power of the Multinational Corporation* (Simon and Schuster, 1974).

22. Gene M. Grossman and Alan B. Krueger, "Environmental Impacts of a North American Free Trade Agreement," Working Paper 3914 (Cambridge, Mass.: National Bureau of Economic Research, 1991), p. 29.

23. Patrick Low, "Trade Measures and Environmental Quality: Implications for Mexico's Exports," paper presented at the Symposium on International Trade and the Environment, World Bank, November 21–22, 1991.

24. A study commissioned by the U.S. Trade Representative estimated that the border would continue to grow at a rate of 5–15 percent without NAFTA, but would be slower if the agreement was approved. This study is cited by Hufbauer and Schott, who concur that industry is more likely to move deeper into Mexico with NAFTA. *North American Free Trade*, p. 138.

25. Grunwald and Flamm, *Global Factory*, p. 161. A more recent estimate by the American Embassy in Mexico found average wages in the *maquiladoras* to be three times the Mexican minimum wage. *Foreign Investment Climate Report*, p. 28.

26. Grunwald and Flamm found that as the wage gap between the United States and Mexico widened, the problem of absenteeism and turnover of labor in the maquiladoras increased. *Global Factory*, p. 179.

27. For a concise summary of the legislation and a discussion of its effects, see Hufbauer and Schott, *North American Free Trade*, pp. 134–53.

28. See Edward Cody, "Mexico Shuts Oil Refinery to Help Save Capital's Air," *Washington Post*, March 19, 1991, p. A22; Robert Reinhold, "Mexico Says It Won't Harbor U.S. Companies Fouling Air," *New York Times*, April 18, 1991, pp. A1, A10; and "Mexico City Pollution Chief Defends Record," *El Financiero International*, May 4, 1992.

29. See Pastor and Castañeda, *Limits to Friendship*, chap. 7.

30. For a detailed analysis of the 1983 plan, see Jan Gilbreath Rich, *Planning the Border's Future: The Mexican-U.S. Integrated Border Environmental Plan* (Austin, Tex.: Lyndon B. Johnson School of Public Affairs, U.S.-Mexican Studies Program, March 1992), pp. 1–3.

31. "White House Fact Sheet: Review of Environmental Effects of Free Trade with Mexico," February 25, 1992.

32. Rich, *Planning the Border's Future*, pp. 26–46.

33. John Audley, "A Critique of the February 21, 1992, Draft of the North American Free Trade Agreement," Sierra Club Center for Environmental Innovation Club, Washington, April 1992, p. 17.

34. Grossman and Krueger, "Environmental Impacts," p. 20. Mexico's per capita GDP in current value was $2,010, but near $5,000 in terms of purchasing power parity. Two other studies cited by Hufbauer and Schott, *North American Free Trade*, p. 131, n.2, arrived at similar conclusions.

35. Mancur Olson, Jr., *The Logic of Collective Action: Public Goods and the Theory of Groups* (Harvard University Press, 1965), and *The Rise and Decline of*

Nations—Economic Growth, Stagflation, and Social Rigidities (Yale University Press, 1982).

36. "Mexico Delays Plans to Dam a Major River," *New York Times*, March 21, 1992.

37. Jan Gilbreath Rich, "FTA Prompts Overhaul at Ecology Secretariat," *El Financiero International*, August 26, 1991, p. 13.

38. *Congressional Record*, May 24, 1991, p. S6799.

39. Tom Barry, ed., *Mexico: A Country Guide* (Albuquerque, N. Mex.: Inter-Hemispheric Resource Center, 1992), p. 183.

40. See "North American Labor Laws: How They Stack Up to Each Other," *El Financiero International*, May 25, 1992, pp. 14–15.

41. "Union Chief Approves Change to Labor Law," *El Financiero Internacional*, June 29, 1992, p. 4.

42. Quoted by Talli Nauman, "Labor Laws Stand before Proposed NAFTA," *El Financiero International*, May 25, 1992, pp. 14–15.

43. See U.S. Department of Labor, Bureau of International Labor Affairs, *Labor Standards in Export Assembly Operations in Mexico and the Caribbean* (Washington, June 1990), p. 7, and *Worker Rights in Export Processing Zones: Mexico* (Washington, August 1990), pp. 17, 67–68; and Pastor and Castañeda, *Limits to Friendship*, p. 199.

44. International Labour Office, *Yearbook of Labour Statistics* (Geneva, 1989–90), cited in Congressional Research Service report, March 25, 1991, p. 40.

45. See, for example, George E. Brown, Jr., J. William Goold, and John Cavanagh, "Making Trade Fair," *World Policy Journal* (Spring 1992), pp. 309–27. Brown is a member of Congress and introduced H.R. 4883, April 9, 1992, calling on U.S. negotiators to include "certain threshold protections regarding worker rights, agricultural standards, and environmental quality." The Charter was published by the Commission of the European Communities, May 1990.

46. Stephen A. Herzenberg, Jorge F. Perez-Lopez, Stuart K. Tucker, "Labor Standards and Development in the Global Economy," a summary of a conference on the subject at the Overseas Development Council, December 1988.

47. *Congressional Record*, October 30, 1991, p. S15524.

48. Hector Aguilar Camin, "World Change and Democracy in Mexico," a lecture given at the National Autonomous University of Mexico, *La Jornada*, reprinted in Foreign Broadcasting Information Service, *Daily Report: Latin America*, April 20, 1992, pp. 6–12. Hereafter FBIS, *Latin America*.

49. The external pressures to which Salinas was referring were not just from the United States. Mario Vargas Llosa called Mexico "the perfect dictatorship." Both quoted in Mark Uhlig, "Mexico's Salinas Rains on His Own Parade," *New York Times*, November 25, 1990, p. E3.

50. Carlos Salinas de Gotari, "State of the Nation Address," November 1, 1991, in FBIS, *Latin America*, November 13, 1991, p. 14.

51. For a good review of the electoral process, see Delal Baer, "The 1991 Mexican Midterm Elections," Center for Strategic and International Studies, Washington, October 1, 1991; Andrew Reding, "The Crumbling of the 'Perfect Dictatorship,'" *World Policy Journal*, Spring 1991, pp. 255–84; and Robert A. Pastor, *Whirlpool: U.S.*

Foreign Policy toward Latin America (Princeton University Press, forthcoming), chap. 14.

52. Miguel Basañez, "Encuesta Electoral, 1991," *Este Pais*, August 1991, p. 6.

53. Salinas, "State of the Nation Address," November 1, 1990, p. 15.

54. Interview with Carlos Salinas de Gortari, Mexico, November 30, 1990.

55. Americas Watch, *Human Rights in Mexico: A Policy of Impunity* (New York, 1990).

56. Interview with Jorge Carpizo and Rosario Green, Atlanta, Ga., September 14, 1990.

57. For a recounting of the arguments on both sides of this debate, see *Update on Recent Developments in Mexico*, Hearing, October 16, 1991.

58. "Rights Group Says Border Agents Abuse Mexicans," *New York Times*, May 31, 1992, p. 12.

59. Inglehart, Nevitte, and Basañez, *Convergence in North America*," chap. 1, p. 1.

60. Interview with Cuauhtemoc Cardenas, Mexico, July 23, 1990.

61. *Congressional Record*, May 24, 1991, pp. S6804-5.

62. Statement on Fast-Track Authority by Representative Richard A. Gephardt, May 9, 1991, Washington.

63. For an elaboration of this point, see Robert Pastor, *Congress and the Politics of U.S. Foreign Economic Policy* (University of California Press, 1980).

64. For a longer discussion of these ideas, see Pastor, *Whirlpool*, chaps. 13–15.

65. For one idea, see Albert Fishlow, Sherman Robinson, and Raúl Hinojosa-Ojeda, "Proposal for a North American Regional Development Bank," paper prepared for a conference sponsored by the Federal Reserve Bank of Dallas, June 14, 1991.

66. Paul Robson, *The Economics of International Integration*, 2d ed. (London: Allen and Unwin, 1984), p. 1.

67. Bela Balassa, *The Theory of Economic Integration* (London: Allen and Unwin, 1962).

68. Robson, *The Economics of International Integration*, pp. 59–61.

69. Victoria Curzon Price aptly reminds us that the free trade area technique has very successfully managed the relationship between the EC and the EFTA countries where this latter group of countries "had no stomach for the highly intensive form of economic integration on which the EC was prepared to embark" and wanted to "keep a free hand, not only in trade policy but in . . . industrial policy." See "Free Trade Areas, The European Experience, What Lessons for Canadian–U.S. Trade Liberalization," Observation no. 31 (Toronto: C.D. Howe Institute, 1987).

70. The only concrete proposal for a higher level of integration was that of President Reagan's for a "North American accord." However, insofar as there was substance to these ideas, they seemed to encompass free (or at least freer) trade combined with common or harmonized policies in areas such as energy, and perhaps more active collaboration in foreign policy. Elements of policy integration or cooperation would thus be combined with elements of market integration. One should not forget the strong negative reactions of President Lopez Portillo and Prime Minister Trudeau to this proposal. See Werner J. Feld and others, "A North American Accord: Feasible or Futile?" *Western Political Quarterly*, vol. 36 (June 1980), pp. 298–311.

71. See Rosemary P. Piper and Alan Reynolds, "Lessons from the European Experience," in Steven Globerman, ed., *Continental Accord: North American Economic Integration* (Vancouver: Fraser Institute, 1991), p. 143.

72. Mexico continues to pursue trade initiatives with other regions. Mexico has recently signed an ambitious cooperative agreement with the EC, a free-trade agreement with Chile, and is planning to sign similar agreements with Colombia, Venezuela, and other countries of Central America.

73. See El Colegio de la Frontera Norte, "Reestructuracion en la Frontera Mexico-Estados Unidos ante el Tratado de Libre Comercio," 1992.

74. Jorge Carrillo, "Transformaciones en la Industria Maquiladora de Exportacion," in Bernardo Gonzalez-Arechiga and Rocio Barajas Escamilla, eds., *Las Maquiladoras: Ajuste Estructural y Desarrollo Regional* (Tijuana: El Colegio de la Frontera Norte—Fundacion Friedrich Ebert, 1988) pp. 37–54.

75. Harley Shaiken, *Mexico in the Global Economy: High Technology and Work Organization in Export Industries*, monograph series 33 (La Jolla, Calif.: University of California, San Diego, Center for U.S.-Mexican Studies, 1990), p. 12.

NAFTA and the Rest of
the World

Carlos Alberto Primo Braga

THE NAFTA negotiations have already generated a voluminous literature, focusing on the potential implications of this minilateral arrangement for the U.S., Mexican, and Canadian economies.[1] The economic implications of NAFTA for the rest of the world (ROW) have also drawn some attention, particularly with respect to the systemic effects of the arrangement—the potential impact of NAFTA on the GATT system.[2] In general, however, this theme has been of secondary importance in the evolving debate on NAFTA.

This paper surveys the literature that deals (explicitly or implicitly) with the potential implications of NAFTA for the ROW. The main questions it addresses are the following:

—What kind of minilateral arrangement will NAFTA be and what are the prevailing perceptions with respect to its potential for discrimination against nonmember countries?

—Will NAFTA significantly affect the welfare of nonmember countries?

—What are the systemic implications of NAFTA for the world trading system and for trade policies of nonmember countries—particularly in the Western Hemisphere?

The paper is organized as follows. In the first section, the nature of NAFTA and the GATT (General Agreement on Tariffs and Trade) rules for minilateral arrangements are discussed. The second section provides a brief theoretical review of the implications of a minilateral arrangement for nonparticipants. The third section surveys several attempts to model the economic implications of NAFTA both at aggregate and sector-specific levels. The fourth section focuses on the implications of NAFTA for Latin

Research assistance from Todd Eisenstadt, Christopher Holmes, and Daniel Lederman is gratefully acknowledged as are the comments and assistance of Drusilla Brown, Susan Collins, Ronald Duncan, Will Martin, Jeffrey Schott, and Horacio Sobarzo.

America and the Caribbean. The final section discusses the systemic implications of NAFTA.

NAFTA, the Issue of Discrimination, and the GATT

NAFTA is often portrayed by its supporters as a trade-expanding development, with minor implications for nonparticipants.[3] The concept of a "North-American Fortress," for instance, has never received much attention in contrast with the notion of "Fortress Europe," which has been prominent in the debate over the European Community "single market program" (EC-92).

It is well recognized that these two minilateral initiatives are very different "animals." NAFTA can be characterized as an "expanded" free trade area, which does not envision—at least in the near future—the same type of "deep" market integration currently pursued by the EC (which, among other major differences from the NAFTA process, includes macroeconomic policy harmonization under the guidance of a supranational institution). Still, the fact that NAFTA's discriminatory effects have not attracted much attention so far elicits a series of questions.

It can be argued, for instance, that this lack of concern simply reflects the low degree of discrimination intrinsic to a preferential arrangement among relatively open economies. At least at the level of trade flows, this proposition seems to be partially supported by the empirical analyses surveyed in the third section of this paper, on quantitative studies. Such an interpretation is consistent with the standard U.S. official position, which has always portrayed U.S. minilateral initiatives as GATT-consistent and designed to foster the ultimate objectives of the multilateral system.[4] Alternatively, it can be argued that the "growth dividend" of NAFTA—that is, its positive impact on growth rates of member countries—is expected to dominate its discriminatory effects, making NAFTA a positive-sum game for member and nonmember countries alike over the long run. Such prospects would provide an incentive for nonmember countries to downplay their immediate concerns with trade diversion.

Another rationale for the apparent lack of concern with the discriminatory effects of NAFTA can be construed as strategic behavior of the potential "victims." Some of them seem to find comfort in the promise that NAFTA will be a first step in the process of building a Western Hemisphere Free Trade Area (WHFTA), as envisioned by the Enterprise for the Americas Initiative (EAI). Accordingly, Latin American countries could be tempering their reservations about trade and investment diversion, with the expectation that they will be able to join the "club" later on. Some countries in Latin America, such as Chile, are actively pursuing this option.

Some exceptions to this rule can be found among the beneficiaries of the U.S.–Caribbean Basin Initiative and Canada's Preferential Trade Scheme for the Commonwealth Caribbean. Their concern reflects the possibility that NAFTA might erode the preferences they currently enjoy under the programs mentioned. Even these countries, however, seem to recognize that their best strategy is to follow the NAFTA negotiations closely, while exploring the opportunities open by the EAI.

Outside the Western Hemisphere, NAFTA has elicited only limited reaction so far. The European Community seems to be too enthralled with its own preferential experiment to be in a position to criticize the arrangement. As for the least developed countries in Africa and Asia (many of which gravitate toward the EC in the context of the Lome Convention), both their trade orientation and pattern of specialization tend to make them relatively indifferent with respect to the agreement's potential implications for outsiders.[5] The Asian newly industrializing economies and Japan are the only major economic partners of NAFTA countries, outside the Western Hemisphere, that seem to be more directly concerned with the possibilities of trade and investment diversion.

It is important to acknowledge, however, that NAFTA—as was true of the Canadian-U.S. Free Trade Agreement (CUSFTA)—will at best be a movement toward freer trade among its members. In other words, it will not establish free trade within North America. It is expected that several nontariff barriers (NTBs) at the sectoral level will continue to exist and that the agreement will introduce a maze of new trade rules for its member countries, such as revised rules of origin for several important industries. In this context, the focus on static trade diversion generated by preferential tariff cuts that characterizes most of the analyses of NAFTA's implications for nonmember countries seems to be missing important dimensions of the problem. Pushing this argument to its limits, one could argue that if NAFTA becomes an experience in managed trade, it may not only increase the level of discrimination against nonmembers (see the section on quantitative studies) but also transform the potential WHFTA into a clutter of managed trade deals.[6] Accordingly, the apparent lack of concern with NAFTA's potential for discrimination could alternatively be interpreted as a sign that the rest of the world has not yet fully grasped (or that it has preferred to overlook) the real contours of NAFTA.

The GATT and Minilateral Arrangements

The multilateral system built on the GATT has at its core the principle of nondiscrimination. Nondiscrimination in the General Agreement is embodied in two concepts: unconditional most-favored-nation (MFN) treatment and national treatment. This paper is not the place to review the history of the evolution of these concepts in the arena of international law.[7] It is sufficient to say that the United States, after a long experience with conditional MFN and national treatment clauses in the context of bilateral trade treaties, chose to support unconditional MFN and national treatment at the multilateral level in the post–World War II period. The U.S. position had a strong influence in framing the original text of the GATT.

U.S. support for nondiscrimination, however, was only partly successful in shaping the multilateral trade system. It is true that some of the old relics of a discriminatory trade era—for example, the commonwealth system of preferences—gradually faded away as the GATT rounds promoted liberalization on an MFN basis. Still, under the GATT umbrella, many new discriminatory trade arrangements appeared, with the EC being the most important one of them.

The GATT's article XXIV spells out the conditions required for member countries to engage in free trade agreements (FTAs), customs unions, or interim agreements expected to develop either into FTAs or customs unions. Basically, it requires the arrangement to cover substantially all trade among its members and that the level of trade barriers against nonmembers not be raised by the agreement. One can rationalize these requirements as an attempt to minimize the degree of discrimination against outsiders that is intrinsic to a preferential arrangement. In reality, however, article XXIV reflected a compromise between the U.S. position in favor of nondiscrimination and the belief of many countries that FTAs and customs unions provided a sound reason to carve an exception to the MFN clause in the General Agreement.[8]

The effectiveness of article XXIV in preventing the expansion of preferential arrangements, however, has been quite limited. It is ironic that by the late 1980s, after a forty-year increase in GATT membership, preferential arrangements influence almost 50 percent of world trade flows.[9]

Over the years more than seventy preferential agreements were notified to the GATT, but in only four cases were the working parties able to reach a consensus concerning their compatibility with article XXIV.[10] Despite this low level of approval, the consensus approach followed by the GATT has limited the relevance of the recommendations of article XXIV–related working parties. It is quite true that the "damage" caused by these preferential agreements in terms of discrimination against outsiders has been qualified by the fact that many of them were not fully implemented. The 1980s, however, witnessed a revival of the interest for minilateral arrangements. Particularly relevant in this context has been the change in attitude of the United States (once the most enthusiastic supporter of the principle of nondiscrimination) with respect to minilateral agreements.[11] Over the last seven years, the United States negotiated FTAs with Israel (the agreement being signed in April 1985) and Canada (the agreement taking effect on January 1, 1989); announced its intent to negotiate an FTA with Mexico in June 1990; and, formally, initiated the negotiations for the NAFTA—in a trilateral format—in June 1991.[12]

NAFTA: An "Expanded" FTA

Although the NAFTA negotiations have so far been characterized by an unusual level of secrecy, the basic structure of the agreement is known.[13] NAFTA is being negotiated as an "expanded" FTA to the extent that it goes beyond the conventional negotiation on tariffs and nontariff barriers, addressing the issue of "market access" in a broad sense. The negotiations encompass the removal of barriers not only to trade in goods but also to trade in services and beyond-the-border policies that may distort trade and competition. Accordingly, a broad array of policies, such as rules of origin, local content requirements, restrictions on establishment, and government procurement practices, as well as divergences between regulatory and legal systems (foreign investment laws, competition policies, intellectual property rights) are on the table. In addition, the NAFTA negotiations also address trade rules—particularly, the use of instruments of contingent protection, such as safeguard, antidumping, and countervailing duties actions—and the establishment of dispute settlement procedures.

The broad format of NAFTA is not surprising. After all, NAFTA is building upon the previous experience of the CUSFTA negotiations.[14] Furthermore, it can be argued that the Uruguay Round had already set the stage for this format by expanding the multilateral agenda to encompass the theme of market access in a broad context.[15] What is surprising in the case of NAFTA is the fact that a developing country (Mexico) took the initiative to launch the process.

The request of the Salinas administration in June 1990 not only meant a dramatic break with the traditional Mexican approach to its northern neighbor (well captured by the saying attributed to Porfirio Diaz: "Poor Mexico! So far from God, and so close to the United States") but also raised many complex economic questions.[16] NAFTA is, to a certain extent, sailing unchartered waters, given the wide income differentials among its participants as well as remaining discrepancies among their legal and political systems.[17]

After a prolonged internal debate, Canada joined the negotiations in June 1991.[18] The trilateralization of the negotiations poses an interesting question: what will be the relationship between NAFTA and CUSFTA? As noted by Whalley, some items of the CUSFTA framework—for example, chapter 8 on "Wine and Distilled Spirits"—have limited relevance for Mexico.[19] At the same time, there are new issues on the negotiating agenda, such as intellectual property rights, that were left out of CUSFTA. These considerations constrain the adoption of the "natural" solution of transforming NAFTA negotiations into a discussion on the terms of accession of Mexico to CUSFTA.

The "hub-and-spoke" problem, in turn, suggests that both Canada and Mexico will favor an explicit accession clause to NAFTA as a way to build the "mythic" WHFTA, if the United States is to pursue this route effectively once NAFTA is finalized.[20] In any case, Canada and Mexico will probably endorse the preservation of strict conditions for countries to qualify for "membership in the club." In this fashion, they will be able to better administer the erosion of their preferences, without being accused of favoring exclusiveness.[21]

Effects of Minilateral Arrangements on Nonmember Countries

It was established long ago that preferential liberalization may not be welfare enhancing for the members of a minilateral arrangement.[22] From a static perspective, the concepts of trade creation (the replacement of a high-cost source of production in one of the members of the agreement by a lower-cost source located in another member) and trade diversion (the replacement of a more efficient source of production in a nonmember by a higher-cost source located in a member of the agreement), introduced by Viner in the context of customs unions, hold the key for the static analysis of the economic implications of minilateral arrangements.

In the conventional static approach, the formation of a preferential arrangement generates a once-and-for-all reallocation of factors of production among the members of the agreement in response to the interplay of trade-creating and trade-diverting effects. In this scenario, the usual presumption is that when trade creation exceeds trade diversion, the preferential arrangement will be welfare improving for its participants.[23]

For nonmembers the implications of the arrangement are partially captured by the trade diversion effect. Nonmembers could also be affected by a deterioration of their terms of trade if the countries in the preferential area are large forces in the world economy. A more direct negative impact may occur if the minilateral arrangement generates an outright increase in the level of protection against outsiders. In this scenario, direct trade suppression would add to the trade diversion effect.

Conventional estimates of trade diversion and creation rely on partial equilibrium models that assume market segmentation and neglect the economywide effects of preferential liberalization.[24] General equilibrium analyses, in turn, try to model these effects explicitly. Some of these models assume perfectly competitive markets and nationally differentiated products—that is, imperfect substitution between imports and the domestic variety of each good (the Armington assumption).[25] More recent efforts in this area, however, have focused on imperfect competition and increasing returns to scale. Dynamic considerations are also sometimes introduced, with the effects of the minilateral agreement on the productive capacity and potential output of its member countries being analyzed.

Economies of scale may generate additional gains for the members of the union. The preferential arrangement, by providing larger markets for the firms of the member countries, allows them to explore economies of scale, which increases their competitiveness—either at the firm or the industrywide level (that is, through positive externalities)—and fosters industry rationalization at the level of the union. Accordingly, nonmember countries will have to cope not only with the conventional trade diversion effect but also with the higher competitiveness of the remaining firms in the member countries.

On a more positive note, once a dynamic perspective is adopted, the growth-enhancing effects of a minilateral arrangement may be significant enough to override its negative impact on outsiders. At the same time, one has to face the prospect of investment diversion from nonmember countries, as capital flows to the union members may increase in response to higher growth expectations.

In practice, the estimation of the economic implications of minilateral arrangements poses several problems. First, the evaluation of the impact of the liberalization of NTBs is a difficult subject. Second, results are sensitive to assumptions concerning market structure, pricing behavior of firms, and capital flows. Third, conventional economic models are ill equipped to deal with broad market access issues (for example, the possibility of contingent protection replacing conventional trade barriers). It is important to keep in mind these qualifications while reviewing the empirical results presented in the following section.

NAFTA and Nonmember Countries: Quantitative Studies

The economic effects of NAFTA on nonmember countries include trade diversion, terms-of-trade changes, investment diversion, and the positive externalities associated with the "growth dividend." Several quantitative studies focusing on NAFTA have appeared lately in a process similar to the one that characterized the debate on CUSFTA.[26] The effect of these studies—particularly, those using computable general equilibrium (CGE) models — on the ongoing negotiations is (to say the least) debatable. In this section, a brief summary of the results derived from some of these models is presented both at aggregate and sectoral levels.

Partial Equilibrium Analyses: The Aggregate Picture

Partial equilibrium analyses of NAFTA suggest that it will not generate significant trade diversion from nonmember countries.[27] Samuel Laird, for instance, calculates that NAFTA (modeled as simply entailing tariff removal among participant countries) would imply a decrease of only 0.72 percent in the value of exports from the other countries in the Western Hemisphere to the United States.[28] For industrialized countries, a NAFTA limited to tariff elimination would mean a decrease of only 0.55 percent of their exports to the United States.

Laird also estimates that the trade expansion effect (that is, the summation of trade creation and trade diversion) under the assumption that NAFTA was to be implemented in tandem with the outcome of the Uruguay Round negotiations of the GATT. His assumptions concerning the results of the multilateral negotiations were the following: a 20 percent reduction in tariffs and NTBs affecting agriculture; the elimination of Multifiber Agreement (MFA) quotas, while textile and clothing tariffs remain at the same level; and tariffs for all other products reduced by 30 percent with remaining NTBs being left untouched. Under these assumptions, trade creation (magnified by the MFN liberalization) completely dominates trade diversion and the developing countries in the Western Hemisphere would experience a 1.8 percent increase in their exports to the United States (a 2.4 percent increase for industrialized countries). If the results of the Uruguay Round are superimposed onto a NAFTA that encompasses the complete removal not only of tariffs but also of NTBs among its member countries, the final outcome would remain marginal: exports to the United States would decrease by only 0.07 percent for Western Hemisphere developing countries (and would expand by 1.6 percent for industrialized countries).

Another aggregate partial equilibrium exercise confirms the limited potential for trade diversion of NAFTA with respect to other Western Hemisphere countries. Focusing on an FTA between Mexico and the United States, Erzan and Yeats find that 94 percent of the total trade diversion associated with this FTA would affect countries outside the Western Hemisphere.[29] And the total amount of trade diversion (estimated to be about $441 million in terms of 1986 trade flows) amounts to roughly only 1 percent of U.S. imports from the ROW.

CGE Models

The results of CGE models for NAFTA are sensitive to their theoretical specifications (particularly, elasticities of demand and supply, market structures, pricing behavior of firms, and assumptions about capital flows). It is also important to keep in mind that the characteristics of the preferential liberalization experiments assumed in these exercises vary significantly.[30]

Available CGE studies (for a detailed review, see the paper by Drusilla Brown in this book) typically find that trade expands among NAFTA member countries as a consequence of the preferential arrangement. Welfare effects are also found to be positive for the participating countries, tending to be larger in models that adopt increasing returns to scale than in those based on constant returns to scale.

The impact on the rest of the world, in turn, may be either negative or positive depending on how the model approaches the interplay between trade diversion, capital flows, and changes in the terms of trade for ROW. It is worth mentioning that the ROW is usually introduced in these models through postulated export supply and import demand functions based on relative prices. Table 1 summarizes the main results for the ROW as established in the models developed by Drusilla Brown, Alan Deardorff, and Robert Stern (BDS); Horacio Sobarzo; and David Cox and Richard Harris.[31] All these models allow for increasing returns to scale and assume that imperfectly competitive firms set prices either by a combination of focal pricing and monopolistic competition (Sobarzo; Cox and Harris) or in a pure monopolistic competitive fashion (BDS).

Preferential liberalization without international factor mobility tends to reduce the volume of trade between NAFTA countries and the ROW. And as illustrated by case 1 of the BDS model, this may result in deterioration in the terms of trade of the ROW as NAFTA's demand for imports from nonmember countries and the supply of exports from NAFTA countries to the ROW fall. The cases summarized in table 1, however, make clear that the size of these changes is not likely to be significant.

The exceptions are provided by those scenarios in which international capital mobility is allowed for (case 2, both in BDS and in Sobarzo) or in which the preferential liberalization is complemented by additional trade barriers against nonparticipants (case 3 in Cox and Harris).

Case 2 in BDS assumes that in parallel with the preferential trade liberalization, Mexico will relax its capital import constraints and as a consequence it will receive a capital inflow from the ROW that will expand its capital stock by 10 percent. The model assumes that current account balances remain at the same level that prevails in the base period. Accordingly, the need to finance interest payments from Mexico to the ROW dictates that Mexico should run a substantial surplus in its balance of trade, an outcome that is basically accommodated by the ROW. It is also worth noting that in this scenario, the ROW experiences an improvement in its terms of trade, a phenomenon related to the large expansion of Mexican exports.

Sobarzo's case 2 assumes a perfectly elastic supply of foreign capital. The Mexican economy in this scenario experiences a much larger increase in gross domestic product than in case 1, a scenario characterized by a fixed capital stock assumption (8.0 percent GDP increase versus 1.9 percent in case 1).[32] This higher level of growth translates into a significant

Table 1. Summary of CGE Results on the Economic Implications of NAFTA for the Rest of the World (ROW)

Percent change unless otherwise specified

Item	Brown, Deardorff, and Stern[a]		Sobarzo[b]		Cox and Harris[c]		
	Case 1	Case 2	Case 1	Case 2	Case 1	Case 2	Case 3
Exports from the ROW							
To NAFTA countries	−0.06	−0.53	...	...	...	...	...
To the United States	...	...	...	...	−0.65	−0.64	−10.9
To Canada	...	...	...	...	0.08	0.07	−2.4
Net exports from the ROW[d]							
To NAFTA countries	0.35[e]	−10.88[e]	...	...	...	...	...
To Mexico	...	...	2.1	17.1	...	...	...
Terms of trade for the ROW	−0.0	0.2	...	...	...	...	...
Welfare[f]							
ROW	−0.0	−0.0	...	...	0.003	0.936	−0.117
Canada	0.7	0.7	...	...	...	...	...
Mexico	1.6	5.0	2.3	2.4	...	...	...
United States	0.1	0.3	...	...	...	...	...

Sources: Drusilla K. Brown, Alan V. Deardorff, and Robert M. Stern, "A North American Free Trade Agreement: Analytical Issues and a Computational Assessment," *World Economy*, vol. 15 (January 1992), pp. 11–30; Horacio E. Sobarzo, "A General Equilibrium Analysis of the Gains from Trade for the Mexican Economy of a North American Free Trade Agreement," ibid., pp. 83–100; and David Cox and Richard G. Harris, "North American Free Trade and Its Implications for Canada: Results from a CGE Model of North American Trade," ibid., pp. 31–34.

a. The Brown, Deardorff, and Stern model (twenty-nine sectors of which twenty-three are tradable goods sectors) assumes that technology in most tradable sectors is characterized by increasing returns to scale and the market structure is monopolistically competitive. Case 1 (BDS' experiment A) assumes complete removal of tariffs among NAFTA members and 25 percent increase of U.S. import quotas that restrain Mexican exports of agriculture, food, textiles, and clothing. Case 2 (BDS' experiment B) maintains the same assumptions plus the liberalization of Mexico's capital import controls, resulting in a 10 percent increase in Mexico's capital stock.

b. The Sobarzo model identifies twenty-seven production sectors and assumes imperfect competition in most of its twenty-one tradable sectors. The model addresses only the impact of a complete removal of tariffs among NAFTA countries. In case 1 (Sobarzo's version 2), a fixed quantity of capital in Mexico is assumed. Case 2 (Sobarzo's version 3), in turn, assumes that capital is mobile between countries.

c. The Cox and Harris model identifies nineteen sectors with ten of them presenting increasing returns to scale. The trade results reported reflect absolute changes in the market share of the ROW in total imports of the United States and Canada. The base for comparison is provided by the CUSFTA situation. Case 1 compares a hub-and-spoke format (with the United States as the hub and Canada and Mexico as the spokes) with CUSFTA. Case 2 compares NAFTA with CUSFTA. Case 3 compares a FAFTA combined with an increase of 10 percent of member countries' ad valorem tariffs against the ROW with CUSFTA. Preferential trade liberalization in all cases reflects only tariff removal.

d. Net exports are defined as exports minus imports.

e. Values in billions of U.S. dollars.

f. Welfare changes are measured in terms of the so-called equivalent variation—that is, they reflect the change in income valued at base prices that would lead to the same change in utility level associated with the liberalization.

deterioration of the balance of trade of Mexico with the ROW, given Sobarzo's ad hoc export supply and import demand functions used to model Mexico's trade relations with North America and the ROW.[33]

Case 3 in Cox and Harris illustrates the negative externalities of NAFTA if it becomes an inward-oriented bloc. In this scenario, the elimination of tariffs among member countries is combined with a 10 percent increase in ad valorem tariffs applied by Canada, Mexico, and the United States against imports from the ROW. As can be seen in table 1, this would bring a significant decrease in trade volumes between NAFTA countries and the ROW through direct trade suppression. An explicit movement toward an inward-oriented trade bloc in North America seems unlikely. After all, as illustrated by the welfare results for Canada, participating countries would also be negatively affected. Still, these results highlight the dangers for the ROW of such a scenario.

Perhaps the main lesson to be derived from these analyses concerns the importance of capital flows in determining the final outcome of NAFTA from the perspective both of member countries and of the ROW. In short, CGE results suggest that barriers to capital flows, as well as the availability of international financing, tend to play a much larger role in shaping the welfare results of NAFTA than does its preferential liberalization component.

Alternative Modeling of the NAFTA

The introduction of imperfect competition into CGE models has helped to shake the conventional wisdom that welfare results associated with trade liberalization are insignificant (a usual outcome of CGE modeling with constant returns to scale). These models cannot, however, adequately capture the effect of trade liberalization on growth rates. The effect of liberalization on capital formation and consumers' savings decisions, industry specialization, and capacity to import specialized inputs are some of the variables emphasized in attempts to model the dynamic implications of minilateral arrangements.[34] As a general rule, these models suggest that the dynamic benefits of liberalization are much higher than the conventional static benefits. Accordingly, one could argue that they strengthen the case for minilateral arrangements to the extent that the "growth dividend" dominates the distortions associated with the preferential liberalization.

Detailed calculations of the dynamic implications of NAFTA on the ROW are not (to my knowledge) available at this time. The only "dynamic" exercise that explicitly addresses the evolution of trade between NAFTA countries and the ROW is provided by Hufbauer and Schott.[35] Their model introduces dynamic considerations by imposing an exogenously determined increase in the rate of Mexican export growth. Linking the success of the NAFTA negotiations to further liberalizing reforms in Mexico, including "sweeping privatization, significant liberalization of the Mexican oil sector, [and continuity of] fiscal and monetary restraint," the authors assume that under these circumstances Mexican exports of goods and nonfactor services will grow at a rate of 11.2 percent a year, a figure that reflects the historical experience of successful liberalization implemented by inward-oriented countries. The failure of the NAFTA negotiations, in turn, is assumed to imply a smaller rate of growth for Mexican exports (7.9 percent), given the authors' assumption that it will foster "policy retrogression" in Mexico. This lower rate of growth is based on historical data for "collapsed liberalizations" and provides the counterfactual scenario used by Gary Hufbauer and Jeffrey Schott in estimating the economic impact of NAFTA.[36]

Their estimates of the NAFTA implications for trade flows among member countries are much larger than the ones found in conventional CGE models. Hufbauer and Schott point out that the "Mexico export gain is 50 percent larger than the most optimistic alternative model, while the U.S. export gain is more than twice as large."[37] The impact of NAFTA on the ROW, however, remains marginal as in the CGE cases (U.S. net exports to the ROW are found to be unaffected by NAFTA, while Mexican net exports decrease by U.S.$3 billion). Unfortunately, the hypotheses used by the authors in performing their calculations (Mexican export and import shares in relation to U.S. shares are fixed at 75 percent) limit the relevance of their results with respect to trade diversion considerations.

Sectoral Analyses

Sectors with relatively high levels of protection in the United States are natural candidates for analyses concerned with trade and investment diversion from the perspective of the ROW. Some interesting cases are provided by the agriculture, textiles and apparel, and steel sectors. Studies focusing on the auto industry are also surveyed in this section, given the importance of that sector in terms-of-trade and investment flows.

AGRICULTURE. Some CGE models focus on the implications for the agricultural sector of an FTA between Mexico and the United States. Sherman Robinson and others, for instance, analyze different combinations of trade liberalization combined with reform of agricultural policies in Mexico and in the United States (including liberalization limited to nonagricultural activities).[38] Their basic conclusion is that, on the aggregate, an FTA would expand bilateral trade under all scenarios. Mexico would experience some trade diversion as imports from the ROW decrease by 2 to 3 percentage points—the exception being the scenario with capital growth in Mexico; in this case, the "growth dividend" would generate a net increase in imports from the ROW. With respect to the United States, the FTA in almost all scenarios implies an increase in imports from the ROW. The results reflect the high level of protection accorded to the Mexican agriculture before the liberalization experiment.[39]

Once the focus of analysis becomes more product specific, one can find cases of trade diversion from the ROW in the U.S. market. Thomas Grennes and others, for instance, use a partial equilibrium model to study the effect of preferential liberalization in the Western Hemisphere on agricultural products.[40] They show that an FTA between the United States and Mexico, by removing restrictions—which amounted to a tariff equivalent of 28 percent in 1988—to Mexican exports of frozen, concentrated orange juice (FCOJ), would divert trade primarily from Brazil. Even in this case, despite the significant growth of Mexican exports of FCOJ to the U.S. market (32 percent), U.S. imports from the ROW would decrease by only 0.5 percent.[41] The situation changes, however, once one assumes that in addition to the tariff removal, NAFTA (and Mexican domestic reforms) will stimulate significant new investments in the Mexican citrus sector. Assuming a doubling of the rate of growth of Mexican FCOJ output, Spreen and others (using a long-term model of the world citrus industry) show that this expansion would basically divert trade from Brazil.[42] By the year 2000, this scenario would imply a decrease of 4.5 percent in the Brazilian production of citrus (a decrease of 14.4 percent in on-tree revenues) as compared with the baseline and much smaller impacts on the Florida citrus sector (a decrease of 0.61 percent in orange production and of 6.34 percent in on-tree revenue).

Analyses of agricultural products for which quantitative restrictions play a major role in controlling access to the U.S. market provide some interesting insights on the potential implications of NAFTA for the ROW. Sugar provides the best example in this context. Brent Borrell and Jonathan Coleman show that bilateral negotiations concerning trade in sugar and corn syrup between the United States and Mexico may have significant effects for the ROW.[43] If, for instance, under an FTA Mexico harmonizes its pricing policy with the one prevailing in the United States and both countries administer a joint quota scheme toward the ROW, this arrangement would impose significant welfare losses upon net exporters (the Caribbean, for instance, would experience a net welfare loss of U.S. $128 million; world net welfare, in turn, would fall by U.S. $241 millions). An even worse scenario can be imagined if the negotiations lead to an exchange of quota rights between Mexican sugar producers (expanding their access to the U.S. market) and U.S. corn syrup producers (who would gain greater access to the Mexican market). Under this scenario, U.S. corn syrup will displace sugar in the Mexican market, which will, in turn, end up in the United States fostering additional trade diversion (world net welfare would fall by U.S. $256 million in this case).

TEXTILES AND APPAREL. International trade in textiles and apparel has been traditionally constrained under the Multifiber Agreement (MFA), which allows developed countries to restrict imports by imposing quotas on a large number of textiles and apparel items. Over the last few years, the United States has gradually liberalized its trade in textiles with Mexico, raising several of its MFA quotas applied to Mexican products. Still, the complete elimination of MFA quotas is often mentioned as a prime objective of Mexican negotiators in the NAFTA talks.

Irena Trela and John Whalley analyze the implications of such a liberalization movement for NAFTA countries and the remaining MFA-restricted countries (which will be identified as the ROW in here).[44] They use a sector-specific CGE model with constant returns to scale, encompassing four textile and apparel product categories and a composite product. Goods are treated as homogeneous across regions, trade in textile and apparel between exporting countries (Mexico and the other thirty-three MFA-restricted countries) is assumed away, and MFA quotas are presumed to be binding. Accordingly, their model is particularly well suited to capture the potential negative effects of NAFTA for the ROW as far as the textiles and apparel industry is concerned.

Trela and Whalley run several liberalization experiments at bilateral (U.S.-Mexican) and NAFTA level in their model. In general their results suggest that Mexico and the United States tend to gain from the liberalization, while Canada and the ROW are losers. The Mexican industry experiences a major outward-oriented expansion with its exports to the U.S. market increasing significantly. The U.S. industry faces a minor adjustment (most of it in its apparel sector), but lower consumer prices guarantee a positive welfare result. Canada, in turn, would experience major market share losses in the U.S. market, given the expansion of Mexican exports. For the countries in the ROW, the negative welfare impact of the liberalization basically reflects the erosion of their quota rents in the U.S. market. NAFTA (that is, the removal of quotas and tariffs on textiles and apparel among member countries) would generate a welfare decrease of 0.03 percent (in terms of GDP) for the ROW.[45]

It is important to keep in mind, however, that the Trela-Whalley model, despite its sophistication, cannot capture an important facet of the NAFTA negotiations. It has been pointed out that the liberalization of tariffs and quotas for the textiles and apparel industry will probably come together with strict rules of origin requirements.[46] Rules of origin are the inevitable counterpart of preferential access in the context of an FTA. It is well known, however, that rules of origin may easily become a protectionist device when they are framed in a way that exceeds the limits required to avoid trade deflection caused by tariff differences among the FTA member countries.[47]

Rules of origin for the textiles and apparel industry are usually defined in terms of changes in tariff nomenclature headings in the productive process, so that a final product using foreign inputs can qualify for "domestic" status (in practice, it is often necessary to complement this procedure with a value-added test). A simple transformation rule requires a single tariff heading change. A double (triple) transformation rule demands two (three) changes in tariff classifications. With clothing, for instance, a simple transformation rule requires that the product be cut and sewn in a member country to qualify as local. Double transformation requires that the inputs into the final product also pass the test—that the fabric be formed in the FTA member countries. Triple transformation requires that all productive processes from yarn forward be implemented within the free trade area.

NAFTA is expected to adopt at least a double transformation rule (as was the case for most textile and clothing products under CUSFTA), with a triple transformation rule being considered the most likely outcome.[48] Bannister and Low point out that the Mexican textiles and apparel industry already displays a high level of dependence on U.S. inputs.[49] Accordingly, compliance with more strict rules of origin should not impose major adjustment costs for Mexico. Strict rules of origin may, however, impair investment from non-NAFTA countries in the Mexican industry, by tying its competitiveness to the efficiency of the U.S. textile sector and discriminating against outsourcing.

STEEL INDUSTRY. The steel industry provides another example of a sector that enjoys protection mainly in the form of quantitative restrictions—typically, voluntary restraint agreements (VRAs). Trela and Whalley have also developed a sector-specific CGE model to analyze the effects of regional liberalization in North America—over a time horizon of forty years—focusing on the steel industry.[50] Their model identifies one importing region (the United States), three exporting regions (Mexico; Canada; and a nineteen-country aggregate of other VRA-affected exporting nations, which represents the ROW), and three commodities-industries (a steel-producing industry; a steel-consuming industry, which is an aggregate of nonsteel manufacturing industries; and an all-other-goods industry).

The results of steel trade liberalization at a bilateral (U.S.-Mexican) and trilateral (NAFTA) level mirror the results obtained in Trela and Whalley's analysis of the textiles and apparel industry. The main impact on the ROW is in the form of smaller quota rents, reflecting terms-of-trade effects. Their analysis, however, illustrates another potential impact for the ROW of preferential liberalization in the context of an intermediate product: as a consequence of lower steel prices, U.S. steel-consuming industries experience an increase in their competitiveness compared with the ROW. This secondary effect contributes to amplify the negative (positive) welfare impact of NAFTA on the ROW (United States).

As with the textiles and apparel industry, even the most sophisticated models cannot capture all dimensions of international trade in steel in North America. The Trela-Whalley model, for instance, assumes that the direction of trade before and after the liberalization is from Mexico to the United States. Accordingly, trade liberalization would bring a contraction of the U.S. steel sector. This forecast seems to be at odds with the "qualified" support offered by the American Iron and Steel Institute to the NAFTA talks.[51] The explanation, however, is simple. The United States is, in reality, a net steel exporter to Mexico. Hence, the preferential liberalization of Mexican steel tariffs, as well as of government procurement policies based on a buy-Mexican provision, is probably attractive enough for the U.S. steel industry for it to accept the preferential quota and tariff removal on the U.S. side.[52] This, in turn, suggests that steel exporters from the ROW will also experience trade diversion in the Mexican market as a result of NAFTA.

THE AUTOMOBILE INDUSTRY. Trade in automobiles and auto parts constitutes the most important component of North American trade. Most of this trade is conducted either duty free or under preferential (low) tariffs. Accordingly, one should not, a priori, expect a major effect of NAFTA on the ROW as far as these trade flows are concerned.

The most detailed sectoral model available, focusing on the auto industry, is provided by Linda Hunter, James Markusen, and Thomas Rutherford (HMR).[53] These analysts approach the production of finished autos, using a four-region CGE model (Canada, Mexico, United States, and the ROW) that is based on two goods (autos and a composite of remaining goods and services) and two factors of production, and that assumes increasing returns to scale in the auto industry (with firms following Cournot behavior) and homogeneous products across countries. Two interesting features of the HMR analysis are its explicit attempt to model the behavior of transnational corporations (TNCs) and the endogeneity in the number of auto plants.

Different liberalization scenarios at the bilateral and trilateral (NAFTA) level are evaluated in HMR. Liberalization basically entails the removal of tariffs. Two scenarios are particularly interesting: free trade at the trilateral level for producers only (a situation that allows producers to maintain price discrimination across borders) and market integration (which allows free trade at the consumer level between the United States and Mexico, while free trade across the U.S.-Canadian border remains limited to producers).

Mexico is the clear "winner" in these exercises as far as welfare results, auto production, and exports are concerned. The effects on Canada, the United States, and the ROW are not significant in relative terms, although some trade diversion is forecasted. In the producers' free trade scenario, Mexican exports increase by 77,000 cars, whereas Canada and the ROW experience a decrease in their exports (9,000 and 32,000 cars, respectively). In the market integration scenario, Mexican exports increase by 157,000 cars, whereas Canadian exports fall by 37,000 and car exports from the ROW fall by 2,000 units as compared with the benchmark situation.

The differences in terms of trade diversion in these two scenarios are explained by the assumptions made by the authors, with respect to the pricing behavior of TNCs. Under market integration, TNCs in Mexico experience a significant decrease in their markups, while the plants located in the United States raise their markup in an attempt to prevent arbitrage between the two markets. This situation even allows the ROW to increase its exports to the United States by 10,000 units above the benchmark, minimizing the trade diversion effects of NAFTA.

The integration scenario, however, suggests that the ROW may be affected in a different way. Although in both scenarios, liberalization does not foster significant rationalization effects in the United States and Canada, it does have a dramatic impact in Mexico, increasing the output per firm by 19.7 percent in the producers' free trade case and by 155 percent in the market integration scenario.[54] There is, however, an important by-product of the rationalization of auto production in Mexico in the integrated scenario. It forces two of the five existing auto producers in Mexico to close their plants. The model does not identify what type of firm would be forced out under these circumstances (there are two types of firms in the HMR model: North American firms and ROW firms), but it calls attention to the possibility that ROW firms in Mexico may be directly affected in this process.

It is interesting to note that the existing five auto producers in Mexico have followed different strategies in terms of their market orientation until recently. The three U.S. automakers (Chrysler, General Motors, and Ford) are outward oriented, exporting mainly to the North American market. The other two producers (Nissan and Volkswagen) followed a much more inward-oriented strategy and only in the last few years (at least in the case of Volkswagen) have they announced investment plans that clearly target the North American market.[55]

It can be argued that those firms that have already established a North American core network strategy (in terms of suppliers and markets) will be in a better position to expand their activities under NAFTA. This argument will be even more relevant if strict local content requirements are adopted by NAFTA. If a 60 to 70 percent standard is confirmed (the North American content requirement under CUSFTA is 50 percent), as seems to be supported by the U.S. automakers, then non-U.S. TNCs will probably have to increase their North American sourcing to qualify for preferential treatment.[56]

A more direct threat to automakers from the ROW, however, seems to be posed by proposals of discriminatory treatment between those companies that have already established plant operations in Mexico and the others. Higher standards in rules of origin for potential newcomers provide a powerful illustration of this concept.[57] Another example is provided by the support given by U.S. automakers to the idea that a phaseout of the Mexican domestic-content law (which requires that no less than 36 percent of the auto parts used in Mexican automobiles be made in Mexico) be implemented in a discriminatory fashion (the decree would continue to apply to eventual newcomers to the Mexican auto industry).[58]

SUMMARY. Quantitative sectoral studies tend to confirm the thesis that NAFTA will not have a great impact on the ROW as far as trade flows are concerned (although some specific industries of nonmember countries may be significantly affected). There is, however, the danger that NAFTA may become a managed trade initiative, characterized by cumbersome regulations with a discriminatory bent. The results may then be different, although one could argue that the NAFTA member countries would probably be the main losers in this scenario.

Investment diversion is another source of concern for the ROW—particularly, for East Asian newly industrialized economies (NIEs) and Japan. Up to now, however, only limited anecdoctal evidence exists in this area.[59] Yet, if NAFTA introduces (explicit or implicit) discrimination against investments from nonmember countries, this threat can become a reality.[60]

NAFTA, Latin America and the Caribbean, and the EAI

Countries in Latin America and the Caribbean (LAC) have followed the NAFTA negotiations with great interest. In some cases, this interest reflects concern with potential trade and investment diversion. In most cases, however, it seems to reflect the perspective that NAFTA will pave the way for WHFTA.

Concern with trade diversion has been more often expressed, at least in the political debate, by those countries that will have their existing preferences eroded by NAFTA—for example, the beneficiaries of the U.S.–Caribbean Basin Initiative—than by countries that receive MFN treatment.[61] This result has an obvious parallel with the misgivings of Lome Convention countries toward the erosion of their preferences in the context of multilateral negotiations. By the end of 1991, however, most Caribbean and all Central American countries had signed framework agreements with the United States, as a first step for the negotiations of FTAs in the context of the Enterprise for the Americas Initiative.

Actually, if the signing of framework agreements, under the EAI, between the United States and other LAC countries is taken as a measure of their interest in building an FTA from "Anchorage to Tierra del Fuego," it would seem that WHFTA receives widespread support in the region—only Suriname, Haiti, and Cuba had not signed framework agreements by December 1991.[62] The inevitable question then is the magnitude of the benefits that these countries can expect to derive from such a minilateral arrangement.

There are no detailed welfare evaluations available of the implications for Western Hemisphere countries of building up WHFTA. Refik Erzan and Alexander Yeats, however, provide some clues in this respect by estimating the potential benefits (in terms of export expansion) for eleven Latin American countries (including Mexico) of negotiating an FTA with the core economy of NAFTA: the United States.[63]

The results are not surprising. Mexico and Brazil would be the ones to appropriate most of the overall trade expansion (roughly, 90 percent) associated with the formation of FTAs between the eleven Latin American countries and the United States.[64] Export expansion would average only 8 to 9 percent, given that most of these countries face relatively low MFN tariffs or already benefit from preferential access under the U.S. generalized system of preferences. The influence of hard-core nontariff barriers is taken into account in a rudimentary fashion by comparing two liberalization movements: in the first case, duties are reduced preferentially to zero in all tariff lines and the existing hard-core NTBs are assumed to adjust to accommodate the preferential trade expansion; in the second case, only tariff lines not affected by hard-core NTBs are considered. A tariffs-only FTA would curtail export expansion from Latin American countries by roughly 20 percent in comparison with the first liberalization scenario mentioned above. This result can be interpreted as a lower-bound estimate of the restrictions imposed by U.S. NTBs on the dynamism of Latin American exports.

The study by Erzan and Yeats also allows a comparison between the hub-and-spoke scenario and the advantages for each one of the eleven countries of signing an exclusive FTA with the United States (that is, without any other country being allowed to negotiate an FTA with the United States).[65] As far as export expansion goes, the erosion of preferences entailed by the multiple FTAs under a hub-and-spoke scenario does not seem to be significant. The total from adding the export expansion of exclusive FTAs is U.S.$2,925 million (in the broad liberalization scenario), which compares with U.S.$2,852.5 million under the hub-and-spoke format. One-third of this decline reflects the erosion of preferences experienced by Mexico, a result that can be interpreted as a *proxy* for the ''losses'' that Mexico will face if NAFTA is followed by additional FTAs in the context of the EAI. The authors also argue that Latin American countries could be significantly affected by the hub-and-spoke format to the extent that their intraregional trade could be disrupted by the preferential access gained by U.S. producers to each one of them.[66]

The potential for trade expansion for LAC countries in the context of a WHFTA does not seem particularly exciting. Actually, the estimates become even less impressive if one adds the possibility of additional MFN tariff and NTB cuts in the context of the Uruguay Round, as discussed in the previous section. It is true that these exercises do not capture potential benefits derived from an eventual "credibility-enhancement" effect for LAC governments of negotiating an FTA with the United States. The favorable "insurance effect" of more stable conditions of access to the U.S. market (presumably, one of the positive by-products of such FTAs for LAC countries) has not been quantified either.

The dangers of overestimating these other benefits, however, should be kept in mind. The significant increase in investment flows from the United States into Mexico is, for instance, often associated with expectations raised by NAFTA. One should not forget, however, the role of the tight Mexican stabilization program in restoring the credibility of the Mexican government from the perspective of foreign investors.[67] In other words, an external agreement is not a substitute for sound domestic economic policies.

The benefits of the so-called insurance effect should also be carefully evaluated. Contingent protection—antidumping (AD) and countervailing dutied (CVD) cases—has been a "growth industry" in the United States in the last decade. It is sometimes claimed that the small fraction of North American trade that is directly affected by these measures should be interpreted as a sign of their irrelevance at least from the perspective of the NAFTA negotiations.[68] One should not, however, underestimate the protectionist bias of these instruments and the fact that at the global level they already affect a significant share of trade flows.[69] Accordingly, the possibility that contingent protection may hinder the benefits of improved market access to the United States under an FTA has to be taken into account. One way to address these fears explicitly is to create binational dispute settlement regimes, as illustrated by chapters 18 and 19 of CUSFTA, in the future FTAs.[70] The extent to which rules will control power in this area is, however, an open question.

The positive response from most LAC countries to the EAI seems to reflect two basic considerations: (1) the limited options they have as to their pattern of insertion in the world economy—particularly in view of the current deadlock in the Uruguay Round negotiations; and (2) the recognition that the EAI (leaving aside conjectures about its effective implementation) represents a positive qualitative change in the focus of U.S. policy for the region.[71]

Systemic Implications

The systemic implications of the expansion of minilateral arrangements have been one of the most hotly debated themes in the recent literature on trade blocs.[72] One way to approach this issue, borrowing from Jagdish Bhagwati, is to ask to what extent NAFTA will be a "building block or a stumbling block" toward further global trade liberalization?[73]

The implications of the NAFTA talks for the final outcome of the Uruguay Round seem to be limited at best.[74] At this point, the main remaining areas of conflict at the multilateral level stand on their own quite independently of the evolution of the NAFTA negotiations. It is difficult to believe, for instance, that the EC position on agricultural trade could be significantly influenced by the evolution of the NAFTA talks. And the relevance of NAFTA as a future model for negotiations on the so-called new themes at the multilateral level is qualified by the fact that the United States, Mexico, and Canada have already achieved a much higher level of "systemic convergence" than the one prevailing at the multilateral level.

The case of intellectual property rights (IPRs) is illustrative in this context. There is no a priori guarantee that a developing country will benefit from strengthening its system of protection of IPRs.[75] Still, for countries following an outward-oriented development strategy, the risk of trade retaliation, combined with the interest in attracting foreign direct investment, may provide enough incentives to move them in that direction. Mexico, for instance, significantly revised its industrial property law in 1991 to "correct" its main weaknesses as perceived by intellectual property owners.[76] Accordingly, the levels of protection already in place in the United States, Mexico, and Canada (despite some important remaining differences with respect to pharmaceutical products) favor a NAFTA outcome that will certainly exceed the standards that may come out of the Uruguay Round negotiations.[77] In this context, the NAFTA negotiations as a model for multilateral intellectual property rights standards seem, at least in the near future, to have limited relevance.

The final outcome of the Uruguay Round may, however, influence the results of the NAFTA talks. Hufbauer and Schott, for instance, argue that a "successful" completion of the round may pave the way for the ratification of NAFTA in the United States by fostering MFN liberalization in sensitive areas (such as textiles and apparel) and deflecting the opposition of interest groups to NAFTA.[78] The lack of results at the multilateral level, in turn, would bolster the case of those who believe the trend toward minilateralism is inevitable. NAFTA would then probably achieve an even higher profile in the trade strategies of its participating countries, a development that could further erode the GATT system.

Hence, although one can debate the precise relationship between the NAFTA and the Uruguay Round results, the future of the multilateral system will clearly be influenced by the final format of NAFTA.[79] This influence may, in theory, be positive, if, as suggested by Bhagwati, NAFTA becomes an exercise in "programmatic" regionalism.[80] In this scenario, NAFTA would evolve into a liberal WHFTA. The Western Hemisphere would then negotiate as a bloc with other regional arrangements (organized around the EC and Japan) the elusive objective of multilateral free trade. Needless to say, the managed trade bias of the NAFTA negotiations does not augur well for this liberal scenario.

One can argue, however, that at least for LAC countries the NAFTA negotiations may foster further trade liberalization. The ongoing liberalization movement in the region was sparked by the macroeconomic developments of the 1980s (the fiscal and the foreign debt crises). Trade liberalization at the unilateral level was pursued in tandem with a renewed interest for minilateral integration at the subregional level. In a clear contrast with past experiences, however, the new minilateral arrangements assumed an outward-oriented profile.[81] Still, the degree of liberalization achieved so far by individual LAC countries varies significantly.

The success of the NAFTA talks is perceived as a necessary condition for the development of the trade component of the EAI—that is, WHFTA. "Progress in achieving open trade regimes" is one of the "indicators of readiness" identified by the Bush administration as a precondition for a country (or a group of countries) to qualify as a candidate for FTA negotiations.[82] Accordingly, it can be argued that the NAFTA talks reinforce the trend toward trade liberalization in the region, at least for those countries more strongly attracted by the U.S. proposal.

The enthusiasm for the EAI, although vivid, is not homogeneous across the region. As Fritsch has pointed out, the willingness of any given country to pursue an FTA with the United States tends to be positively correlated with the importance of the U.S. market for its exports and the degree of liberalization that it has already achieved.[83] The EAI (even if limited to an exercise in rhetoric) tends to support the liberal bias of current subregional integration schemes by providing additional bargaining chips for "liberal" countries engaged in these arrangements. Those countries are now in a stronger position to promote liberalization at the minilateral level, since they can always refer to the EAI, at least in principle, as a fallback position in their regional agenda.

In sum, NAFTA may well become a building block for a more liberal multilateral trade order. One can, however, easily imagine the opposite scenario, in which NAFTA becomes a managed trade initiative, promoting further discrimination against the ROW. Such a scenario would have one ironic implication for other countries in the Western Hemisphere. They would probably benefit more from the pursuit of the preconditions established by the United States in the EAI (macroeconomic stability, outward-oriented trade policies, GATT membership), than from the formation of an FTA with the United States in itself. Actually, if NAFTA sets the stage for a regional experiment in managed trade, excluded countries may fare better than the participants in this minilateral initiative.[84]

Final Remarks

The basic conclusion of the literature surveyed in this paper is that the overall impact of NAFTA on the rest of the world should not be significant if the agreement fosters freer trade among its participants. A danger exists, however, that NAFTA will become more a managed trade initiative (emphasizing the discriminatory administration of rules of origin and quotas) than one designed to liberalize trade on a preferential basis. In this scenario, NAFTA may have significant negative implications for both member and nonmember countries.

The systemic implications of NAFTA will essentially depend on the final format of the arrangement. If one perceives NAFTA as a trade-liberalizing movement, it is easier to argue that it will serve as a building block for a more liberal world trade order. The potential for harm, however, should not be underestimated.

Finally, in terms of the evolving research agenda on the implications of NAFTA for the rest of the world, the following themes deserve further attention: the role played by capital flows in the context of the NAFTA; the effect of discriminatory rules of origin on the firms of nonmember countries; and the influence of NAFTA on the investment strategies of transnational corporations.

Comment by Susan M. Collins

Primo Braga's paper provides a clear, interesting, and useful summary of some of the likely implications for NAFTA on countries in the rest of the world. These considerations suggest that, overall, NAFTA will have very small effects on nonmembers. I agree with most of the points Primo Braga raises. However, I have a nagging feeling that some of the more provocative and potentially important aspects of the question have been left out—issues that are not easily incorporated into computable general equilibrium models. A closer look at these additional issues may help to explain why some countries and some interest groups so actively oppose the agreement. Alternatively, playing devil's advocate may help to debunk some of the concerns raised by NAFTA opposition. In my comments, I first briefly summarize the main conclusions of the paper and then turn to a more speculative discussion of some of these omitted issues.

The paper reaches three conclusions. First, the economic effects of NAFTA on nonmembers as a group are likely to be small. The paper clearly explains this conclusion, pointing out that the implied liberalization of tariffs and nontariff barriers is unlikely to generate significant trade diversion. Second, however, the agreement could have a significant effect on producers or consumers in a few industries such as sugar and textiles. The paper could have gone into more depth to explain what these outcomes are likely to depend on. Third, the impact on specific country groups should be evaluated in terms of continuing economic relationships with NAFTA members. In particular, concerns that the Caribbean countries will be hurt by NAFTA may have been overstated in light of the fact that CARICOM (Caribbean Community) and Central American countries have already signed framework agreements with the United States—the first step for negotiating free trade agreements within the Enterprise for the Americas Initiative. This is an important point that has often been buried in the debate on this issue.

The paper basically implies that NAFTA is simply not a big concern for other countries. I share this view for the most part. However, some countries are less sanguine, and I doubt that this discussion goes far in convincing those who are initially nonbelievers. In the remainder of my comments, I take an alternative approach and ask the question: if NAFTA were to present problems for the rest of the world, from what areas would they be likely to come? There are at least three areas in which such difficulties could emerge: (1) the political economy of trade policy in the United States; (2) the implications of NAFTA for factor mobility (capital as well as labor); and (3) the implications for the terms of trade of non-members. I discuss each in turn, suggesting areas that could be interesting to explore further.

The paper does touch on some political economy considerations. It makes it clear that much of the action in negotiating NAFTA will concentrate on a few protected sectors, such as agriculture, where access to markets is key. It also provides some discussion of systemic trade-offs between regional and GATT trade negotiations. Let me raise a related issue: the outcome of trading negotiations between Western Hemisphere developing (WHD) countries and the United States may depend on whether NAFTA is in place, or more generally on the order in which various agreements are negotiated. It is possible that negotiating an agreement with Mexico first will result in a less favorable outcome for WHD countries than if Mexico and these countries came to the table together. Perhaps negotiating issues that are domestically sensitive has a high fixed cost in the United States so that addressing problem areas once (for Mexico) reduces the chances of a second change in the status quo in the near future. After Mexico has reached an agreement, its interests may conflict with those WHD countries seeking greater access to these U.S. markets. Of course, this might go the other way. Negotiation of NAFTA may pave the way for easier negotiations for WHD countries. I have seen relatively little analysis of these bargaining issues, and it is difficult to assess how important they are in practice.

A second potential problem area is factor migration. I focus here on the ability of WHD countries to attract foreign direct investment. In my view, economists know quite a bit about the conditions a country needs to make it attractive to foreign capital owners. Among other factors, these typically include a stable macroeconomic and political environment, protection of property rights, and the ability to repatriate earnings. Considerably less is known about the sufficient conditions to generate a direct foreign investment (DFI) inflow, however, and some countries remain unsuccessful despite the implementation of significant domestic adjustments. (Bolivia provides one such example.) This suggests to me the existence of inefficiencies and information problems in international capital markets. Investments may well be characterized by bandwagon and other effects.

In terms of the present discussion, the relevant question is whether these characteristics imply that having Mexico form an FTA with the

United States first has a negative impact of private capital flows from the United States to WHD countries. Additional empirical analysis on the determinants of DFI, and the extent to which flows to different recipients are substitutes or complements, could help to assess whether this concern is a valid one or not.

The third issue concerns terms of trade. It is well known that FTAs have a beggar-thy-neighbor aspect. When two countries form a free trade agreement, those countries that are left out tend to suffer a terms-of-trade deterioration, even in the absence of any changes in trade barriers with nonmembers. Let me raise a specific version of this terms-of-trade effect to illustrate the more general point that might deserve further attention.

In a world of restricted access to financing for external imbalances, real exchange rates play a critical adjustment role. For many Caribbean and Latin American countries, tourism is a major export. In this context, the concern is as follows. Suppose NAFTA (all else equal) causes a reorientation of U.S. and Canadian tourists toward Mexico and away from other vacation sites, such as Venezuela and Jamaica. That would cause a deterioration in the current accounts of these countries, perhaps requiring real depreciations and associated cuts in domestic living standards. In contrast, if all WHD countries negotiated FTAs together, such a shift in tourist destinations would be unlikely. Would NAFTA cause such a reorientation of tourism? On the one hand, some redirection is a likely response to the increased media focus on Mexico as negotiations proceed. On the other hand, most analysts expect the Mexican peso to sustain a real appreciation as a result of NAFTA. More expensive Mexican vacations could offset the effects of increased advertising. The potential for tourism diversion has received relatively little attention in discussions of trade diversion due to NAFTA. This is also an area in which additional empirical analysis could prove interesting and useful.

Overall, Primo Braga's conclusion that NAFTA would not have major implications for the rest of the world is about right. However, I would like to see much more discussion and analysis of issues that the CGE models do not tend to address. One or more of those issues may turn out to be very important.

Comment by Jeffrey J. Schott

NAFTA has sparked significant interest in its effect on the rest of the world, or "third countries," but surprisingly few have expressed concern about the potential implications of the agreement for their trading interests. Three types of countries could be affected by the NAFTA preferences:

—Countries that live in glass houses and thus are not going to throw stones at trade preferences similar to those they grant to their neighbors. Examples abound, since most countries participate in some type of preferential trading arrangement or another; most notable are the European Community, most countries in Latin America, and Australia and New Zealand.

—Countries that are concerned about the erosion of their existing preferences in the U.S. market, including the Caribbean countries and Canada. Indeed, concern about the erosion of preferences under the Canadian-U.S. Free Trade Agreement explains at least in part Canada's schizophrenic reaction to being one of the protagonists in the NAFTA negotiation.

—Countries that are beginning to voice concern about NAFTA because of potential trade or investment diversion. These are predominantly countries in East Asia (Japan, Korea, and Taiwan) that are not members of any preferential club and are not sure whether their rights are going to be protected under the multilateral trading system.

One can classify third-country concerns into three categories: trade diversion, investment diversion, and implications for the world trading system. Primo Braga includes one other category, the increased competitiveness of the countries involved in the preferential trading pact, but I regard that issue as a prominent part of the concern about investment diversion. The following sections provide some brief comments on each category of concern.

Trade Diversion

Concern that NAFTA will lead to a substantial diversion of trade has been relatively muted, for two reasons. First, existing barriers to the U.S. market (which accounts for about 85 percent of the North American region) are quite low. Indeed, under the Canadian-U.S. agreement, some firms have ignored the CUSFTA preferences, because the paperwork to qualify for the reduced tariffs was more expensive than paying the minimum duty!

The margin between the most-favored-nation rate that third countries pay, and the preferential (zero) rate applied under CUSFTA, is very small in most sectors—and is going to be reduced further by the GATT Uruguay Round reforms. Even in the textiles and apparel sector, the applied rates on Mexican exports to the United States are in the range of 6 to 8 percent because of the extensive U.S. duty drawback programs and preferences under the generalized system of preferences. In most cases, NAFTA preferences will not be a significant obstacle to third-country trade in North America.

Second, NAFTA is likely to cause very limited trade diversion *if* there is a successful Uruguay Round. The main areas of potential trade diversion are in the textiles and apparel, automobile, and agricultural sectors. Trade in these product sectors will be subject to extensive liberalization in the Uruguay Round if and when a GATT package of agreements is put together. For example, the draft final act of the Uruguay Round calls for the elimination of textile and apparel quotas over a ten-year period and for substantial tariff reductions (including the auto sector, where U.S. levies are already very low except for light trucks). Agriculture is the one area in which there could be some significant trade diversion because of uncertainty about how far the Uruguay Round (or NAFTA, for that matter) will go in terms of liberalization.

However, one cannot conclude a discussion of potential trade diversion without referring to the threat posed by rules of origin. In free trade areas, these rules are designed to prevent transshipment of imports from low-tariff to high-tariff countries and to determine which goods qualify for preferential treatment. The potential for abuse is large: negotiators are often tempted to construct backroom deals to appease sectoral interests by crafting special and more restrictive origin rules for specific industries that mask increased protection against third-country competition. That is already the situation in the NAFTA negotiations on textiles, in which the negotiators have seemingly reached an agreement on a triple transformation test that makes the already protectionist rule of origin on textiles in the CUSFTA seem liberal by comparison.

If the origin rule for textiles and apparel becomes a precedent for special rules for the auto, computer, and other sectors, then I think the worst fears of third countries will be realized. This problem should be the focus of much more attention than the concern raised by Primo Braga about the abuse of contingent protection laws. If anything, NAFTA is likely to provide some protection against the abuse of countervailing and anti-dumping duty practices by extending the special dispute settlement provisions of chapter 19 of CUSFTA to Mexico as well as Canada, and by instituting new disciplines on subsidies. In this area, NAFTA is likely to be a positive force—not toward changing existing laws, but toward ensuring that existing laws are administered properly and that future statutory and regulatory changes move in a liberalizing direction.

Investment Diversion

Third countries are right to worry about investment diversion, but most of the concern is inappropriately placed at the door of NAFTA. Investment diversion is more a function of the comprehensive economic reforms (including macroeconomic stabilization, deregulation, and privatization, as well as trade and investment liberalization) that are attracting investors to move into Mexico and other countries following a similar path of policy reform. The trade agreement is only a small part of the package of reforms that is influencing the investment decision.

In essence, countries are now competing in a global beauty contest to see which have the most desirable economic policies. The judging is being done by investors—both domestic and foreign—who vote with their capital. That is why Mexico has already capitalized on large inflows of funds, even before the free trade agreement has been negotiated and implemented. I think NAFTA will reinforce those trends.

On the other hand, the failure to achieve a free trade agreement (after a huge buildup of expectations) could send a shock wave through the capital markets that could cast doubts on the sustainability of the Salinas reform program and subsequently lead to a stabilization or even a reversal of those inflows critical to the financing of Mexico's growing current account deficit. That is a point that deserves much more attention than it has received.

Systemic Effects

Let me conclude with two quick points relating to the nexus between NAFTA and the Uruguay Round. First, if the Uruguay Round concludes before NAFTA, it should provide a strong base for crafting the final provisions of NAFTA—particularly in the areas of subsidies, intellectual property, and agriculture. In particular, it would greatly facilitate drafting a North American agreement on farm reform if the parameters of the commitments to subsidy reductions in the multilateral deal were known.

However, if NAFTA precedes the conclusion of the Uruguay Round (as now seems entirely possible), there is a danger that the provisions of NAFTA—especially the rules of origin—could be crafted with a more managed trade focus, at least in certain sectors. The rationale behind such an approach (at least in the textiles and apparel sectors) would be to defuse some of the opposition to an eventual deal in the Uruguay Round by limiting foreign competition in the North American market. However, if NAFTA precedes the Uruguay Round, it will be more difficult to reach North American deals on agriculture and intellectual property. In the latter case, for example, the Canadians would have a problem in making a concession on compulsory licensing of pharmaceutical patents in the North American context (recall they refused to do so in CUSFTA); it would be a lot easier politically for them to do so in a multilateral context.

Finally, in light of such concerns about managed trade, GATT members should take a close look at the consistency of NAFTA with the spirit and letter of GATT obligations. With regard to the letter of the law—that is, the requirements of GATT article XXIV to qualify to grant discriminatory trade preferences to FTA partners despite the MFN obligation of GATT article I—NAFTA is likely to pass muster as well as any other FTA that has been notified to the GATT. The problem is that GATT article XXIV reviews are lackluster and provide little discipline on the preferences accorded under FTAs and customs unions. As a result, enforcement of GATT requirements is lax and ineffective.

The proliferation of preferential trading arrangements in Europe, North America, and Latin America makes it increasingly important that GATT obligations under article XXIV and GATT reviews of FTAs and customs unions are strengthened. In particular, there is a strong need to institute formal multilateral monitoring of all preferential trade pacts—not just in North America but also in the evolving European economic area.

The GATT's new trade policy review mechanism (TPRM) could be used to examine prospective preferential trade pacts under negotiation by the country subject to review, and then to monitor the implementation of the final agreement over time to ensure that it does not adversely affect the trading interests of third countries. The TPRM could analyze both the schedule of trade liberalization and the trade rules (for example, rules of origin and dispute settlement procedures) to guard against opaque protectionism hidden in the agreement. Enhanced multilateral monitoring of FTAs is essential to ensure the consistency of preferential trading arrangements with the GATT.

Notes

1. For simplicity, the term "minilateralism" is used to characterize any type of preferential arrangement (free trade areas, custom unions, common markets, and so on). A minilateral arrangement is a treaty negotiated among trading partners, which violates the most-favored-nation rule—unilateral concessions, such as the generalized systems of preferences of industrialized countries, are not considered in this context. The term multilateralism, in turn, is used as synonymous with the General Agreement on Tariffs and Trade (GATT).

2. See, for example, Gary C. Hufbauer and Jeffrey J. Schott, *North American Free Trade: Issues and Recommendations* (Washington: Institute for International Economics, 1992); Jagdish Bhagwati, *The World Trading System at Risk* (Princeton University Press, 1991); and Sidney Weintraub, "A North American Free Trade Area and the Rest of the World," in G. E. Lich and J. A. McKinney, eds., *Region North America: Canada, United States, Mexico* (Baylor University, 1990).

3. See, for example, Hufbauer and Schott, *North American Free Trade*; Sidney Weintraub, *A Marriage of Convenience: Relations between Mexico and the United States* (Oxford University Press, 1990); and Rudiger Dornbusch, "U.S.-Mexican Trade Relations," Testimony before the Subcommittee on Trade of the House Committee on Ways and Means, June 14, 1990.

4. William E. Brock, former U.S. Trade Representative, summarized this position in 1984 in the following way: "Without any diminution in its adherence to or support for the GATT, the United States is proceeding with various groups of countries or individual countries to explore trade liberalization on a basis less comprehensive than GATT. . . . The reasoning behind these efforts is that additional trade-creating, GATT-consistent liberalization measures should not be postponed while some of the more inward-looking contracting parties contemplate their own economic malaise." See William E. Brock, "U.S. Trade Policy toward Developing Countries," in Ernest H. Preeg, ed., *Hard Bargaining Ahead: U.S. Trade Policy and Developing Countries* (Washington: Overseas Development Council, 1985), p. 38.

5. More than sixty former European colonies and dependencies benefit from almost tariff-free access, as well as reduced levies under the Common Agricultural Policy, to the EC market under the Lome Convention. For further details, see, for example, Christopher Stevens, ed., *EEC and the Third World: A Survey 4—Renegotiating Lome* (London: Hodder and Stoughton, 1984).

6. This perspective is discussed in John Whalley, "Regional Trade Arrangements in North America: CUSFTA and NAFTA," paper presented at a World Bank-CEPR Conference on New Dimensions in Regional Integration, Washington, April 1992.

7. For an analysis of this evolution, see, for example, Rodney de C. Grey, *Concepts of Trade Diplomacy and Trade in Services*, Thames Essays (London: Trade Policy Research Centre, 1990).

8. Article XXIV does not rely on the conventional concepts of trade creation and trade diversion, often used to evaluate the economic adequacy of a minilateral arrangement. That should come as no surprise, since these concepts were formally

introduced by Jacob Viner three years after the draft of the General Agreement. See Viner, *The Customs Union Issue* (New York: Carnegie Endowment for International Peace, 1950). For a summary review of the historical developments that led to the inclusion of article XXIV in the GATT, see Bhagwati, *World Trading System at Risk*, pp. 63–66; and J. Michael Finger, "GATT's Influence on Regional Arrangements," paper presented at a World Bank–CEPR Conference on New Dimensions on Economic Integration, Washington, April 1992.

9. For further details on the dimensions of international trade conducted under minilateral arrangements, see C. A. Primo Braga and Alexander J. Yeats, "The Simple Arithmetic of Existing Minilateral Trading Arrangements and Its Implications for a Post–Uruguay Round World," International Trade Division working paper (Washington: World Bank, 1992).

10. According to Jeffrey Schott, the following agreements were found compatible with article XXIV: the South Africa–Rhodesia customs union (1948); the Nicaragua–El Salvador FTA (1951); the Nicaraguan accession to the Central American Free Trade Area (1958); and the Caribbean Community and Common Market. "More Free Trade Areas?" in Jeffrey J. Schott, ed., *Free Trade Areas and U.S. Trade Policy* (Washington: Institute for International Economics, 1989), p. 25. It is worth mentioning that the recently released report of the working party on the Canada-U.S. Free Trade Agreement has kept the tradition, to the extent that it was unable to conclude on the consistency of this agreement with the GATT. See "Report on Canada-US FTA Adopted," *Focus*, November–December 1991, p. 5.

11. The reasons behind this change in attitude are discussed, for example, in Schott, "More Free Trade Areas?" and J. Bhagwati, "Regionalism vs. Multilateralism: An Overview," paper presented at a World Bank–CEPR Conference on New Dimensions in Regional Integration, Washington, April 1992.

12. Also on June 27, 1990, the Bush administration announced the EAI, raising the possibility of additional FTA negotiations with other countries in the Western Hemisphere.

13. For a detailed presentation of the working groups in the NAFTA negotiations, see Whalley, "Regional Trade Arrangements in North America," pp. 13–23.

14. Hufbauer and Schott, *North American Free Trade*, chap. 2, as well as Whalley, "Regional Trade Arrangements in North America," sec. 2, analyze the links between CUSFTA and NAFTA.

15. On this point, see Bernard Hoekman, "Market Access and Multilateral Trade Agreements: The Uruguay Round Services Negotiations," Discussion Paper 294 (University of Michigan, Institute of Public Policy Studies, 1992).

16. In reality, since 1987 a series of bilateral agreements—such as the 1987 Framework Understanding—were paving the way for a closer economic relationship between the United States and Mexico. For a list of these agreements, see, for example, U.S. International Trade Commission, *The Likely Impact on the United States of a Free Trade Agreement with Mexico*, USITC 2353 (Washington, 1991), pp. 1–8 and 1–9.

17. As pointed out by Hufbauer and Schott, *North American Free Trade*, pp. 7–10, the EC expansion to incorporate Greece, Spain, and Portugal posed similar problems. Yet, insofar as the discrepancy in income levels for NAFTA is larger, and since

the agreement does not consider the possibility of income transfers or regional subsidies to the weaker member (in a clear contrast with the EC experience), NAFTA has a unique character.

18. For detailed analyses of the main reasons that led the United States, Mexico, and Canada to engage in the NAFTA talks, see the collection of papers of the "Symposium on North American Free Trade," Gustavo Vega, ed., in *World Economy*, vol. 14 (March 1991), pp. 53–111.

19. Whalley, "Regional Trade Arrangements in North America," p. 14.

20. For a discussion of the hub-and-spoke concept, see Ronald J. Wonnacott, "U.S. Hub-and-Spoke Bilaterals and the Multilateral Trading System," in *Commentary* (Toronto: C. D. Howe Institute, 1990). David Cox and Richard G. Harris suggest that Canada would be basically indifferent—as far as welfare, trade volumes, and real wages are concerned—between a hub-and-spoke format and NAFTA. "North American Free Trade and Its Implications for Canada: Results from a CGE Model of North American Trade," *World Economy*, vol. 15 (January 1992), pp. 31–44.

21. An alternative scenario for the evolution of FTAs in the Western Hemisphere is presented by Sylvia Saborio. The growing perception in Latin America and the Caribbean that Washington does not have yet a well-defined post-NAFTA agenda paves the way for a "NAFTA + Mexico Hub-and-Spoke" structure, as other countries in the region negotiate separate FTAs with Mexico in an attempt "to be where the action is." See "Statement by Sylvia Saborio before the Joint Economic Committee, Congress of the United States," Washington, April 2, 1992, p. 5.

22. For further details, see Viner, *Customs Union*; and Paul Wonnacott and Mark Lutz, "Is There a Case for Free Trade Areas?" in Schott, ed., *Free Trade Areas and U.S. Trade Policy*. It is worth pointing out that Kemp and Wan have shown that customs unions can always be designed in such a way as to generate a Pareto-superior outcome from the point of view of member countries. Murray C. Kemp and Henry Wan, Jr., "An Elementary Proposition Concerning the Formation of Customs Unions," *Journal of International Economics*, vol. 6 (February 1976), pp. 95–98.

23. In reality, as shown by Meade, a trade-diverting customs union is not necessarily welfare-worsening, if substitution in consumption is allowed. Collier has shown that a trade-creating union does not need to be welfare-increasing in a multigood world. See James E. Meade, *The Theory of Customs Unions* (Amsterdam: North Holland, 1955); and Paul Collier, "The Welfare Effects of Customs Unions: An Anatomy," *Economic Journal*, vol. 89 (March 1979), pp. 84–95.

24. For an example of a partial equilibrium analysis of the economic effects of FTAs between the United States and Latin American countries, see Refik Erzan and Alexander Yeats, "Free Trade Agreements with the United States: What's in It for Latin America?" Working Paper 827 (Washington: World Bank, 1992).

25. See, for example, Bob Hamilton and John Whalley, "Geographically Discriminatory Trade Arrangements," *Review of Economics and Statistics*, vol. 67 (August 1985), pp. 446–55.

26. For a review of the main quantitative studies focusing on CUSFTA, see Drusilla Brown and Robert M. Stern, "Some Conceptual Issues in the Modeling and Computational Analysis of the Canada-U.S. Free Trade Agreement," paper presented at the 1991 Annual Meeting of the International Agricultural Trade Research Consortium, New Orleans, December 1991.

27. For a description of the standard partial equilibrium model used for trade creation and trade diversion calculations, see, for example, William Cline and others, *Trade Negotiations in The Tokyo Round—A Quantitative Assessment* (Brookings, 1978). An analysis of some of the shortcomings of this approach is provided in Samuel Laird and Alexander J. Yeats, "Two Sources of Bias in Standard Partial Equilibrium Trade Models," Working Paper 374 (Washington: World Bank, 1990).

28. Data for 1983 trade flows were used in this exercise. See Samuel Laird, "U.S. Trade Policy and Mexico: Simulations of Possible Trade Regime Changes," International Trade Division working paper (Washington: World Bank, 1990).

29. The U.S.-Mexican FTA was assumed to entail zero duties for all tariff lines and adjustment of prevailing hard-core NTBs to accommodate the preferential trade expansion. See Erzan and Yeats, "Free Trade Agreements," p. 44.

30. This section focuses on CGE models that explicitly address NAFTA. There are many other CGE exercises that focus, for instance, on a U.S.-Mexican FTA. Their results, however, are not at odds with the main conclusions presented above, as far as the economic implications for the ROW are concerned. See, for example, Raúl Hinojosa-Ojeda and Sherman Robinson, "Alternative Scenarios of U.S.-Mexico Integration: A Computable General Equilibrium Approach," Working Paper 609 (University of California, Berkeley, Department of Agricultural and Resource Economics, April 1991); and Carlos Bachrach and Lorris Mizrahi, "The Economic Impact of a Free Trade Agreement between the United States and Mexico: A CGE Analysis" (Washington: KPMG Peat Marwick, February 1992).

31. Drusilla K. Brown, Alan V. Deardorff, and Robert M. Stern, "A North American Free Trade Agreement: Analytical Issues and a Computational Assessment," *World Economy*, vol. 15 (January 1992), pp. 11–30; Horacio E. Sobarzo, "A General Equilibrium Analysis of the Gains from Trade for the Mexican Economy of a North American Free Trade Agreement," *World Economy*, vol. 15 (January 1992), pp. 83–100; and Cox and Harris, "North American Free Trade and Its Implications."

32. Sobarzo, "General Equilibrium Analysis," p. 93. Note that the welfare impact of both scenarios is approximately the same (see table 1). This is explained by the fact that despite the larger expansion of the Mexican economy in case 2 compared with case 1, the additional income generated by the use of foreign capital does not belong to Mexican nationals.

33. Ibid. Mexico's overall trade balance experiences an 18.3 percent deterioration, reflecting an 18.9 percent deterioration with the rest of North America (United States and Canada) and a 17.1 percent deterioration with the ROW.

34. See, for example, Leslie Young and Jose Romero, "A Dynamic Dual Model of the Free Trade Agreement," paper presented at the conference "North American Free Trade," Federal Reserve Bank of Dallas, June 1991; and Timothy J. Kehoe, "Modeling the Dynamic Impact of North American Free Trade," Working Paper 491 (Federal Reserve Bank of Minneapolis, March 1992.

35. See Hufbauer and Schott, *North American Free Trade*, chap. 3.

36. Historical data on liberalization experiments are derived from Demetris Papageorgiou, Michael Michaely, and Armeane M. Choksi, eds., *Liberalizing Foreign Trade: Lessons of Experience in the Developing World*, vol. 7. (Cambridge, Mass.: Basil Blackwell for the World Bank, 1991).

37. Hufbauer and Schott, *North American Free Trade*, p. 60.

38. Sherman Robinson, Mary E. Burfisher, Raúl Hinojosa-Ojeda, and Karen E. Thierfelder, "Agricultural Policies and Migration in a U.S.-Mexico Free Trade Area: A Computable General Equilibrium Analysis," Working Paper 617 (University of California, Berkeley, Department of Agricultural and Resource Economics, 1991).

39. Accordingly, they recommend gradualism in the liberalization of Mexican agriculture to avoid "large rural outmigration from Mexico." See Robinson and others, "Agricultural Policies," p. 33.

40. Thomas Grennes and others, "An Analysis of a United States-Canada-Mexico Free Trade Agreement," International Agricultural Trade Research Consortium, November 1991.

41. Ibid., p. 41.

42. See Spreen and others, in American Farm Bureau Federation, *NAFTA: Effects on Agriculture*, vol. 4 (Park Ridge, Ill., 1991).

43. Brent Borrell and Jonathan R. Coleman, "Gains from Trade in Sugar and the U.S.-Mexico Free Trade Agreement," working paper (Canberra: Centre for International Economics, 1991).

44. See Irena Trela and John Whalley, "Trade Liberalisation in Quota Restricted Items: US and Mexico in Textiles and Steel," *World Economy*, vol. 15 (January 1992), pp. 45–64.

45. Ibid., table 5.

46. See, for example, Hufbauer and Schott, *North American Free Trade*, pp. 160–61; and Geoffrey Bannister and Patrick Low, "North American Free Trade in Textiles and Apparel: A Case of Constrained Liberalization," World Bank, International Trade Division, Washington, 1992.

47. See, for example, Jan Herin, "Rules of Origin and Differences between Tariff Levels in EFTA and in the EC," Occasional Paper 13 (Geneva: EFTA Secretariat, 1986).

48. According to Hufbauer and Schott, *North American Free Trade*, p. 161, the American Apparel Manufacturers Association even defended a "down to the cotton ball" rule of origin for NAFTA, which could be interpreted as a quadruple transformation rule.

49. Bannister and Low, "North American Free Trade in Textiles and Apparel."

50. See Trela and Whalley, "Trade Liberalisation in Quota Restricted Items."

51. See Hufbauer and Schott, *North American Free Trade*, p. 250.

52. For details on the U.S. and Mexican structures of protection with respect to the steel industry, see U.S. International Trade Commission, "Review of Trade and Investment Liberalization Measures by Mexico and Prospects for Future United States–Mexican Relations," USITC 2326 (Washington, 1990), pp. 2–23.

53. See Linda Hunter, James R. Markusen, and Thomas F. Rutherford, "U.S.-Mexico Free Trade and the North American Auto Industry: Effects on the Spatial Organisation of Production of Finished Autos," *World Economy*, vol. 15 (January 1992), pp. 65–81.

54. The U.S. and Canadian results are explained in terms of the domination of the industry by TNCs. According to the authors, imports from Mexico are not interpreted as a loss of market by the U.S. TNCs, given the pattern of plant ownership in the industry. See Hunter, Markusen, and Rutherford, "Free Trade and the Auto Industry," p. 80.

55. Taking into account vehicles, engines, and auto parts, exports accounted, respectively, for 48.4 percent, 68.4 percent, and 81.5 percent of the total sales by GM, Ford, and Chrysler Mexican operations in 1987. The totality of these exports in the case of Chrysler and Ford went to North America (60 percent in the case of GM). Exports from Volkswagen and Nissan, in turn, were estimated to represent at most 35 percent of their sales, with a more diversified trade orientation (for instance, only 20 percent of the Mexican Volkswagen exports went to North America). See United Nations Centre of Transnational Corporations, *World Investment Report, 1991: The Triad in Foreign Direct Investment* (New York, 1991).

56. See UNCTC, "Foreign Direct Investment and Industrial Restructuring in Mexico," UNCTC Current Studies 18 (New York, 1992), p. 78.

57. For details, see Hufbauer and Schott, *North American Free Trade*, p. 231.

58. See "Major Automakers Are Divided over Free Trade Rules of Origin," *U.S.-Mexico Free Trade Reporter* 1 (December 16, 1991), p. 7.

59. Zenith Eletronics Corporation, a U.S. company, has announced its decision to transfer a manufacturing plant from Taiwan to Mexico. This resolution has been interpreted as an evidence of the role played by expectations about NAFTA in the allocation of resources of TNCs. UNCTC, "FDI and Industrial Restructuring in Mexico," p. 78.

60. The debate in the U.S. Congress concerning the grant of fast-track authority for NAFTA negotiations, for instance, provides evidence that there is support for discriminatory rules of origin in the United States. See *Proposed Negotiation of a Free Trade Agreement with Mexico*, Hearings before the Subcommittee on Trade of the House Committee on Ways and Means, 102 Cong. 1 sess. (Government Printing Office, 1991), pp. 531, 632–33.

61. In a survey of the 114 statements presented at the hearings before the two committees that have a decisive say in the United States for the granting of fast-track authority (the House Ways and Means Committee and the Senate Finance Committee), CBI countries were the ones most often mentioned as potential losers from NAFTA.

62. Julio Nogues and Rosalinda Quintanilla, "Latin America's Integration and the Multilateral Trading System," World Bank-CEPR Conference on New Dimensions in Regional Integration, Washington, April 1992, p. 41.

63. See Erzan and Yeats, "Free Trade Agreements."

64. The countries considered were Argentina, Bolivia, Brazil, Chile, Colombia, Ecuador, Mexico, Paraguay, Peru, Uruguay, and Venezuela. See Erzan and Yeats, "Free Trade Agreements," p. 32.

65. Ibid., pp. 32–34.

66. Ibid., pp. 39–42.

67. On this theme see Liliana Rojas-Suarez, "From the Debt Crisis toward Economic Stability: An Analysis of the Consistency of Macroeconomic Policies in Mexico," International Monetary Fund working paper, Washington, 1992.

68. See, for instance, the comments on the relative importance of AD investigations made by Michael Stein, as quoted in Hufbauer and Schott, *North American Free Trade*, p. 30.

69. According to the SMART data bank, the percentages of total exports to the United States covered by these actions in 1989 were the following: AD duties (3.12 percent), AD investigations (11.58 percent), CVDs (0.62 percent), CVD investigations

(4.06 percent), price undertakings linked to AD cases (0.67 percent). Voluntary export restraints (often an outcome of contingent protection investigations) affected 7.59 percent of total exports to the United States.

70. Chapter 18 provides a dispute resolution process to address eventual disagreements in the interpretation or implementation of the CUSFTA provisions. Chapter 19, in turn, provides for the review of AD or CVD determinations taken either by the United States or Canada. For a review of the use of CUSFTA's dispute settlement regime, see Judith H. Bello, Alan F. Holmer, and Debra A. Kelly, "Midterm Report on Binational Dispute Settlement under the United States-Canada Free Trade Agreement," *International Lawyer*, vol. 25 (Summer 1991), pp. 489–516.

71. This second point is discussed in further detail by Peter Hakim, "President Bush's Southern Strategy: The Enterprise for the Americas Initiative," *Washington Quarterly*, Spring 1992, pp. 93–106. It is also worth remembering that the EAI has an investment component and a debt-relief component (besides its trade aspect), which, despite their limitations, have attracted the attention of some LAC countries.

72. See, for example, Bhagwati, *Trade System at Risk*; and Paul Krugman, "Is Bilateralism Bad?" in Elhanan Helpman and Assaf Razin, eds., *International Trade and Trade Policy* (Cambridge, Mass.: MIT Press, 1991).

73. See Robert Z. Lawrence, "Emerging Regional Arrangements: Building Blocks or Stumbling Blocks?" in Richard O'Brien, ed., *Finance and the International Economy*, vol. 5 (Oxford University Press, 1991).

74. It is sometimes argued that NAFTA may be used as "a prod for the multilateral process and as a model for GATT provisions in new areas such as intellectual property rights." See Hufbauer and Schott, *North American Free Trade*, p. 43.

75. See C. A. Primo Braga, "The Developing Country Case for and Against Intellectual Property Protection, in W. E. Siebeck, ed., *Strengthening Protection of Intellectual Property in Developing Countries: A Survey of the Literature*, World Bank Discussion Paper 112 (Washington, 1990).

76. For details, see Roberto Villarreal Gonda, "The New Mexican Law on Industrial Property," *Industrial Property*, November 1991, pp. 436–45.

77. For analyses of potential outcomes for IPRs negotiations at the NAFTA and multilateral levels, see Robert M. Sherwood, "Intellectual Property and Free Trade in North America," paper presented at the conference How is Free Trade Progressing? Fraser Institute, Toronto, November 1991; Jacques J. Gorlin, "Update on International Negotiations on Intellectual Property Rights," paper presented at the conference The Global Dimensions of Intellectual Property Rights in Science and Technology, National Research Council, Washington, January 1992.

78. See Hufbauer and Schott, *North American Free Trade*, p. 43.

79. In response to the pressure of interest groups in the United States, the Bush administration submitted to the Congress an action plan addressing environmental and labor issues linked to the NAFTA negotiations. Although the negotiations on these themes are supposed to evolve on a different track from the NAFTA talks, this development underscores the growing complexity of trade negotiations. It also suggests that it will become increasingly difficult to avoid the inclusion of nontrade issues— particularly, the environment—in the multilateral negotiations. On the Bush administration's action plan, see Laura Rawlings, "The North American Free Trade Agreement," *Policy Focus*, vol. 2 (Washington: Overseas Development Council, 1992).

80. See Bhagwati, "Regionalism vs. Multilateralism," p. 33.

81. For details concerning the history of minilateral arrangements in Latin America, see, for example, C. A. Primo Braga, "U.S. Policies and the Prospects for Latin American Economic Integration," in Werner Baer and Donald V. Coes, eds., *United States Policies and the Latin American Economies* (Praeger, 1990); and Nogues and Quintanilla, "Latin America's Integration."

82. See Jeffrey J. Schott and Gary C. Hufbauer, "Free Trade Areas, the Enterprise for the Americas Initiative, and the Multilateral Trading System: Implications for Latin America," paper presented at the OECD-IDB International Forum on Strategic Options for Latin American Trade in the 1990s, Paris, November 1991.

83. Winston Fritsch, "Hemispheric Integration: Will Trade Discrimination Pay?" Inter-American Dialogue working paper, Washington, 1992.

84. Whalley, "Regional Trade Arrangements," p. 50.

Panel
Discussion

Discussion by Carlos Bazdresch Parada

Instead of summarizing the many valuable opinions from the interesting debate on NAFTA, I would like to emphasize some specific points. The first concerns the magnitude of the economic benefits of signing NAFTA. As Drusilla Brown summarizes in her paper, several applied general equilibrium models show these benefits to be small. Of course, their benefits are greater for Mexico than for the United States. Besides, these benefits increase as one assumes more consequences associated with NAFTA. Thus the dynamic models that consider the effect of the capital flows NAFTA could cause point to much larger benefits than the static ones. However, the dynamic models have much less empirical content, so their results are less reliable.

These results seem puzzling. Why, given its low projected impact, is there so much concern about NAFTA? Was the expectation of much larger benefits wrong? Perhaps, as Robert Pastor suggests, NAFTA is just another aspect of a larger integration process, so that interest in it is fueled also by noneconomic concerns?

I do not think one should be surprised that the static benefits are projected to be small. First, as Sherman Robinson pointed out at the conference, the Mexican economy is small relative to the U.S. economy, so that whatever happens in Mexico will not have a "large" proportional effect in the United States. Besides, both economies have already reduced tariffs significantly. The static benefits of eliminating low tariffs cannot be very large.

On the other hand, ever since Tibor Scitovsky underestimated many years ago the static economic benefits of integrating Europe as a 1–2 percent increase in joint GDP, economists have been aware that this kind of analysis tends to yield very low figures.[1] The reason, as Scitovsky pointed out later, is that this analysis does not include the competitiveness gains that the participating economies may obtain through the integration process, nor the positive contributions of various associated dynamic effects.

Some of these effects are considered in the Young-Romero model, which includes the impact of the capital inflows that Mexico may receive as a consequence of NAFTA. In this way their model projects much larger benefits for Mexico than the other models. I think Young and Romero are on the right track, because to me it is clear that the important NAFTA effects will occur only in the long run. However, one should be conscious of the speculative nature of this work.

Even if results obtained up to now with the AGE models are not surprising, this work should continue. At the very least, the model-building activity introduces more economists—from both sides of the border—to the Mexican and U.S. economies, and to one another.

In addition, these models are useful in quantifying well-known effects, so that research may concentrate on the less obvious consequences of NAFTA. As an example, I would highlight the assertion of Hinojosa and Robinson that one should not expect the migration of low-wage Mexican labor into the United States to end with NAFTA. Many have suspected this fact, but Hinojosa and Robinson provide data to substantiate this belief.

The results already obtained with the AGE models indicate that more detailed models are needed to explore the flows of capital and labor that may result from NAFTA. Here I would like to point out that no one has studied the potential flows of skilled labor from the United States and Canada into Mexico. I think that this migration, even if temporary, may be substantial and may have important effects on both countries.

Also, it is important to study the short-run transitional problems that may arise, mainly in Mexico, when the NAFTA mechanisms are introduced. The present evolution of the Mexican economy suggests that these difficulties may not be trivial.

The general assumption is that NAFTA will result in an increase in competition, at least in the Mexican economy. However, as Carlos Alberto Primo Braga warns, this is not necessarily true. NAFTA may be the framework for a set of managed trade deals.

This point needs to be investigated, or, at least, recognized as a possibility. Considering the present situation of the Mexican economy, with its high degree of oligopolization, the big companies—American or otherwise—may not like the idea of competing with one another. With a market of that size, competition may not seem worth the effort. Therefore, despite NAFTA, large companies may prefer to protect their sales through negotiated deals, not market competition.

What would happen in that situation? The question concerns not only trade diversion but those who would benefit from this diversion. Further, what would be the reaction of the companies whose headquarters are located outside NAFTA? Would they attempt to restrict their sales also? Or, perhaps, would they try to seize new NAFTA opportunities by expanding their sales?

The answer will depend on many factors, but in any case one should be aware that managed trade practices may creep in unless all countries involved maintain a strong desire for free trade. Of course, not having more competition within the Mexican economy would imply a serious reduction of the benefits that Mexico could obtain from NAFTA.

It is true that many Mexicans expect that signing NAFTA will greatly reduce the danger of arbitrary U.S. and Canadian contingent protectionism. Maybe that assumption is too optimistic, but I still think that Barry Bosworth is right in asserting that at least in the long run the United States–Canada, even more—will abide by the law even if it has to be reasserted by the panels established to resolve conflicts. Obviously, this aspect of NAFTA will depend heavily on how the dispute resolution issue is handled in the NAFTA text, but I do not agree with Primo Braga that "there is little scope for rules to control power in this area."

In contrast with these doubts, the evolution of cooperation in the non-trade areas has been encouraging. The greater attention paid by both the U.S. and Mexican governments—especially the latter—to environmental and labor regulation issues constitutes a good and somewhat surprising side effect of the NAFTA negotiations. As Pastor pointed out, NAFTA is merely part of a much wider change in relations between Mexico and the United States. This widening integration, which has yet to be officially recognized in the policy agendas of both governments, tends to demand more cooperation than both governments are currently able to manage.

One implication of this shift is that along with the trade issue, other issues, most of them concerning public policy, will keep appearing. Accordingly, all NAFTA observers should be prepared to focus their attention on those issues, as well as on more immediate questions of trade policy.

Discussion by Sylvia Ostry

All the contributions in this book have interpreted NAFTA research as a comparison of different econometric models designed to estimate and analyze the impact of NAFTA on the three participating countries. In this summary, I introduce a different context, shifting from models to political economy. Since NAFTA is widely regarded as evidence of a broader trend to regionalization in the international trading system, it is useful to situate the North American developments within a framework of a regional taxonomy based on the nature and extent of integration, both economic and political. The spectrum of integration runs from the European Community, a region of progressively deepening integration in multiple dimensions— political, economic, and institutional—to the primarily economic, or "natural" integration of North America and east Asia, which differ in some significant ways related to the primary integrating element of factor flows. The purpose of this comparative analytic approach is to highlight issues that are likely to help determine the future evolution of NAFTA and hence merit both further research and policy analyses.

Because the EC is the most advanced (indeed the only) example of deep regional integration, the essential elements of the European paradigm are worth spelling out in some detail.

The European Community: Deep Integration

The original impetus to the formation of the European Community (and before it, the European Coal and Steel Community) was *political*: to reconcile countries that had fought bitter wars over the previous century. This *political* contract between France and Germany was, and continues to be, the foundation for European cohesion. The *means* chosen to achieve this cohesion were economic: initially trade and agriculture, though the ultimate economic objective was far more ambitious—the achievement of the four freedoms enshrined in the Treaty of Rome, the free movement of goods, services, capital, and people. After years of piecemeal fiddling and stop-go moves, the goal often seemed out of reach until an astonishing momentum to deepening integration developed in the 1980s. The spark that lit the fire in 1985 (marked by the publication of the Commission White Paper) was an external economic development. The impact of the OPEC (Organization of Petroleum Exporting Countries) price shocks exposed serious structural rigidities in European economies, causing rising unemployment and serious pressure on profits. A new disease called Eurosclerosis was diagnosed, along with an accompanying disorder termed Europessimism, which reflected deep fear of declining competitiveness vis-à-vis the United States.

In response to this crisis, Europe's business elite rallied to create a new organization, the European Roundtable, with a channel of communication to the European Commission in Brussels and especially to the dynamic, newly appointed president, Jacques Delors, as well as to key political figures in member states. The essence of the business response to external challenges was an urgent call for the completion of the internal market to create the internal capabilities required to compete abroad.

The vision of a competitive Europe became the consensus driver that led to the Single European Act in 1986, a major amendment to the Treaty of Rome that launched Europe 1992, the removal of all barriers to mobility within Europe. Helping to forge the consensus was Delors's vision of the European social market economy, in which a social Europe was integral to a competitive economic union. The elements of a social Europe took longer to spell out than those of the economic union and only emerged five years later at Maastricht, in December 1991, though without agreement by the United Kingdom.

Thus it is clear that the force behind the 1980s' momentum for completing the internal market was mainly a response to a global economic challenge. (Paradoxically, the external trading environment was not a consideration and, indeed, virtually no information on the external trade implications was provided for several years, thus creating suspicions about Fortress Europe.) So, the EC paradigm of the 1980s is an *external shock* followed by a coherent *response of elites* that leads to the creation of a *consensus driver* focused primarily on internal capabilities and an emerging shared vision of a *social market economy*. But underlying all that, it is important to remember, was the original political ties that created the Treaty of Rome.

To illustrate the nature of deep integration, it is useful to enumerate the main elements of the Single European Act. First is microconvergence. The act provided for qualified majority voting for most Commission directives and regulations necessary for the removal of nearly 300 internal border barriers. But the act also provided the means of harmonizing domestic regulations in the member states, that is, product standards, pollution safeguards, financial regulations, government procurement—or microconvergence. It established the European Technology Community, which gave the Commission enhanced powers in the fields of research and development, education, and training to promote coordination in science and technology policy, reflecting the originating emphasis on competitiveness. Finally, it strengthened and reinforced the Commission's role in competition policy not only with respect to the private sector but also for government subsidies (with specific and clearly defined exceptions such as regional policy) to create a meaningful level playing field.

Of course, the progressively deeper integration of the EC did not stop with the 1992 project. A three-stage passage to full monetary union was adopted at the meeting in Maastricht in December 1991. The economic and monetary union (EMU) program will impose strict conditions for membership (so-called nominal, or macroeconomic convergence) involving satisfactory performance in fiscal policy and inflation. The punishment for not achieving these rigorous goals of fiscal and monetary rectitude will be exile from EMU, not a veto over its implementation.

Another significant development of Maastricht that deserves mention here was the launch of the European Environmental Community. The word *environment* did not even appear in the Treaty of Rome; if it had, the meaning would be quite different from that of today. The first environmental program of the EC was established in 1973. Thus twenty years of supranational policy development preceded the Maastricht amendment to the treaty, and that amendment reflects the heightened political importance of environmental issues in many European countries (and especially in the European Parliament). It will give the Commission significant new powers to represent the Community in negotiations on the environment with both international organizations and third countries. Moreover, environmental measures proposed by the Commission will be approved by majority vote of the Council of Ministers, which will greatly strengthen the harmonization process. In addition, member states will not be allowed to set measures that are more restrictive than those of the EC. This requirement will be especially contentious since not all member states are the same shade of "green."

Indeed, environmental harmonization has proved to be one of the more difficult tasks of the EC, and the Maastricht decisions represent a large step forward. Elaborate consultative mechanisms involving industry, workers, consumers, and environmentalists have been established by the Commission as well as mechanisms to involve a range of commissioners other than the head of the Environment Directorate to increase policy integration with fields such as transport, energy, and R&D. Further, the Maastricht conference agreed to establish a cohesion fund to finance the structural impact of this environmental initiative on the poorer member states. Yet with all these elaborate and complex institutional and financial arrangements, and after twenty years of policy experience, no one expects environmental harmonization to be easy. The contrast with NAFTA, to which I turn shortly, could hardly be more striking.

As a concluding footnote to this brief account of the EC in the 1980s, one might speculate on the impact of deepening integration on the global system. The fears of Fortress Europe have largely dissipated. But the lack of concern about the external trading environment that was so clear at the launch of Europe 1992 has to some degree been amplified by the EC's role in the Uruguay Round, which was first characterized by stalling to delay the launch and then by an inability or unwillingness to come to terms with the need for fundamental reform of the common agricultural policy. At the very least one might say it would be unwise to look to the EC, now more than ever preoccupied with problems of widening versus deepening and fears of the disintegration of the former Soviet Union, to play a lead role in rescuing the GATT.

Equally important, however, has been the use or abuse of antidumping policy and the manipulation of rules of origin in the 1980s to induce Japanese, Korean, and even American investment in the electronics sector. While the debate about strategic industries has not yet been resolved in the Community (though a considerable range of R&D programs have been launched by the Commission), the use of trade policy not to create a fortress but to create a magnet for ''good'' investment sets a dangerous precedent for the growing number of Americans who would advocate the same approach. A recent proposal from Senator Max Baucus, for example, would set 70 percent local content for autos and ''could serve as a model to help other industry sectors, such as machine tools, steel, semiconductors and electronics.''[2]

Turning from the EC to North America, one finds the nature of the regionalization to be very different.

North America: Natural Integration Plus Nongovernmental Harmonization

The first move to regionalization in North America was the launch of negotiations in 1985 on a Canadian-U.S. Free Trade Agreement (CUSFTA). But the integration of the Canadian-U.S. economies began in the nineteenth century, when Canada introduced its protectionist national policy aimed at building a Canadian industrial base behind tariff walls. This move erected a branch plan economy as American firms jumped the barriers, first to serve the small local market and later, as tariffs were reduced, to serve the American market in some sectors. Another government action in the 1960s, the Auto Pact, created an integrated North American automobile sector for the big three American producers— General Motors, Ford, and Chrysler. Finally, integration accelerated in the first half of the 1980s as the Canadian dollar followed the U.S. dollar's overvaluation, though with some lag and gap. Because of these developments, and also, of course, because Canada and the United States are "natural" trading partners by reason of geography, the degree of integration by the time of the launch of the negotiations in 1985 was for Canada, the smaller economy, much higher than for the EC. This integration can be illustrated in many ways. Thus, for example, the ratio of the U.S. export share to Canada to its share of Canadian GDP is more than double the same measure for the EC.[3] Well over 70 percent of Canadian exports go to the United States and nearly 70 percent of imports come from the United States (the comparable figures for the United States are, of course, much smaller—about 20 percent—because of the relative size of the two economies). Nearly 80 percent of Canada's stock of foreign direct investment (FDI) is American. Nearly 50 percent of Canadian imports and more than 50 percent of exports of goods are intraenterprise. In business services, the comparable figures are 54 percent and 37 percent.

So, in contrast to the EC, Canada and the United States experienced 100 years of integration, led by investment flows, before establishing any institutional arrangement. The CUSFTA paradigm is thus investment first, then trade, then politics and institutions.

The 1988 Canadian-U.S. Free Trade Agreement spanned a wide range of issues: tariffs, a new set of procedures for resolving bilateral disputes concerning countervailing and antidumping duties, and a series of arrangements and disciplines covering sectoral and other matters. Because of both the very high degree of trade and investment integration that already exists and the low-tariff barriers governing most trade between the two countries, the agreement is, in itself, unlikely to affect the degree of regional integration significantly. Moreover, it excludes the three most heavily protected sectors: agriculture, textiles and apparel, and steel. The agreement has not, at this stage, markedly curtailed U.S. use of trade remedy laws or, from Canada's viewpoint, U.S. unilateralism, the latest example being the dispute over the rules of origin as applied to exports from Honda's Canadian plant.

The most significant new element in the agreement was the dispute settlement procedure covering trade remedy laws, pending further agreement to achieve harmonization in a five- to seven-year negotiated process. This decision is significant because it could presage a limited form of deeper integration if the negotiations prove to be successful. It was regarded by some Americans at the time of the negotiations as an unacceptable incursion on sovereignty despite its limited scope, which is simply to make determinations about whether a trade remedy action taken by either country is compatible with its domestic law.

But I would argue that over the longer run the real significance of the CUSFTA is not the agreement itself but the fact that it marked a fundamental change in U.S. trade policy. The new trade policy was announced in a speech by President Ronald Reagan on September 23, 1985, the day after the Plaza Accord signaled a new policy for the dollar. For the first time in the postwar period, American trade policy was multitrack: continuing efforts to launch the GATT round; bilateral free trade agreements where appropriate; and more active self-initiation of the little-used section 301 of the 1974 Trade Act to deal with other countries and unfair trade practices, through retaliation if necessary. This multitrack policy has continued and evolved over the past seven years.

On the bilateral track, the next stage of regionalization in North America was the initiative of the trilateral NAFTA in the spring of 1991. Negotiations are now going on, with daily speculation on how and when they will conclude.

Like Canada, Mexico is strongly integrated with the United States in trade (70 percent of imports and exports) and investment (64 percent of Mexican FDI). There is very limited linkage in either trade or investment between Canada and Mexico. U.S. corporations have not developed an integrated North American or Western Hemisphere strategy but have invested bilaterally in each country. Except for the auto industry, integrated between Canada and the United States by government policy, this "shallower" integration contrasts with regionalization in the Pacific, led by Japanese FDI. Will NAFTA spur corporate restructuring similar to that in Japan? Such restructuring would probably occur first in automobiles, but what other sectors would be candidates is not clear. A key issue in NAFTA will be the treatment of investment, especially for third countries. More broadly, the thorny issue of rules of origin (and locational competition for investment), already evident in the EC, will be key to the NAFTA negotiations. Indeed, in regionalization, the emphasis today, and in the foreseeable future, is investment more than trade.

Two features of the NAFTA negotiations are unique and possibly of singular importance over the long run, whatever the shape of the final package. The most important concerns the issue of the environment and the role of private interest groups in setting the agenda. The heightened political importance of the green movement has already strongly affected the nature of the EC integration. But the pressure for gradual harmonization over a longer period of time and, equally important, for major financial adjustments has been accommodated by an existing and now reinforced institutional structure. To some extent, too, the green movement in Europe has chosen the political rather than the pressure group route, which has most likely improved the process of accommodating what, in the future, will be a profound and highly disputatious transformation of both domestic and international policymaking. Seen in this light, it is somewhat surprising that the Bush administration underestimated the importance of the environmental issue at the start of the negotiations. And the administration's response, thus far, seems once again to underestimate the influence of the environmental lobby on Congress. Unless some reasonably robust institutional mechanism is included in the agreement and adequate financial provisions made for environmental problems, the future viability of NAFTA will remain in doubt.

The other unique feature of North American, or rather U.S.- Mexican, integration has been the importance of labor flows across the border from Mexico to the United States. Labor flows have not been a major feature of Canadian-U.S. integration, consisting, as they have over the twentieth century, mainly of a small, continuing migration of Canadians to the United States (a steady brain drain of the better educated and more entrepreneurial seeking broader horizons in the larger country). But Mexican migration to the United States has been of great importance: as has been pointed out by Hinojosa and Robinson, it is estimated that in recent years 10 percent of the U.S. labor force growth has been due to Mexican migration. Given that wage convergence is a very slow, long-run phenomenon, NAFTA is not only unlikely to constrain migration but likely to increase it because of the restructuring of the Mexican economy (especially agriculture) and because of the enormous demographic bulge that is occurring in Mexico. The impact of this migration in the United States will create downward pressure on unskilled wages and result in growing wage dispersion in the United States. The political, economic, and social consequences in the United States could be highly significant, at the very least creating continuing demands for "harmonization" of labor standards and even wages: microconvergence by nongovernmental pressure groups. Integration by factor flows is thus very different for investment than it is for labor.

Finally, what is the likelihood of the CUSFTA or NAFTA following, albeit over some time, an EC path of progressive and multidimensional integration? The odds are stacked against it, in my view. The main reason has to do with U.S. dominance. U.S. GNP is 85 percent of the combined North American total and its population is 70 percent of the total. The erosion of sovereignty involved in the EC model, an issue that has created and will continue to create problems in Europe, palls beside the political fallout that would erupt in Mexico and Canada! No strong political foundation exists, as in the EC, for deepening integration in North America. Moreover, no shared consensus paradigm like the social market economy exists. Indeed, Canada is much more European than American in this respect. That may also turn out to be true of Mexico as well once an economic growth trajectory is established.

Moreover, the degree of income disparity between Mexico and the other two countries is far greater than that between Spain and Portugal and the EC average. And even in the EC, the tension now evident in changing its budget to increase adjustment funds suggests how unlikely it would be for the United States, in its present and future fiscal position, to agree to assume the major portion of adjustment costs for Mexico, whose population today equals one-third that of its two northern neighbors.

What could be a more likely evolution in North America is an intensified economic integration led by investment and continuing labor flows, with further refinement of institutional mechanisms focused on trade remedies, rules of origin, local content, and the environment as well as, perhaps, labor standards. The present policy thrust of NAFTA seems ill designed to proceed on this evolutionary path.

East Asia: Natural Integration
Japanese Style

Intraregional trade in east Asia (the four newly industrializing countries and the Association of Southeast Asian Nations, or ASEAN) has grown rapidly in the second half of the 1980s (almost doubling between 1986 and 1989) and is about the same proportion of total world trade as that of intraregional North America trade. A prime factor triggering this development was the appreciation of the yen in 1985, after the Plaza Accord.

To offset their higher costs of exports, Japanese firms quickly restructured by relocating operations throughout the area. Japanese investment in east Asia increased sixfold between 1985 and 1989. This trend is likely to continue. In a survey of Japanese firms' investment intentions conducted in 1990, the Export-Import Bank of Japan reported that nearly 50 percent of FDI planned for the first half of the decade would be directed to Asia.

This Japanese investment is unlike U.S. investment in North America, which is not based on an integrated continental strategy. Japanese companies do not simply seek lower cost production but are developing a complex strategy of integrated and flexible production that serves the regional market, the Japanese market, and the North American and European markets. The Asia-based Japanese corporations tend to sell finished goods to the United States and Europe but largely semifinished goods to Japan. Thus the pattern of investment-led integration in Asia so far suggests a form of hierarchical investment that is "tighter" than that yet apparent in the other blocs. It should be noted, however, that host country policies have also played a more significant role in these locational decisions than in North America. Further, and more recently, Taiwan, Singapore, and Korea have started to replicate Japanese corporate strategies in ASEAN and south Asian economies.

So the process of regionalization in the Pacific is driven by economics, with investment as the driver and little sign yet of an institutional development. The region is also divided by history, religion, language, culture, and forms of government. Politics is not a glue, as in the EC, but a divider. Further, the important economic and security role of the United States in the Pacific would lessen the possibility of a more formal arrangement. True, the Asia-Pacific Economic Cooperation Council (APEC) was launched in 1989 with a modest mandate of seeking a common voice at the GATT. Although APEC may expand its mission (especially if the Uruguay Round fails), the prospects for a significant institutional development—an Asian free trade agreement, for example—seem pretty remote.

Conclusion

When one moves from econometrics to political economy, a very different list of questions about the implications of NAFTA arises. Some concern NAFTA itself: will the agreement and, equally important, the domestic policies of the U.S. administration provide the means for flexible adaptation to pressures arising from the environmental movement and the political fallout of growing income inequality in the United States?

But, other questions, arguably more important, relate to the trading system as a whole. NAFTA and regionalization more broadly are primarily political phenomena—as is true of all trade policy. There would be less cause for concern if the political will were rallied to conclude the Uruguay Round and to create a new multilateral trade organization that could start to deal in a multilateral framework with the urgent problems of trade and the environment, investment competition, and other aspects of deeper integration. In system terms, the concern about NAFTA is that it may add (by accident, not by design) yet another barrier to the ethos of inter-nationalism in a global milieu characterized increasingly by formidable obstacles to international cooperation.

Notes

1. Tibor Scitovsky, *Economic Theory and Western European Integration* (London: Unnin University Books, 1967), p. 67.

2. *International Trade Reporter*, February 26, 1992, p. 344.

3. See estimates by Lawrence Summers presented in Paul Krugman, "Regionalism vs. Multilateralism," World Bank and CEPR Conference on New Dimensions in Regional Integrations, Washington, April 2–3, 1992, p. 36.

Principal Contributors

Drusilla K. Brown is associate professor of economics at Tufts University. Her research and publication efforts have focused primarily on the application of computable general equilibrium techniques to the study of preferential trading areas and the theory of trade policy in the presence of imperfectly competitive goods markets.

Raúl Hinojosa-Ojeda is assistant professor of planning in the graduate school of architecture and urban planning at the University of California, Los Angeles. Various articles he has written focus on the political economy of regional integration dynamics in different parts of the world, including debt, trade, and migration relations among the United States, Mexico, and other Latin American countries.

Tim Josling has been professor at the Food Research Institute at Stanford University since 1978, after teaching at the London School of Economics and the University of Reading, England. He has been a consultant to various international institutions and governmental bodies on agricultural policy. His research and publications have focused on domestic and trade policies relating to agricultural products, particularly in industrial countries, international policies in the agricultural area, and world food problems.

Robert A. Pastor is professor of political science at Emory University and fellow at Emory's Carter Center. A Fulbright Professor at El Colegio de Mexico, he was coauthor of *Limits to Friendship: The United States and Mexico*. His most recent book is *Whirlpool: U.S. Foreign Policy toward Latin America and the Caribbean* (Princeton University Press, 1992).

Carlos Alberto Primo Braga is an economist with the trade division of the World Bank. Previously he was assistant professor of economics at the University of Sao Paulo and senior researcher at the Fundacao Instituto de Pesquisas Economicas (FIPE). Since 1988 he has been visiting professor at the Johns Hopkins School of Advanced International Studies. His main research interests and publications encompass international economics, the economics of science and technology, intellectual property rights, industry studies (steel, frozen concentrated orange juice), and the economics of education.

Sherman Robinson is professor in the department of agricultural and resource economics at the University of California, Berkeley. Before teaching at Berkeley he worked for six years as an economist in the research department of the World Bank. His research and publications have been concerned mostly with the economics of developing countries, focusing on issues of trade policy, income distribution, and the choice of development strategy. He is a visiting scholar at the Congressional Budget Office for the 1992–93 academic year.

Sidney Weintraub is Dean Rusk Professor of International Affairs at the Lyndon B. Johnson School of Public Affairs, University of Texas at Austin, and distinguished scholar at the Center for Strategic and International Studies. He also serves as an economic consultant to the Mexican and U.S. governments, as well as to several multinational institutions. He has participated in negotiations of the General Agreement on Tariffs and Trade and in discussions at the Organization for Economic Cooperation and Development and at many United Nations agencies. He has written extensively about the Canadian-U.S. and Mexican-U.S. trade relationships.

Discussants and Panelists
with their affiliations at the time of the conference

Carlos Bazdresch Parada
Centro de Investigación y Docencia Económicas

Susan M. Collins
Harvard University

Robert W. Crandall
Brookings Institution

Timothy J. Kehoe
University of Minnesota

Anne O. Krueger
Duke University

Robert Z. Lawrence
Harvard University

Darryl McLeod
Fordham University

Sylvia Ostry
University of Toronto

Michael Piore
Massachusetts Institute of Technology

Jaime Ros
University of Notre Dame

Jeffrey J. Schott
Institute for International Economics

Gustavo Vega-Canovas
El Colegio de México

Index